THE MIDDLE MAN

VOLUME 1

Created & Written by
Javier Grillo-Marxuach

Illustrated by
Les McClaine

Published by Viper Comics
9400 N. MacArthur Blvd., Suite 124-215
Irving, TX 75063

First edition: January 2006
ISBN: 0-9754193-7-4

This volume collects issues 1-4
of the series The Middleman.

JESSIE GARZA PRESIDENT & PUBLISHER
JIM RESNOWSKI EDITOR-IN-CHIEF & CREATIVE DIRECTOR

VIPER COMICS | **WWW.VIPERCOMICS.COM** | **EST. 2001**

INTRODUCING THE MIDDLEMAN
By Paul Dini

Okay, this introduction is supposed to be covert, so I'll whisper. Pssst! Hey, Bud! Yeah, I'm talking to you, meat-sock! C'mere…closer! Lift the lid on this hatch thingee and jump in, no one'll see you. There ya go! Now it's time I laid the straight dope on you about THE MIDDLE-MAN and the cats that give him his super-secret marching orders.

First off, you can take it from me that one of the great joys of working in both TV and comics is that you get to meet those unique individuals whose imaginations make those mediums truly special. Not only do they know how to tell a hell of a story, but their affection for what they do comes through in every frame and on every page.

That was the feeling I got when I first walked into the LOST writer's room that fateful February day in 2004 and met Javier Gillo-Marxuach. Getting to know Javi and working alongside him in those early days of the show's creation was, to borrow a term from Javi himself, "Fahn-*tahstic!*" I found him to be both a gentleman and a geek of the first order, a polite, razor-sharp young man who spoke of writing technique, the current political climate and C-list Star Wars bounty hunter 4-Lom with equal ease and expertise. Rare is the man who can pepper casual conversation with references to obscure works of 70's Korean gangster cinema like "The Beating of Frankie Han." Okay, so Javi made up that last one (which became for a time a running joke in the writer's room) but for as much as Javier references pop culture, the boy knows how to give it back. His many outstand-ing scripts to the LOST mythos prove that, as does his stellar work on such genre shows as SEAQUEST, CHARMED and JAKE 2.0, to name a few.

So when Javi somewhat hesitantly asked if I would read his unpro-duced script THE MIDDLEMAN that he was considering turning into a comic series, I enthusiastically agreed. I knew it would be a good story and I was not disappointed. On Puckishly twisted Javiworld, humankind is constantly threatened by a legion of monsters and other horrors that lurk just at the fringes of our consciousness. Set squarely between our blissfully ignorant selves and the evil forces that would destroy us is The Middleman, a highly-trained and dangerously outfitted troubleshooter. The fact that he also shoots demons and ghouls is equally good news for us clueless mortals.

I found the dialogue smart and funny, the action exciting, and as Javi had figured, perfect material for an on-going comic series. The Middleman himself I took to be a refreshing callback to such heroes as The Phantom and Zorro. He's a classic Dirk Strongjaw (a Javi term, not the character's actual name) who assumes the mantle of duty from the similarly-named heroes who have gone before him. His slogan "Fighting evil so you don't have to," recalls, perhaps with a knowing wink, the Ghostbusters' motto, "We're ready to believe you," itself a sly jibe at the gung-ho slogans of a more innocent era. The inspired post-modern spin on the concept is the addition of the Middleman's partner, a jaded, wise-cracking Playstation-weaned bohemian named Wendy Watson. You get the idea that in her twenty years or so of disenfranchised youth, Wendy has seen it all, so the idea of fighting genetic freaks and hit-man apes falls perfectly in line with her unflappable "Whatever, dude" attitude. Her many hours at the game console have made her a great shot, a definite asset when you are up to your neck in pug-uglies.

Wendy is one of the most appealing new heroines to come along in a while, due in no small part to the talents of artist Les McClaine. Already known to indy comic fans for his HIGHWAY 13 series and his on-line comic JOHNNY CROSSBONES, Les is an excellent choice to render the usually fearsome, sometimes funny world of the Middleman. Imagine a scene out of H. P. Lovecraft directed by Tex Avery and you have some small idea of the horror/humor fusion that Les brings to the book. It doesn't hurt that he draws very cute girls and guys, either.

Now, thanks to the good folks at Viper Comics, Volume One of THE MIDDLEMAN is in your hands and you can enjoy the saga from the very beginning. If you experience half the fun and excitement I did when I first read Javi's script, then it's mission accomplished for Javi, Les, Wendy and the Middleman.

It is, in a word, "Fahn-*tahstic!*"

Paul Dini
October, 2005

CHAPTER 01

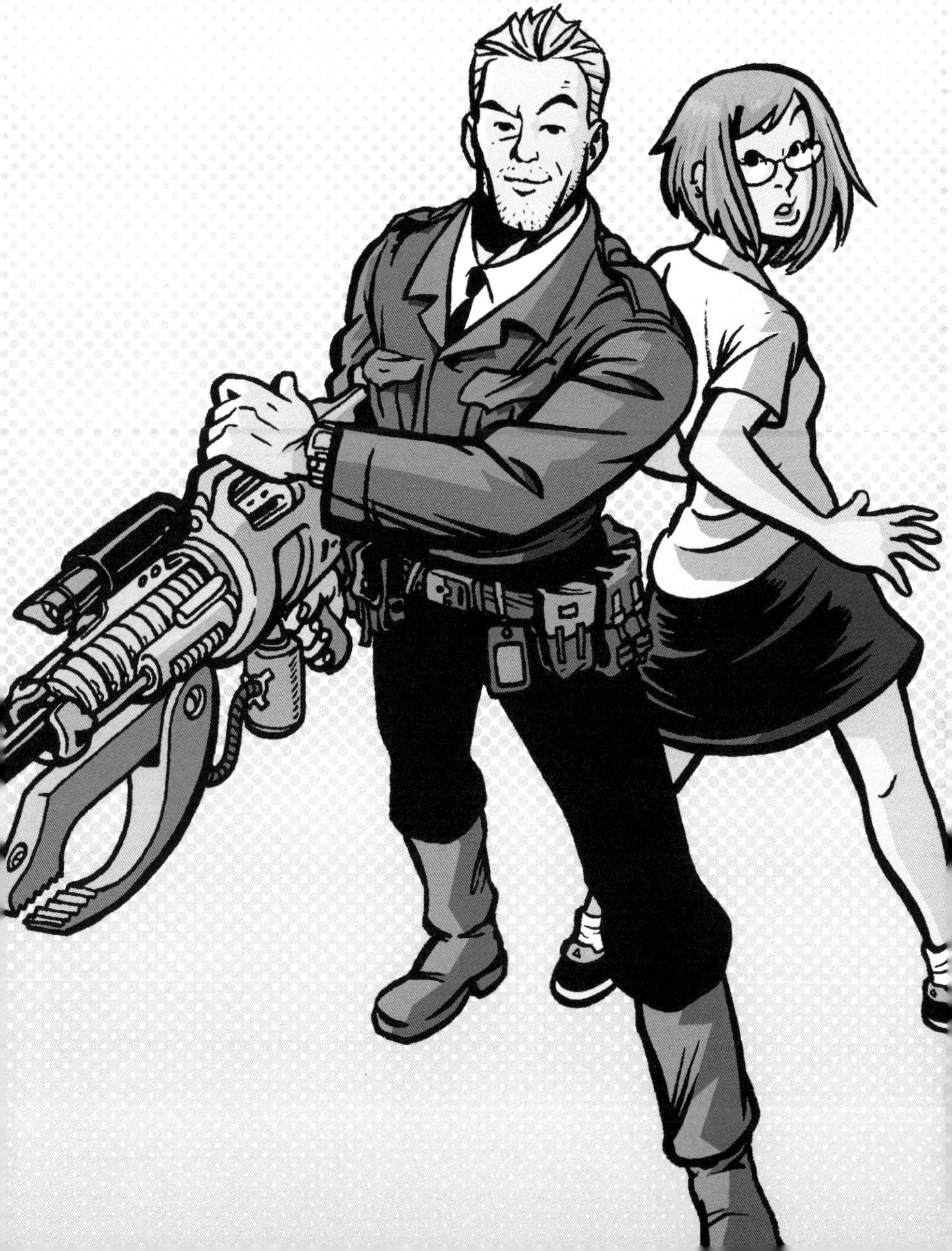

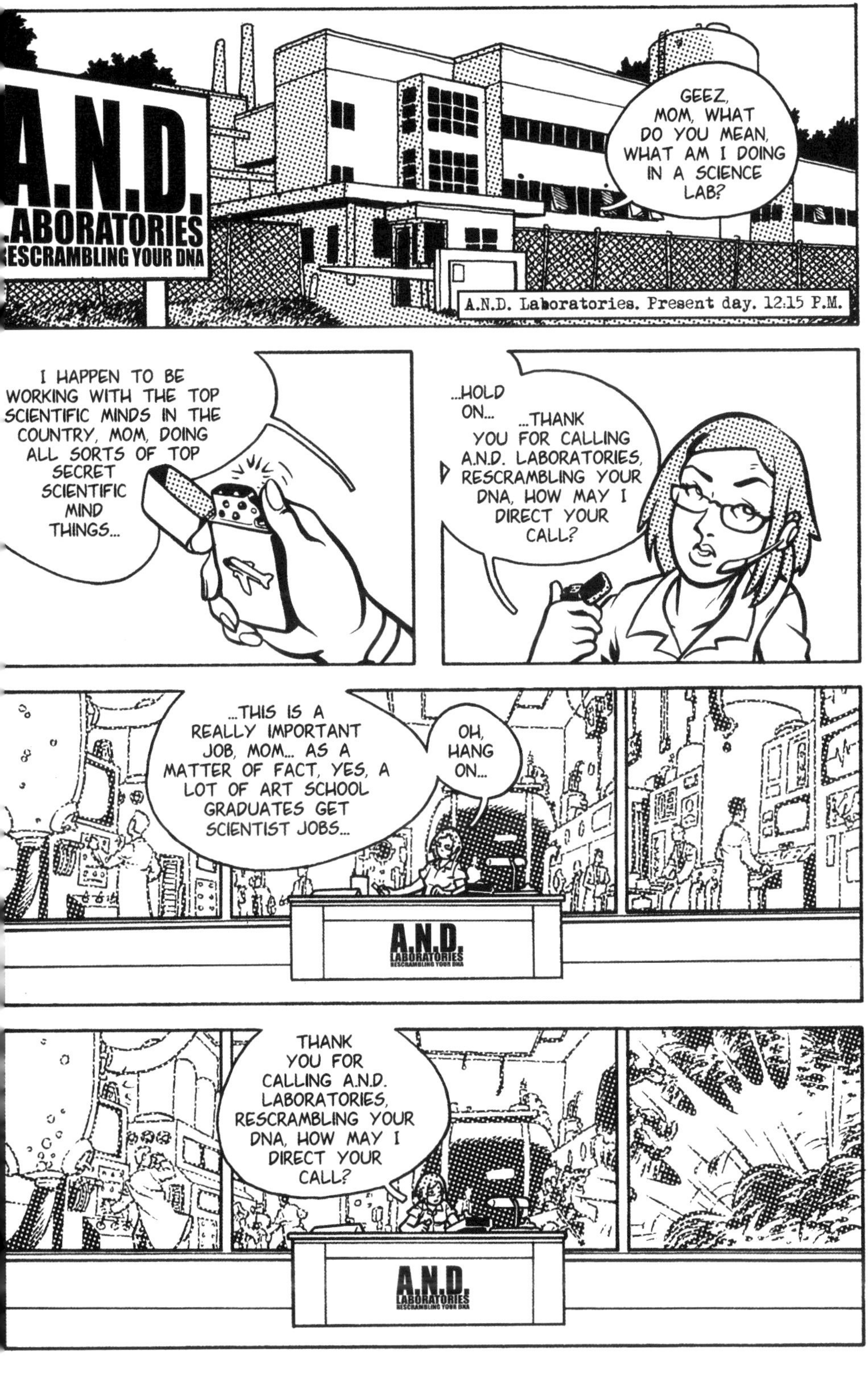
A.N.D. LABORATORIES RESCRAMBLING YOUR DNA
GEEZ, MOM, WHAT DO YOU MEAN, WHAT AM I DOING IN A SCIENCE LAB?
A.N.D. Laboratories. Present day. 12:15 P.M.
I HAPPEN TO BE WORKING WITH THE TOP SCIENTIFIC MINDS IN THE COUNTRY, MOM, DOING ALL SORTS OF TOP SECRET SCIENTIFIC MIND THINGS...
...HOLD ON...
...THANK YOU FOR CALLING A.N.D. LABORATORIES, RESCRAMBLING YOUR DNA, HOW MAY I DIRECT YOUR CALL?
...THIS IS A REALLY IMPORTANT JOB, MOM... AS A MATTER OF FACT, YES, A LOT OF ART SCHOOL GRADUATES GET SCIENTIST JOBS...
OH, HANG ON...
A.N.D. LABORATORIES RESCRAMBLING YOUR DNA
THANK YOU FOR CALLING A.N.D. LABORATORIES, RESCRAMBLING YOUR DNA, HOW MAY I DIRECT YOUR CALL?
A.N.D. LABORATORIES RESCRAMBLING YOUR DNA

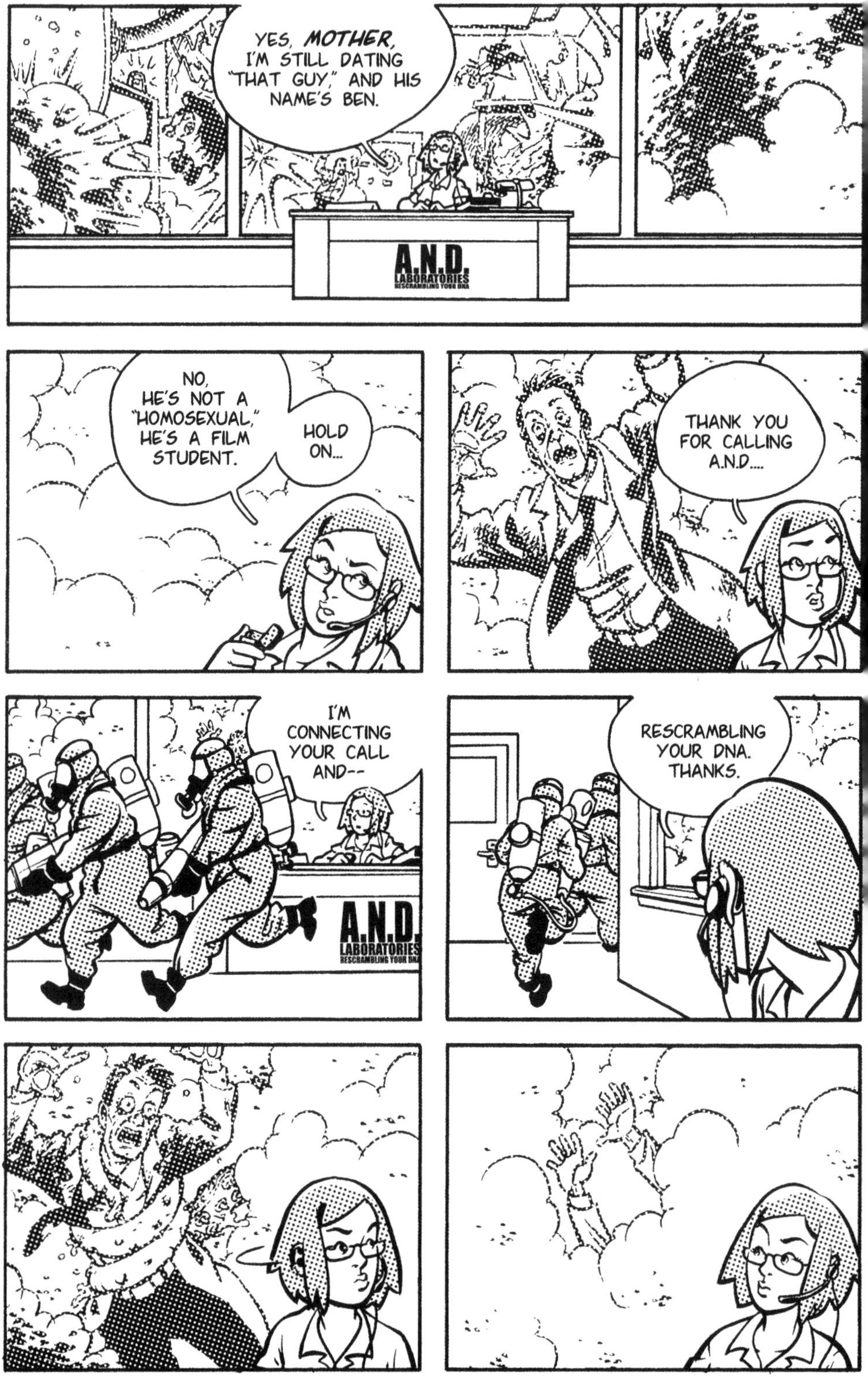
YES, *MOTHER*, I'M STILL DATING "THAT GUY," AND HIS NAME'S BEN.
A.N.D. LABORATORIES RESCRAMBLING YOUR DNA
NO, HE'S NOT A "HOMOSEXUAL," HE'S A FILM STUDENT.
HOLD ON...
THANK YOU FOR CALLING A.N.D....
I'M CONNECTING YOUR CALL AND--
A.N.D. LABORATORIES RESCRAMBLING YOUR DNA
RESCRAMBLING YOUR DNA. THANKS.

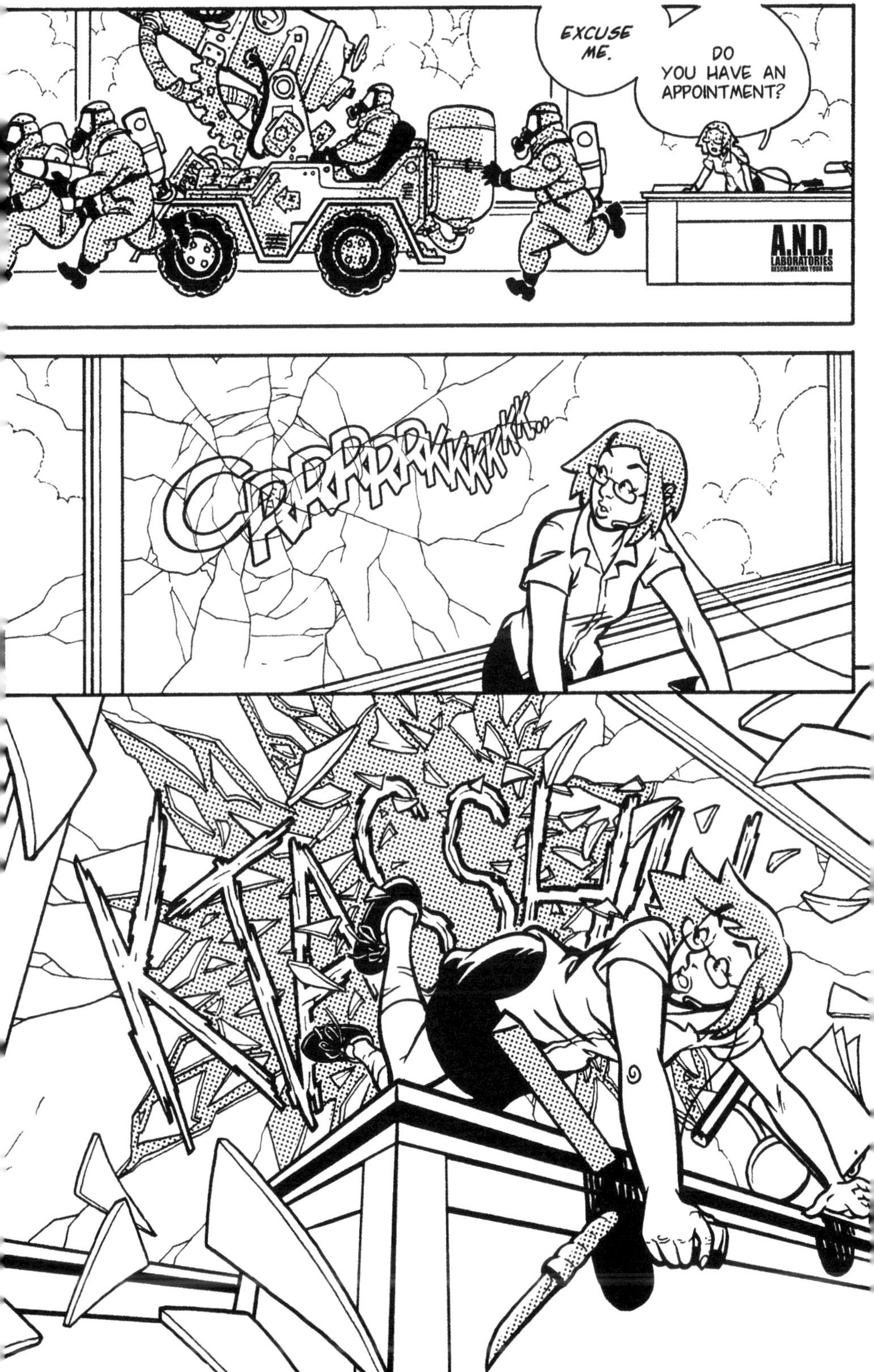
EXCUSE ME.
DO YOU HAVE AN APPOINTMENT?
A.N.D.
LABORATORIES
KTASCH

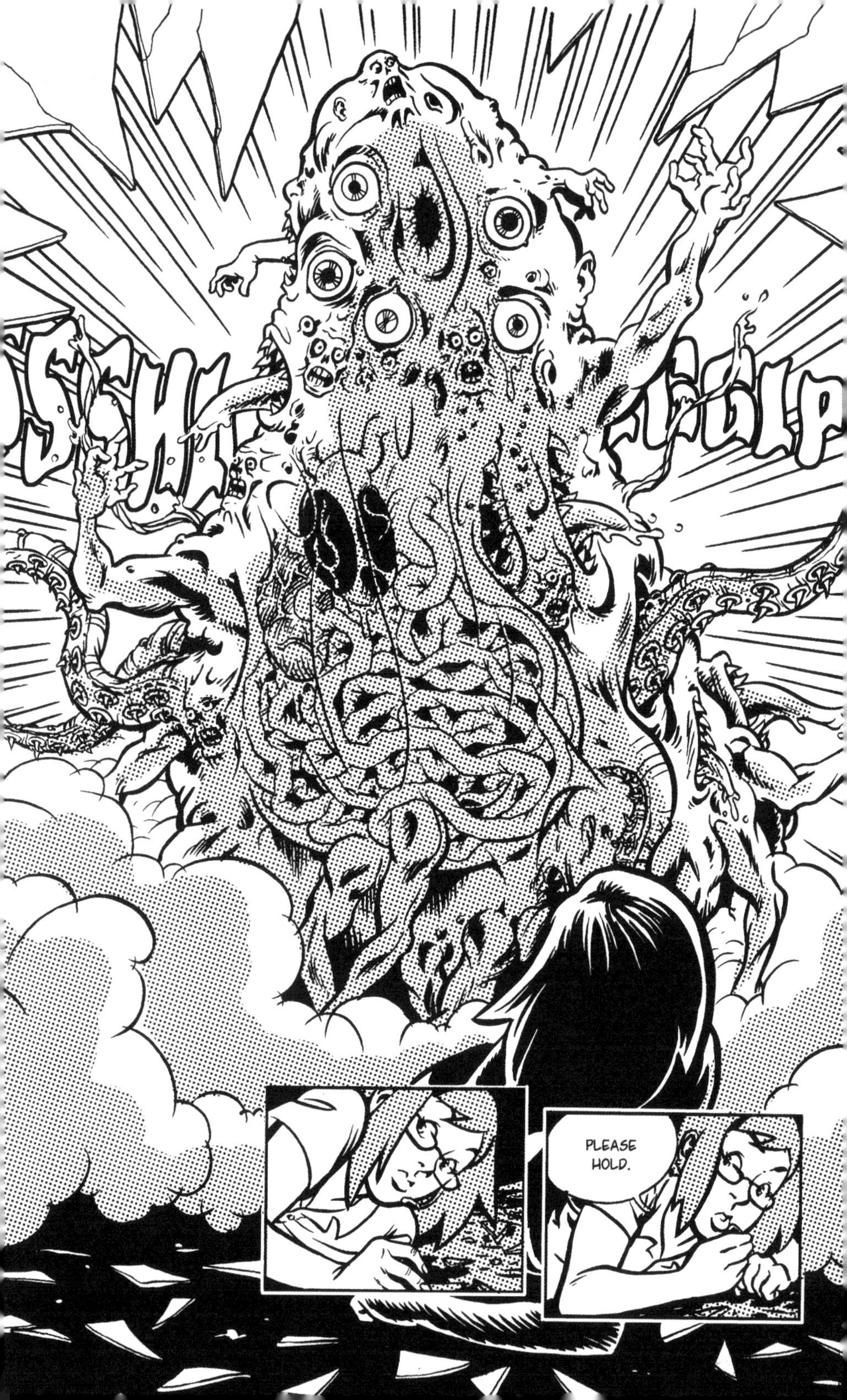
PLEASE HOLD.

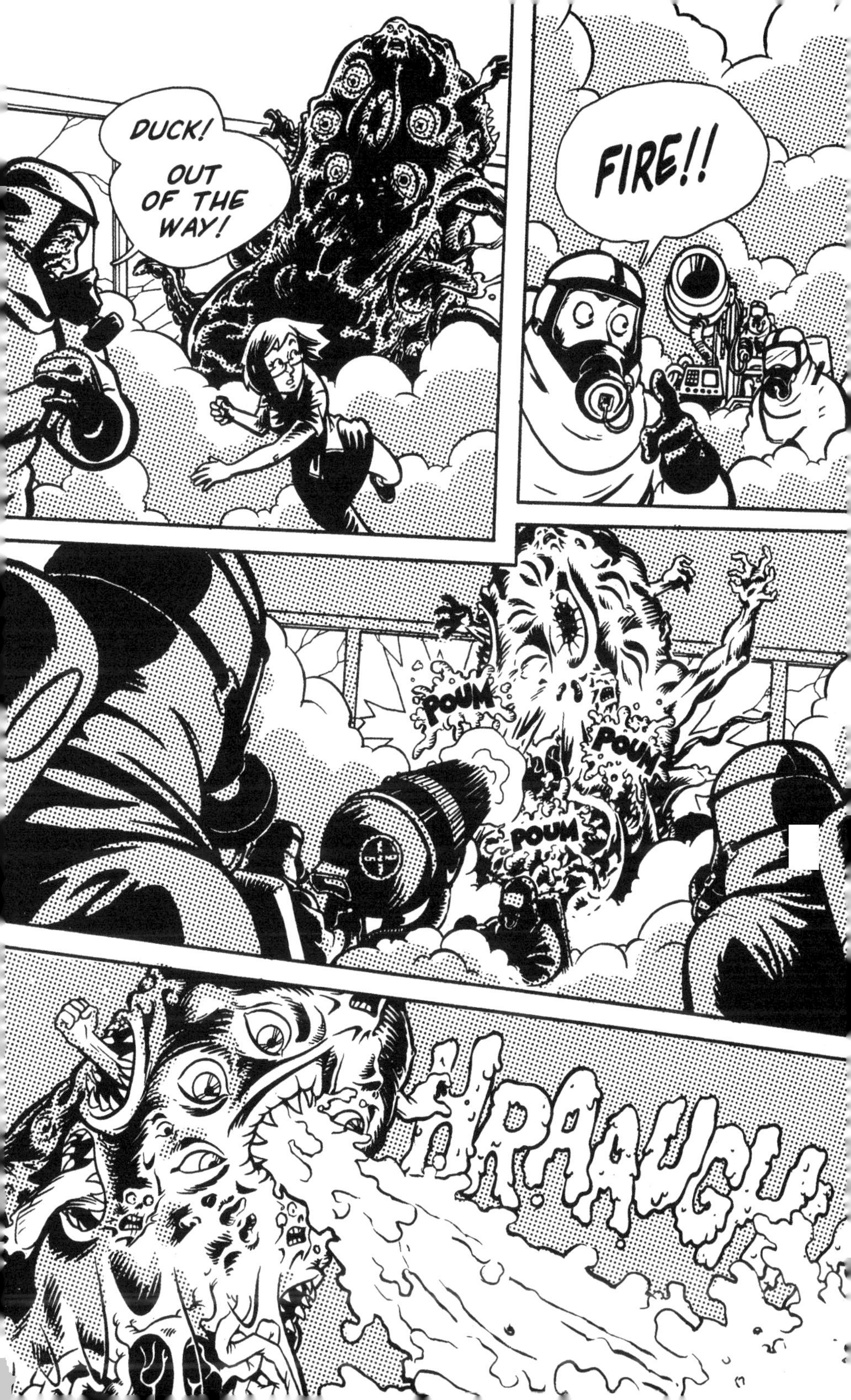
DUCK! OUT OF THE WAY!
FIRE!!
POUM
POUM
POUM
HRAAUGH

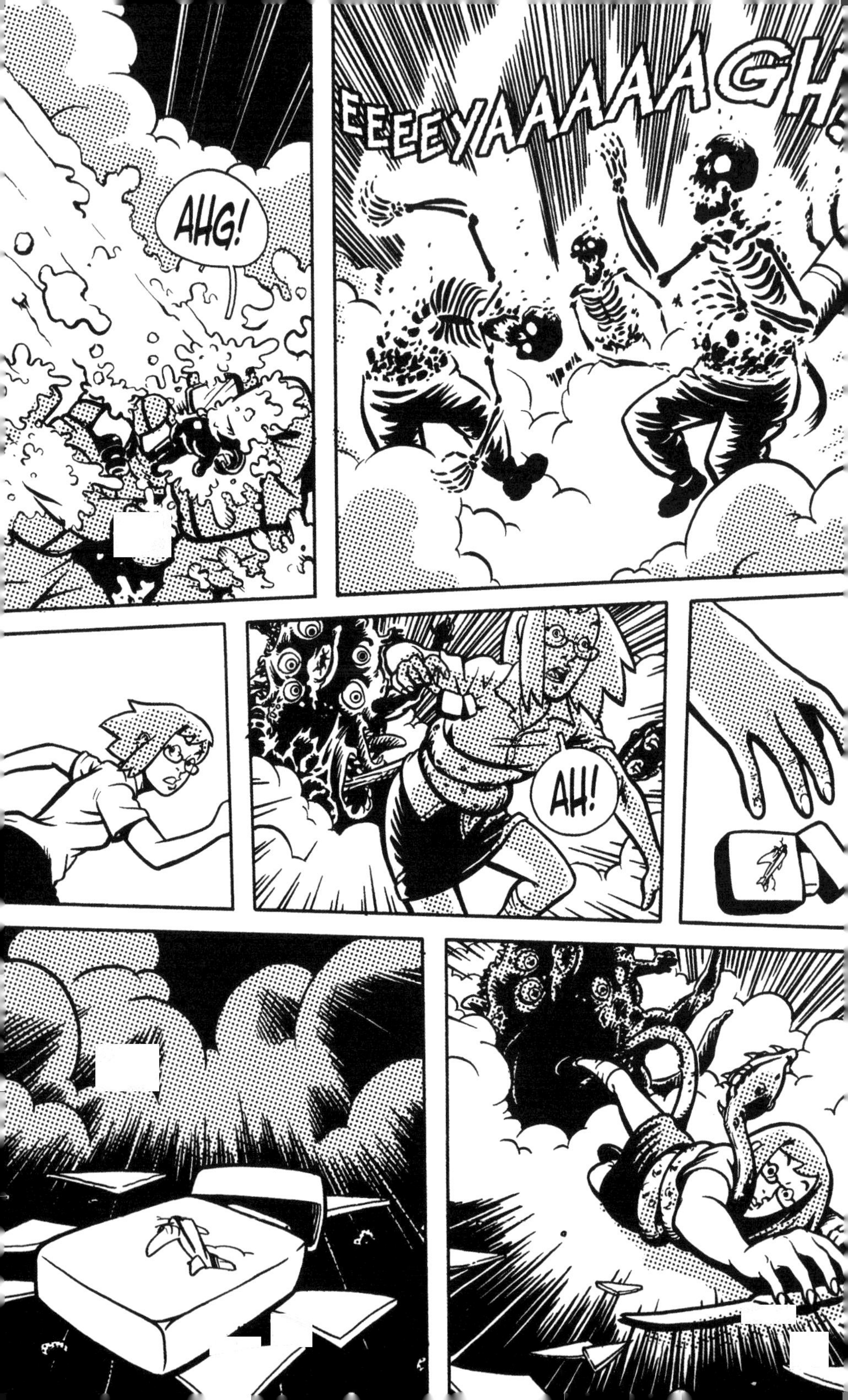
AHG!
EEEEYAAAAAGH!
AH!

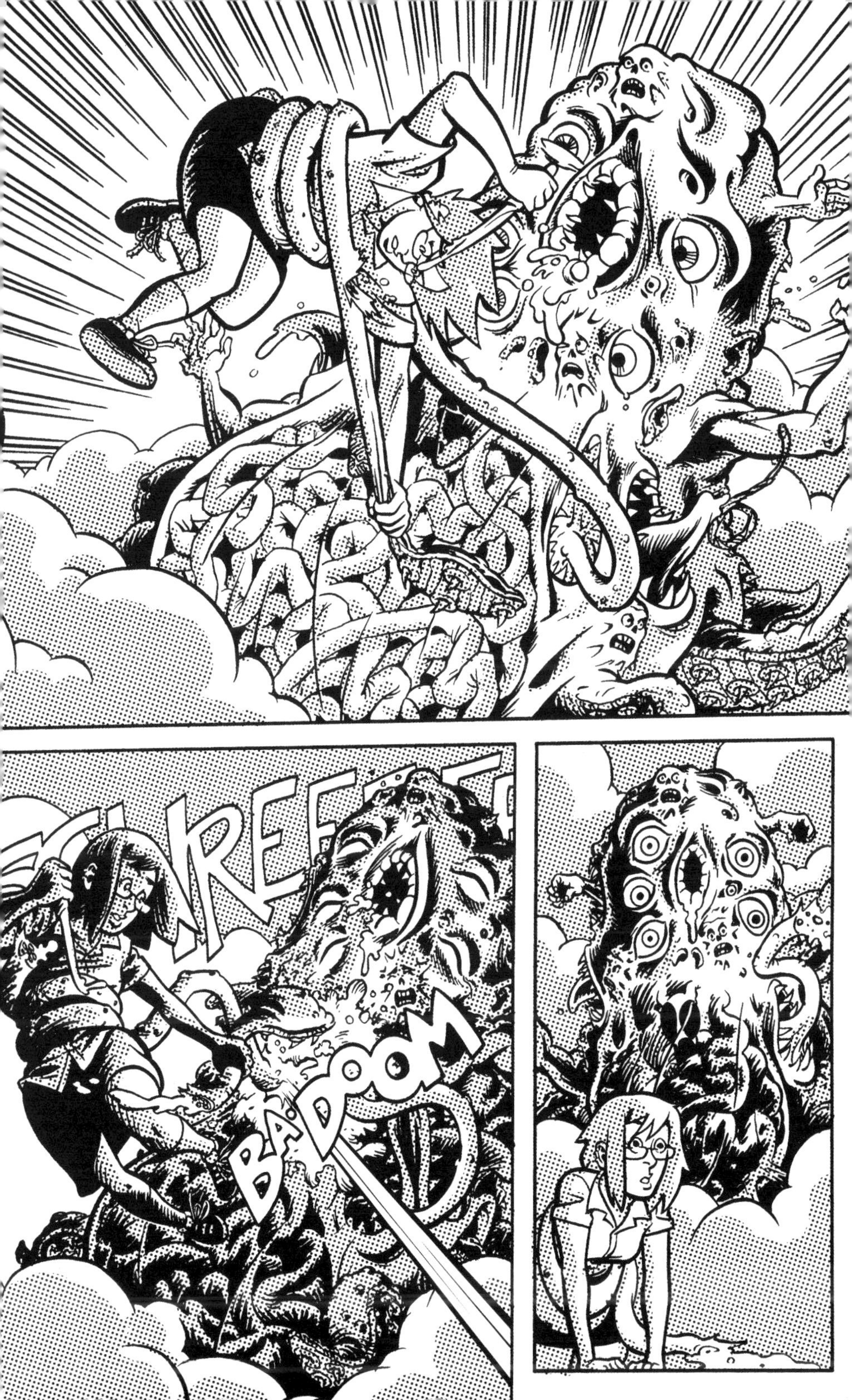
BADOOM

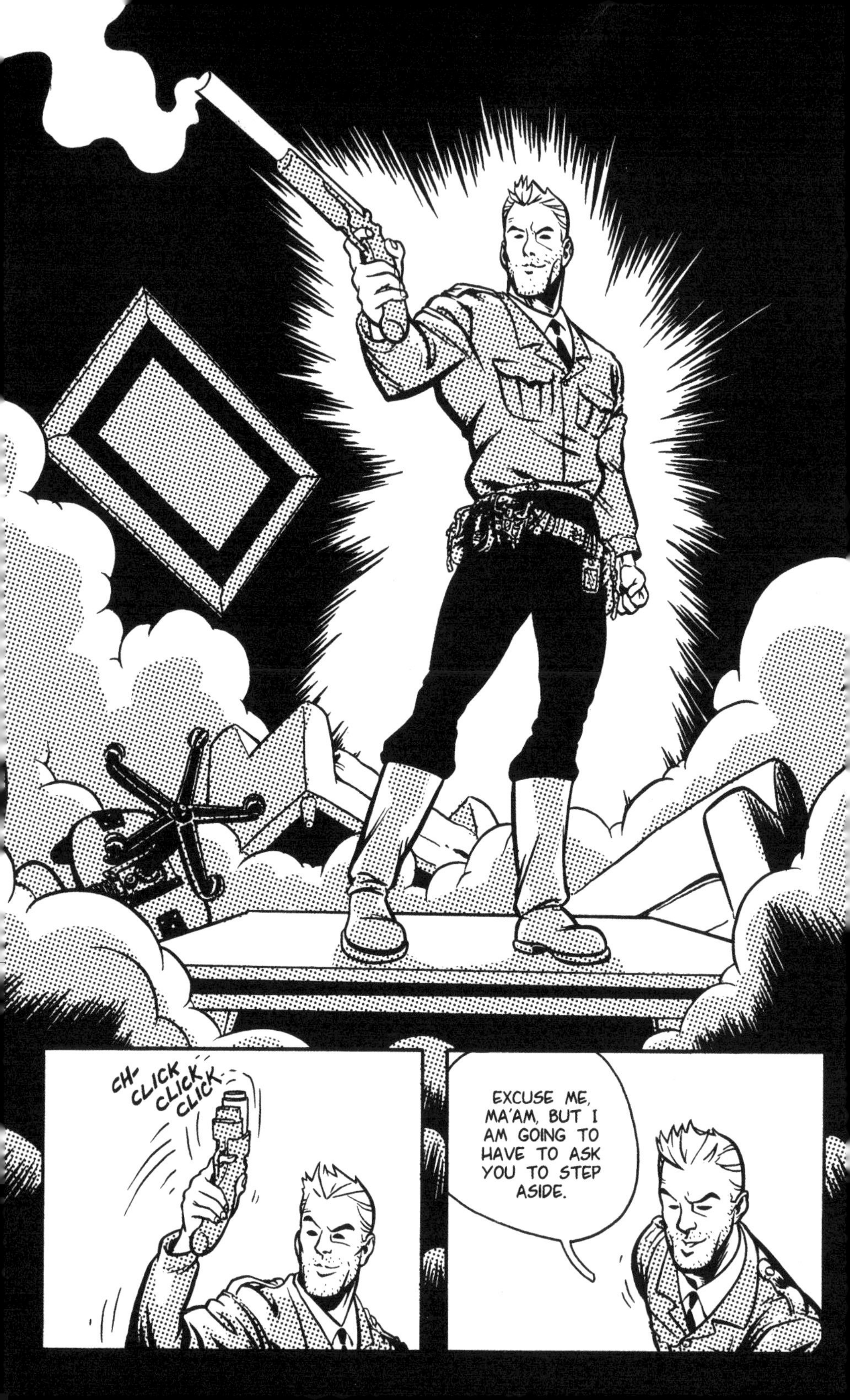
CH-CLICK CLICK CLICK
EXCUSE ME, MA'AM, BUT I AM GOING TO HAVE TO ASK YOU TO STEP ASIDE.

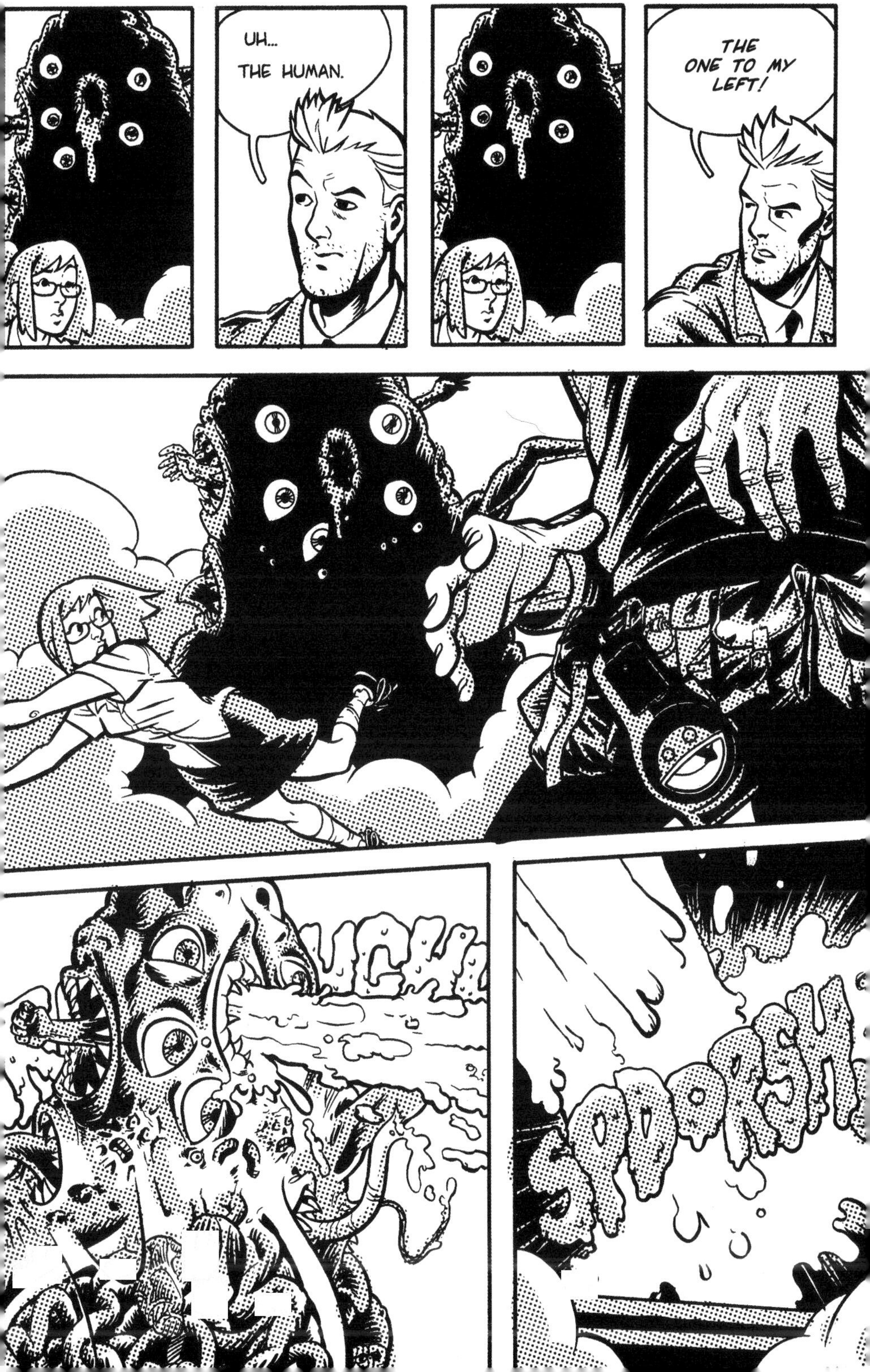
UH...
THE HUMAN.
THE ONE TO MY LEFT!

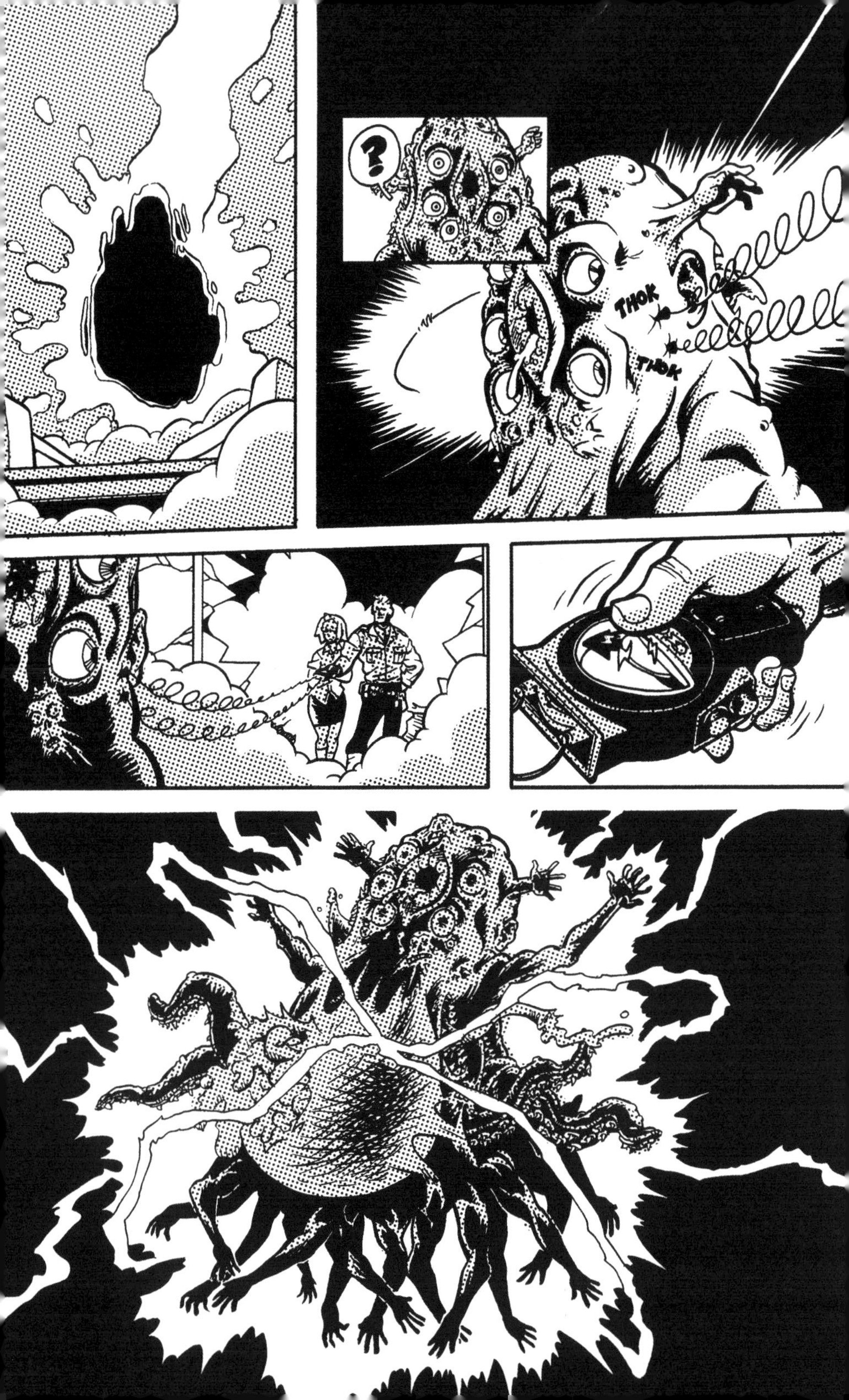
?
THOK
THOK

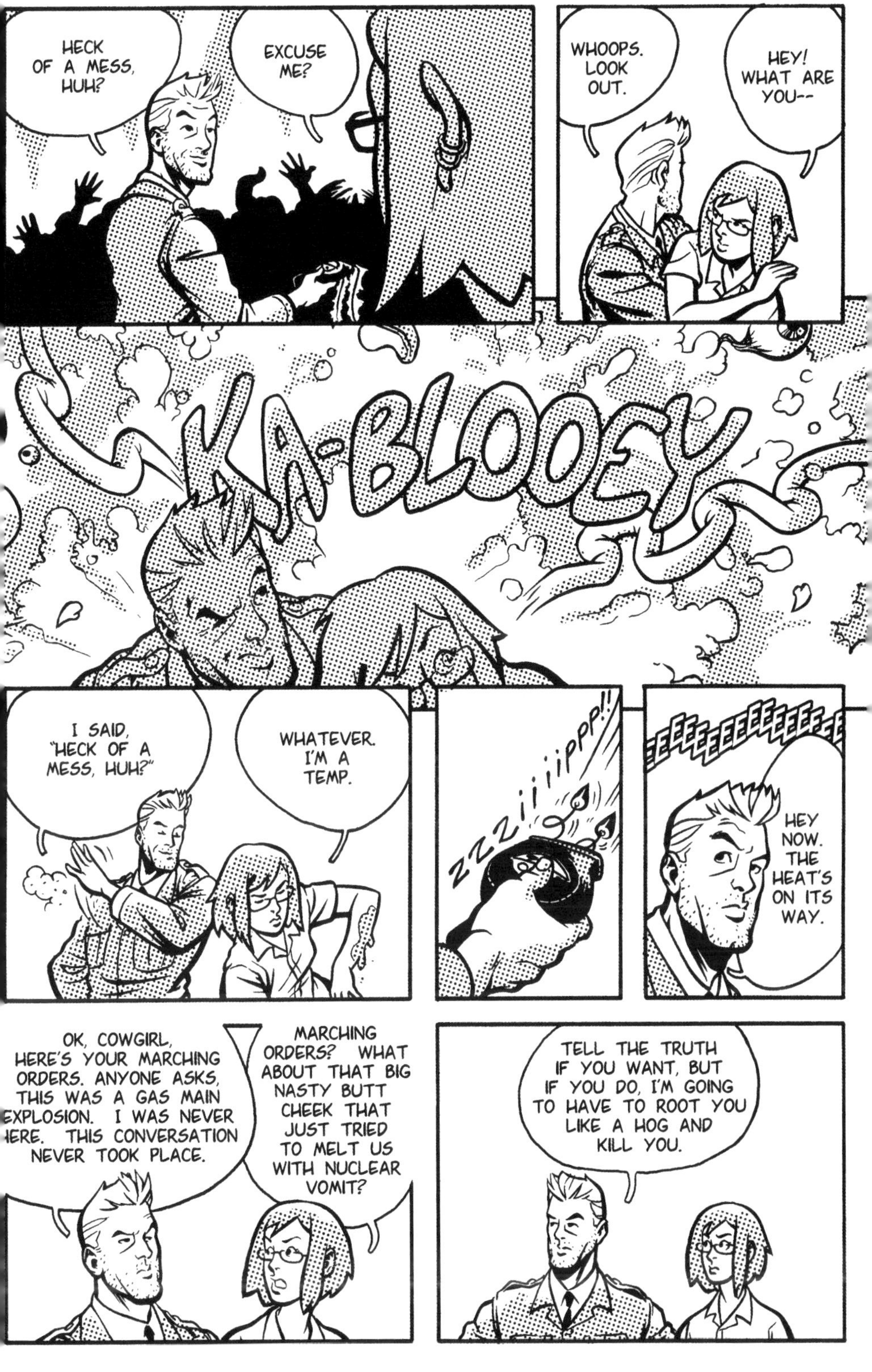
HECK OF A MESS, HUH?
EXCUSE ME?
WHOOPS. LOOK OUT.
HEY! WHAT ARE YOU--
KA-BLOOEY
I SAID, "HECK OF A MESS, HUH?"
WHATEVER. I'M A TEMP.
ZZZIIIIIPPP!!
EEEEEEEEEEEEEEEEEE
HEY NOW. THE HEAT'S ON ITS WAY.
OK, COWGIRL, HERE'S YOUR MARCHING ORDERS. ANYONE ASKS, THIS WAS A GAS MAIN EXPLOSION. I WAS NEVER HERE. THIS CONVERSATION NEVER TOOK PLACE.
MARCHING ORDERS? WHAT ABOUT THAT BIG NASTY BUTT CHEEK THAT JUST TRIED TO MELT US WITH NUCLEAR VOMIT?
TELL THE TRUTH IF YOU WANT, BUT IF YOU DO, I'M GOING TO HAVE TO ROOT YOU LIKE A HOG AND KILL YOU.

SORRY.

SO WHAT'S IT GONNA BE? KEEP THE SECRET OR DEATH?

WHAT DO YOU THINK?

MA'AM, SPECIFICITY IS THE SOUL OF ALL GOOD COMMUNICATION.

YES. DUH!

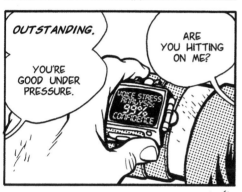

OUTSTANDING.

YOU'RE GOOD UNDER PRESSURE.

VOICE STRESS ANALYSIS: 90% CONFIDENCE

ARE YOU HITTING ON ME?

JUST MAKING AN OBSERVATION.

HELLO! NUTJOB, PARTY OF ONE.

NO, MA'AM.

I'M JUST MIDDLEMAN

CRASH

ARE YOU ALL RIGHT?

UH... YES... I--

...

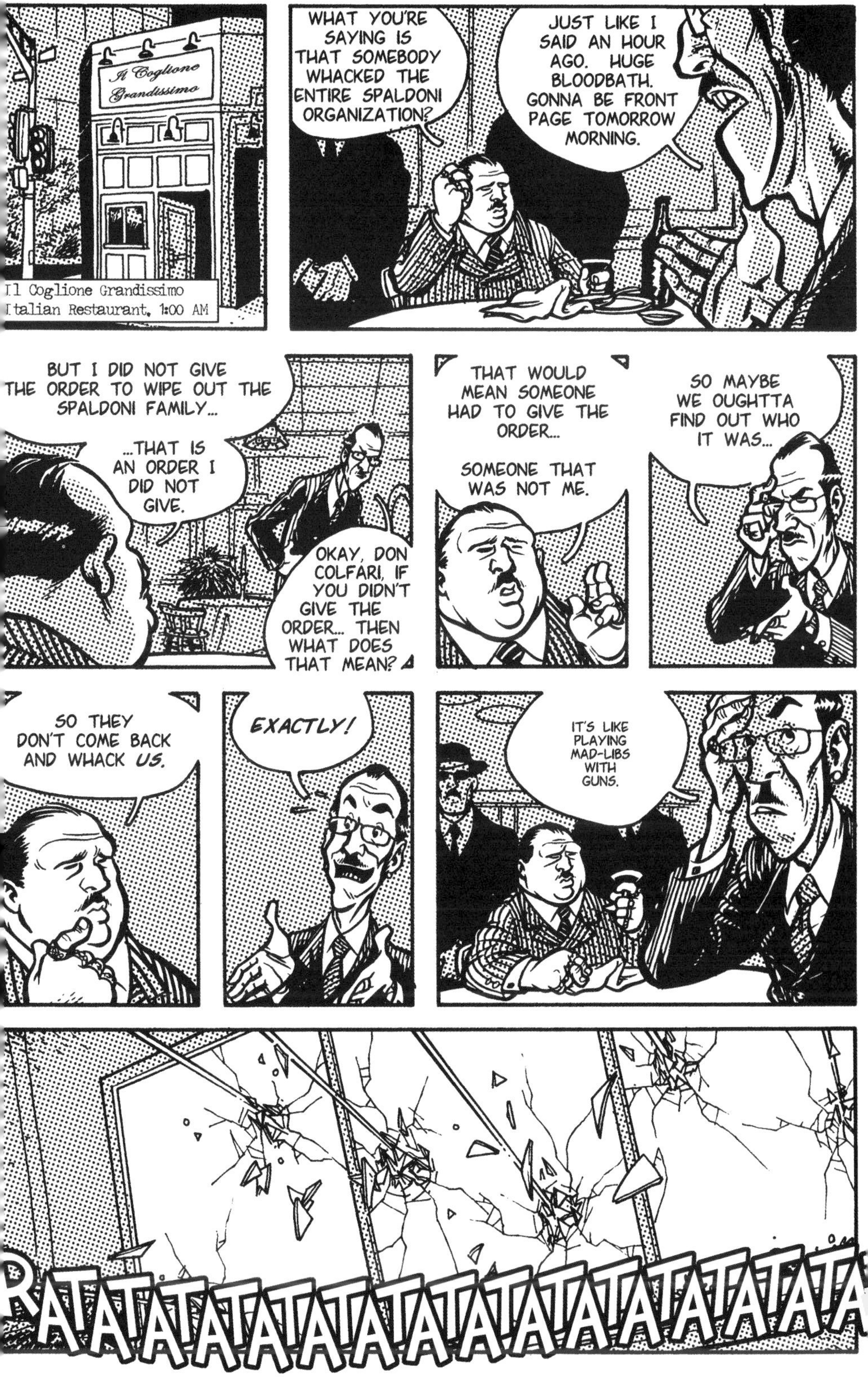

Il Coglione Grandissimo
Il Coglione Grandissimo Italian Restaurant, 1:00 AM
WHAT YOU'RE SAYING IS THAT SOMEBODY WHACKED THE ENTIRE SPALDONI ORGANIZATION?
JUST LIKE I SAID AN HOUR AGO. HUGE BLOODBATH. GONNA BE FRONT PAGE TOMORROW MORNING.
BUT I DID NOT GIVE THE ORDER TO WIPE OUT THE SPALDONI FAMILY...
...THAT IS AN ORDER I DID NOT GIVE.
OKAY, DON COLFARI, IF YOU DIDN'T GIVE THE ORDER... THEN WHAT DOES THAT MEAN?
THAT WOULD MEAN SOMEONE HAD TO GIVE THE ORDER...
SOMEONE THAT WAS NOT ME.
SO MAYBE WE OUGHTTA FIND OUT WHO IT WAS...
SO THEY DON'T COME BACK AND WHACK *US.*
EXACTLY!
IT'S LIKE PLAYING MAD-LIBS WITH GUNS.
RATATATATATATATATATATATATATATATATATATA

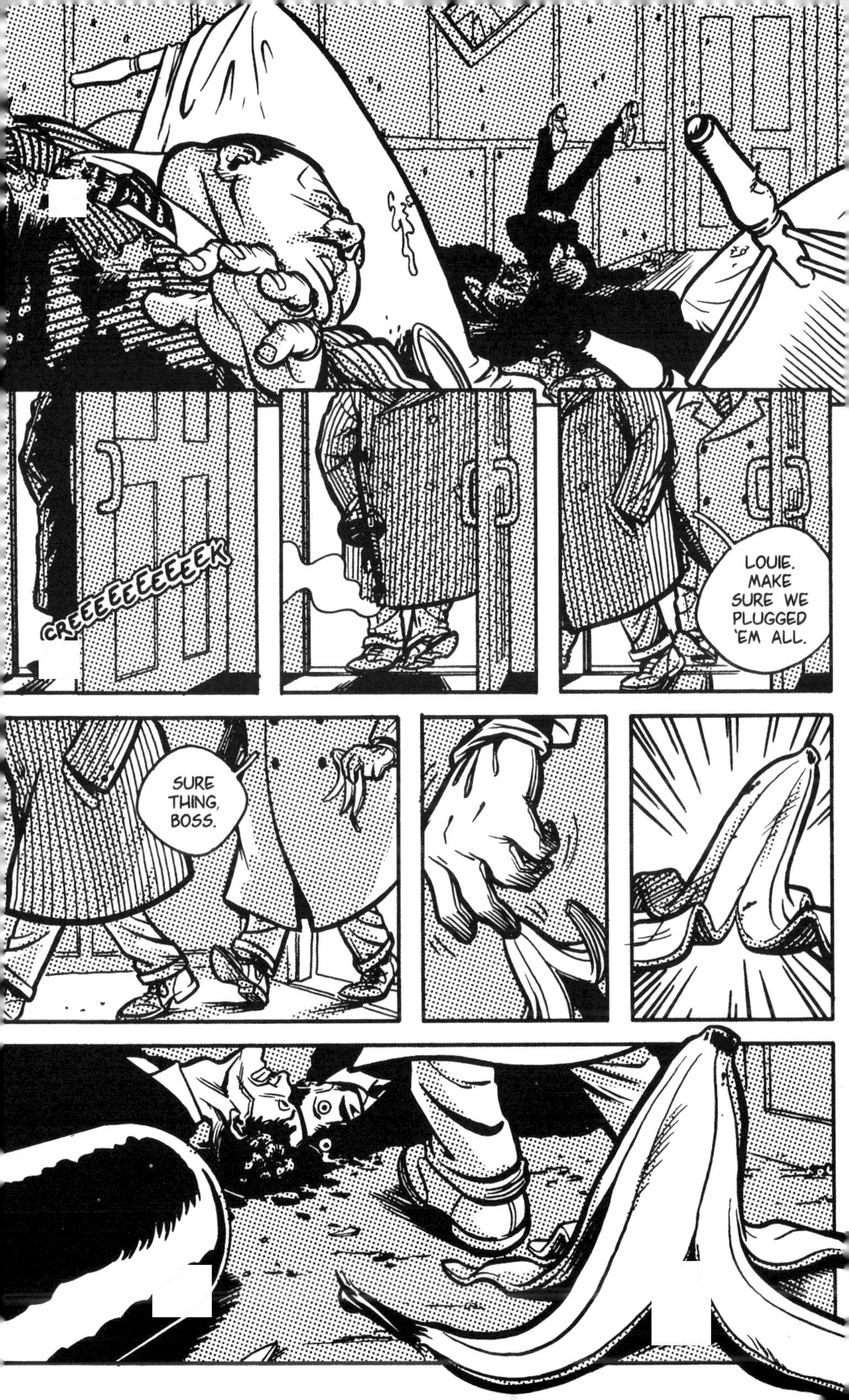
CREEEEEEEEEEK
LOUIE. MAKE SURE WE PLUGGED 'EM ALL.
SURE THING, BOSS.

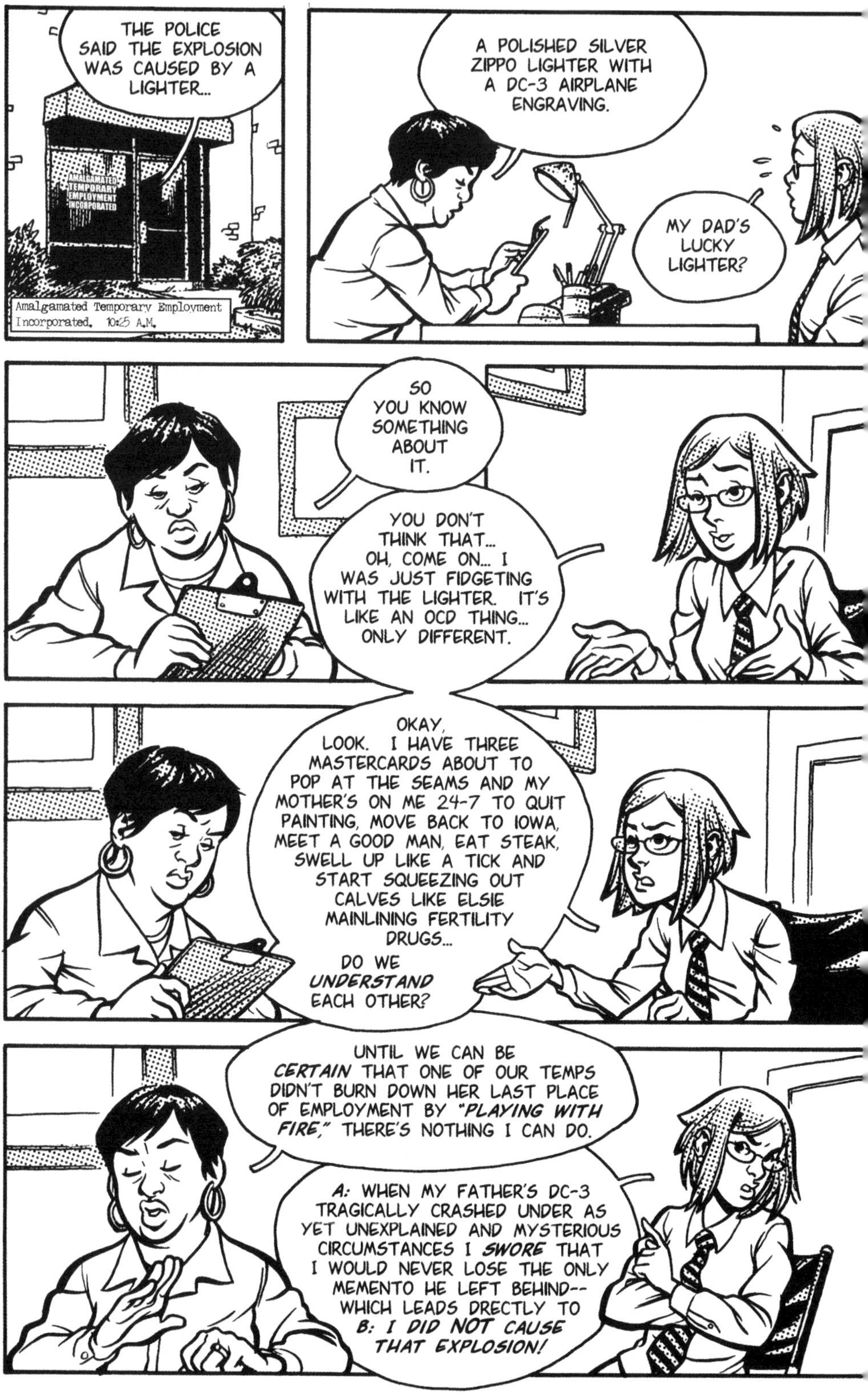
THE POLICE SAID THE EXPLOSION WAS CAUSED BY A LIGHTER...
AMALGAMATED TEMPORARY EMPLOYMENT INCORPORATED
Amalgamated Temporary Employment Incorporated, 10:25 A.M.
A POLISHED SILVER ZIPPO LIGHTER WITH A DC-3 AIRPLANE ENGRAVING.
MY DAD'S LUCKY LIGHTER?
SO YOU KNOW SOMETHING ABOUT IT.
YOU DON'T THINK THAT... OH, COME ON... I WAS JUST FIDGETING WITH THE LIGHTER. IT'S LIKE AN OCD THING... ONLY DIFFERENT.
OKAY, LOOK. I HAVE THREE MASTERCARDS ABOUT TO POP AT THE SEAMS AND MY MOTHER'S ON ME 24-7 TO QUIT PAINTING, MOVE BACK TO IOWA, MEET A GOOD MAN, EAT STEAK, SWELL UP LIKE A TICK AND START SQUEEZING OUT CALVES LIKE ELSIE MAINLINING FERTILITY DRUGS...
DO WE *UNDERSTAND* EACH OTHER?
UNTIL WE CAN BE *CERTAIN* THAT ONE OF OUR TEMPS DIDN'T BURN DOWN HER LAST PLACE OF EMPLOYMENT BY *"PLAYING WITH FIRE,"* THERE'S NOTHING I CAN DO.
A: WHEN MY FATHER'S DC-3 TRAGICALLY CRASHED UNDER AS YET UNEXPLAINED AND MYSTERIOUS CIRCUMSTANCES I *SWORE* THAT I WOULD NEVER LOSE THE ONLY MEMENTO HE LEFT BEHIND-- WHICH LEADS DRECTLY TO *B: I DID NOT CAUSE THAT EXPLOSION!*

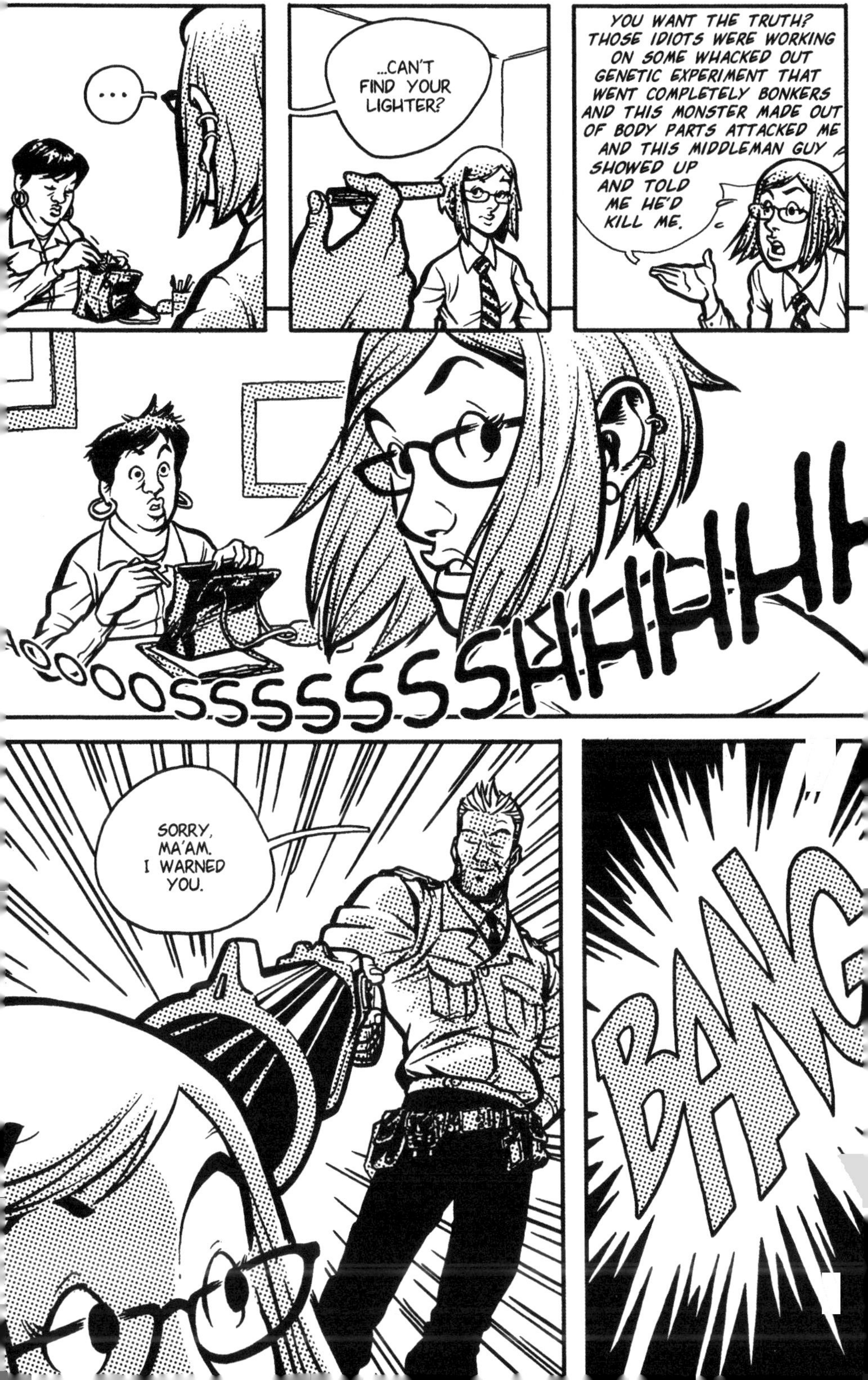
...
...CAN'T FIND YOUR LIGHTER?
YOU WANT THE TRUTH? THOSE IDIOTS WERE WORKING ON SOME WHACKED OUT GENETIC EXPERIMENT THAT WENT COMPLETELY BONKERS AND THIS MONSTER MADE OUT OF BODY PARTS ATTACKED ME AND THIS MIDDLEMAN GUY SHOWED UP AND TOLD ME HE'D KILL ME.
OOOOSSSSSSSSHHHHHHH
SORRY, MA'AM. I WARNED YOU.
BANG

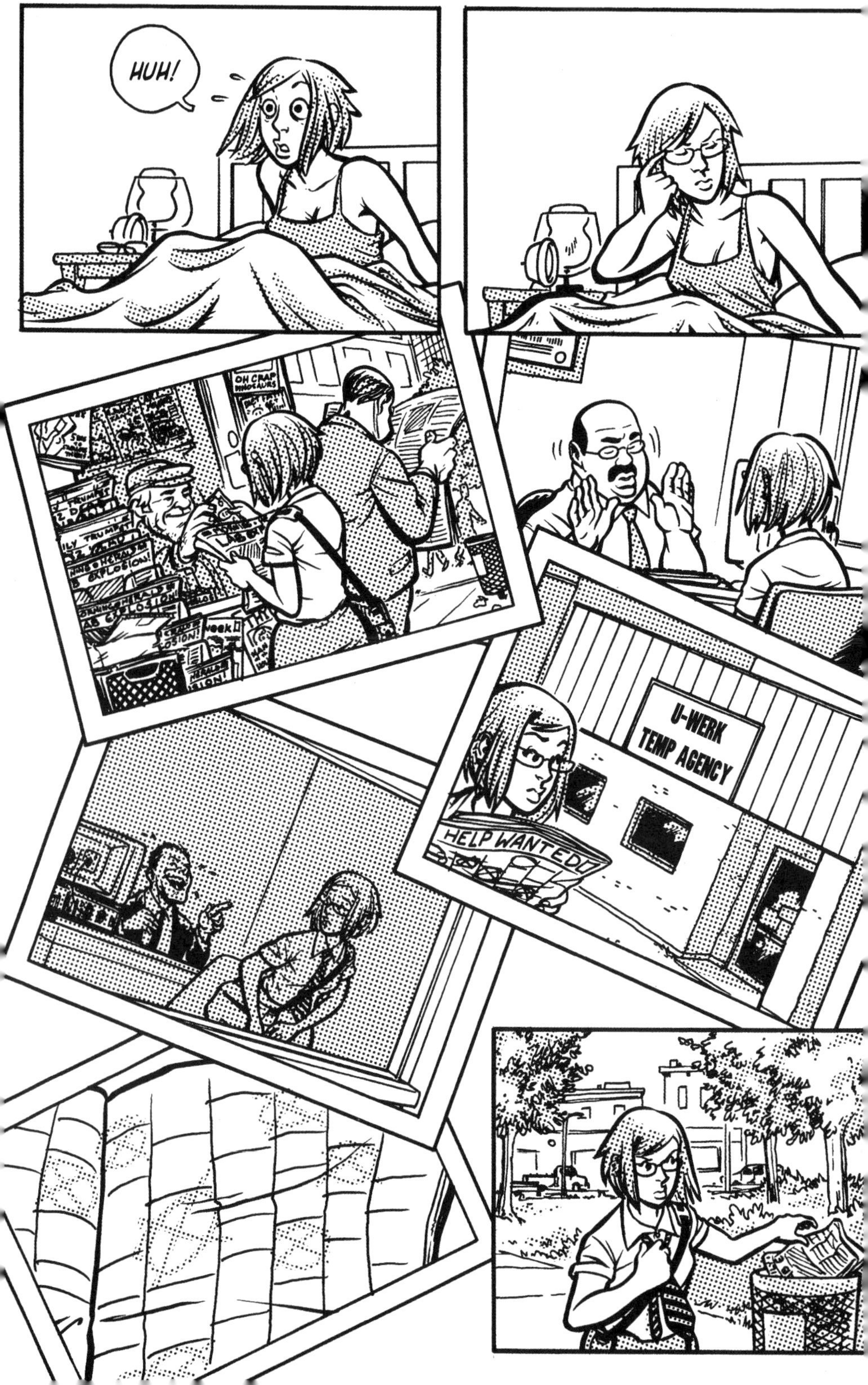
HUH!
OH CRAP DINOSAURS
U-WERK TEMP AGENCY
HELP WANTED

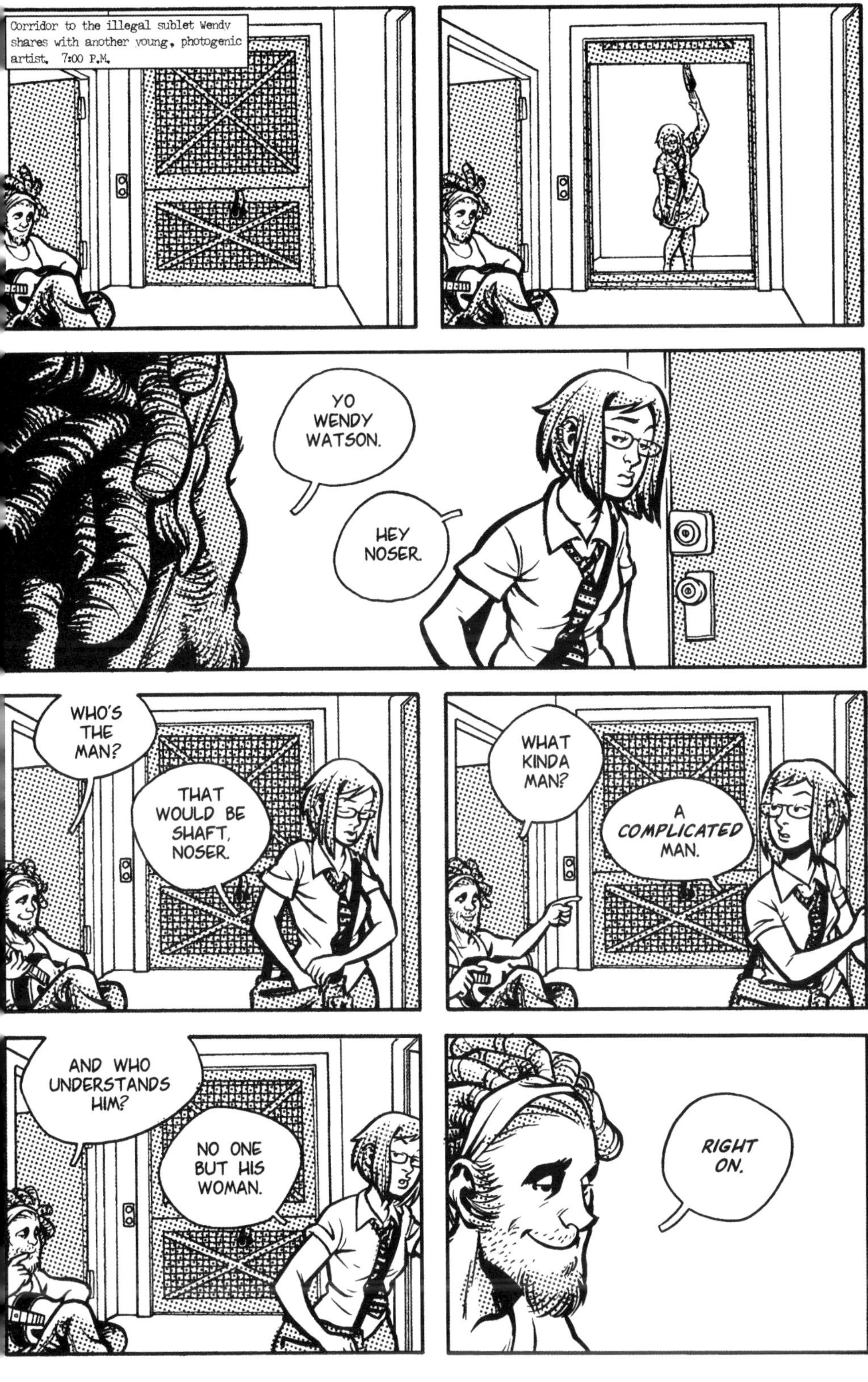
Corridor to the illegal sublet Wendy shares with another young, photogenic artist. 7:00 P.M.
YO WENDY WATSON.
HEY NOSER.
WHO'S THE MAN?
THAT WOULD BE SHAFT, NOSER.
WHAT KINDA MAN?
A COMPLICATED MAN.
AND WHO UNDERSTANDS HIM?
NO ONE BUT HIS WOMAN.
RIGHT ON.

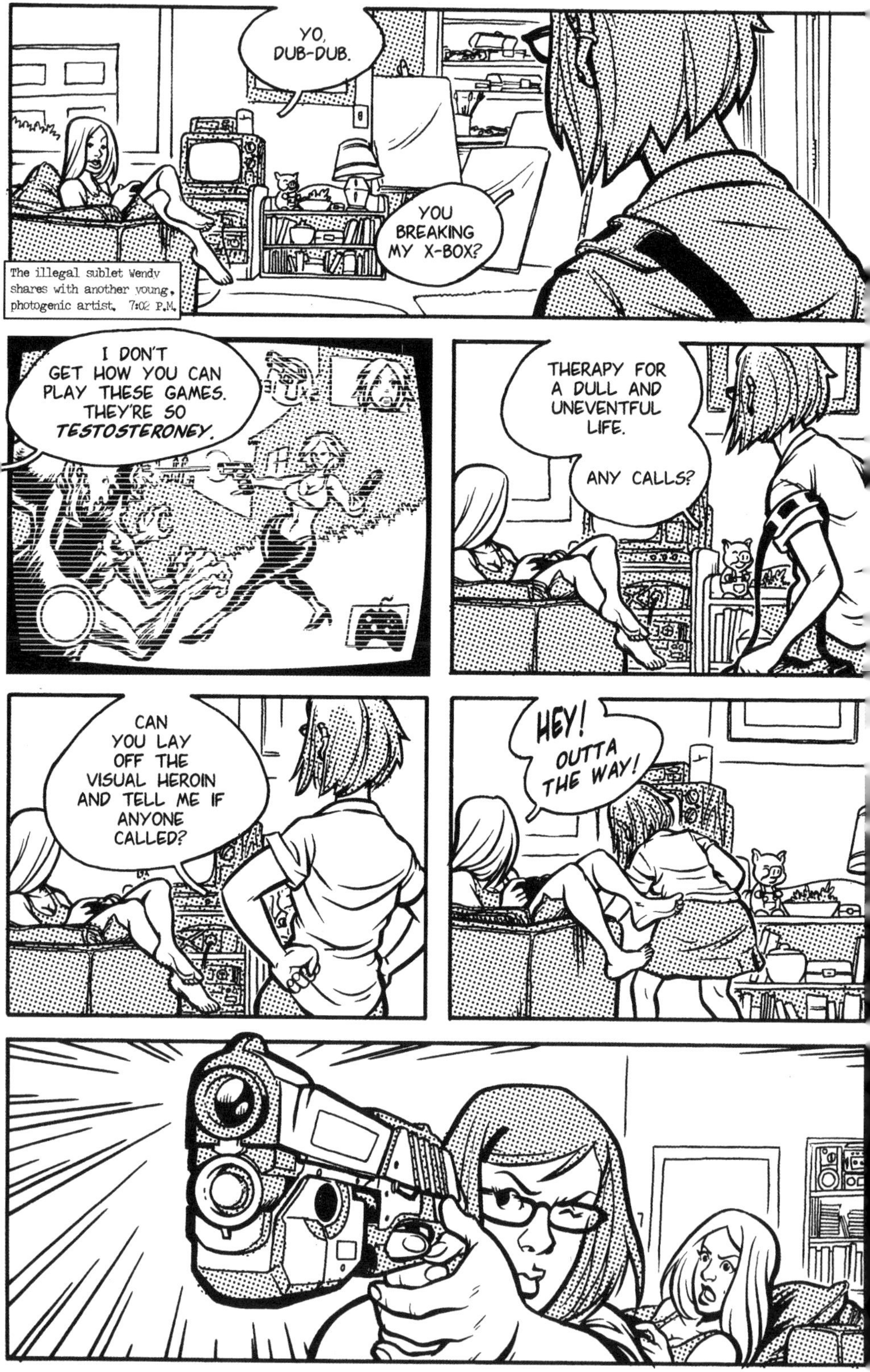
YO, DUB-DUB.
YOU BREAKING MY X-BOX?
The illegal sublet Wendy shares with another young, photogenic artist. 7:02 P.M.
I DON'T GET HOW YOU CAN PLAY THESE GAMES. THEY'RE SO TESTOSTERONEY.
THERAPY FOR A DULL AND UNEVENTFUL LIFE.
ANY CALLS?
CAN YOU LAY OFF THE VISUAL HEROIN AND TELL ME IF ANYONE CALLED?
HEY! OUTTA THE WAY!

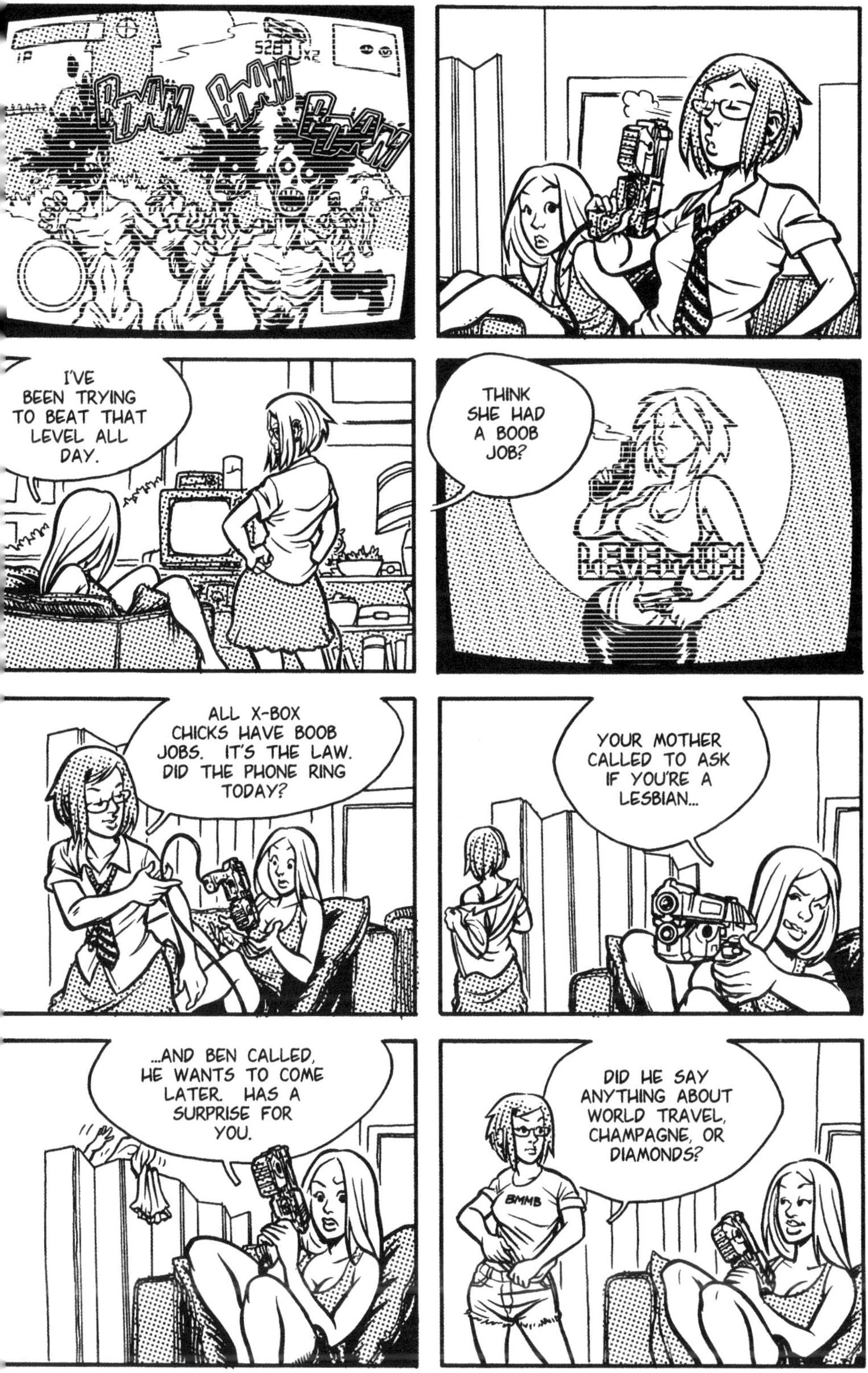
I'VE BEEN TRYING TO BEAT THAT LEVEL ALL DAY.
THINK SHE HAD A BOOB JOB?
ALL X-BOX CHICKS HAVE BOOB JOBS. IT'S THE LAW. DID THE PHONE RING TODAY?
YOUR MOTHER CALLED TO ASK IF YOU'RE A LESBIAN...
...AND BEN CALLED, HE WANTS TO COME LATER. HAS A SURPRISE FOR YOU.
DID HE SAY ANYTHING ABOUT WORLD TRAVEL, CHAMPAGNE, OR DIAMONDS?
BMMB

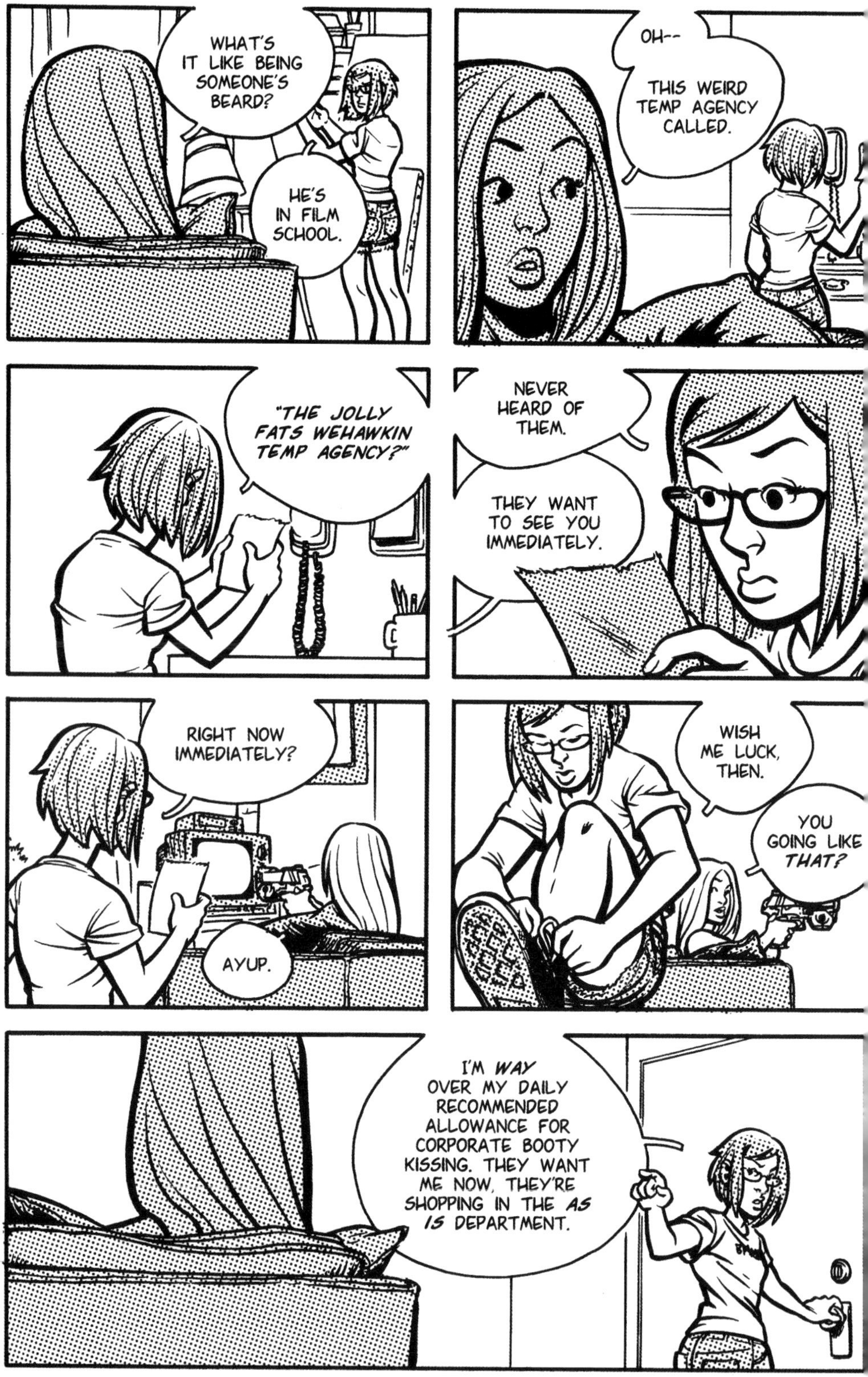
WHAT'S IT LIKE BEING SOMEONE'S BEARD?
HE'S IN FILM SCHOOL.
OH--
THIS WEIRD TEMP AGENCY CALLED.
"THE JOLLY FATS WEHAWKIN TEMP AGENCY?"
NEVER HEARD OF THEM.
THEY WANT TO SEE YOU IMMEDIATELY.
RIGHT NOW IMMEDIATELY?
AYUP.
WISH ME LUCK, THEN.
YOU GOING LIKE *THAT?*
I'M *WAY* OVER MY DAILY RECOMMENDED ALLOWANCE FOR CORPORATE BOOTY KISSING. THEY WANT ME NOW, THEY'RE SHOPPING IN THE *AS IS* DEPARTMENT.

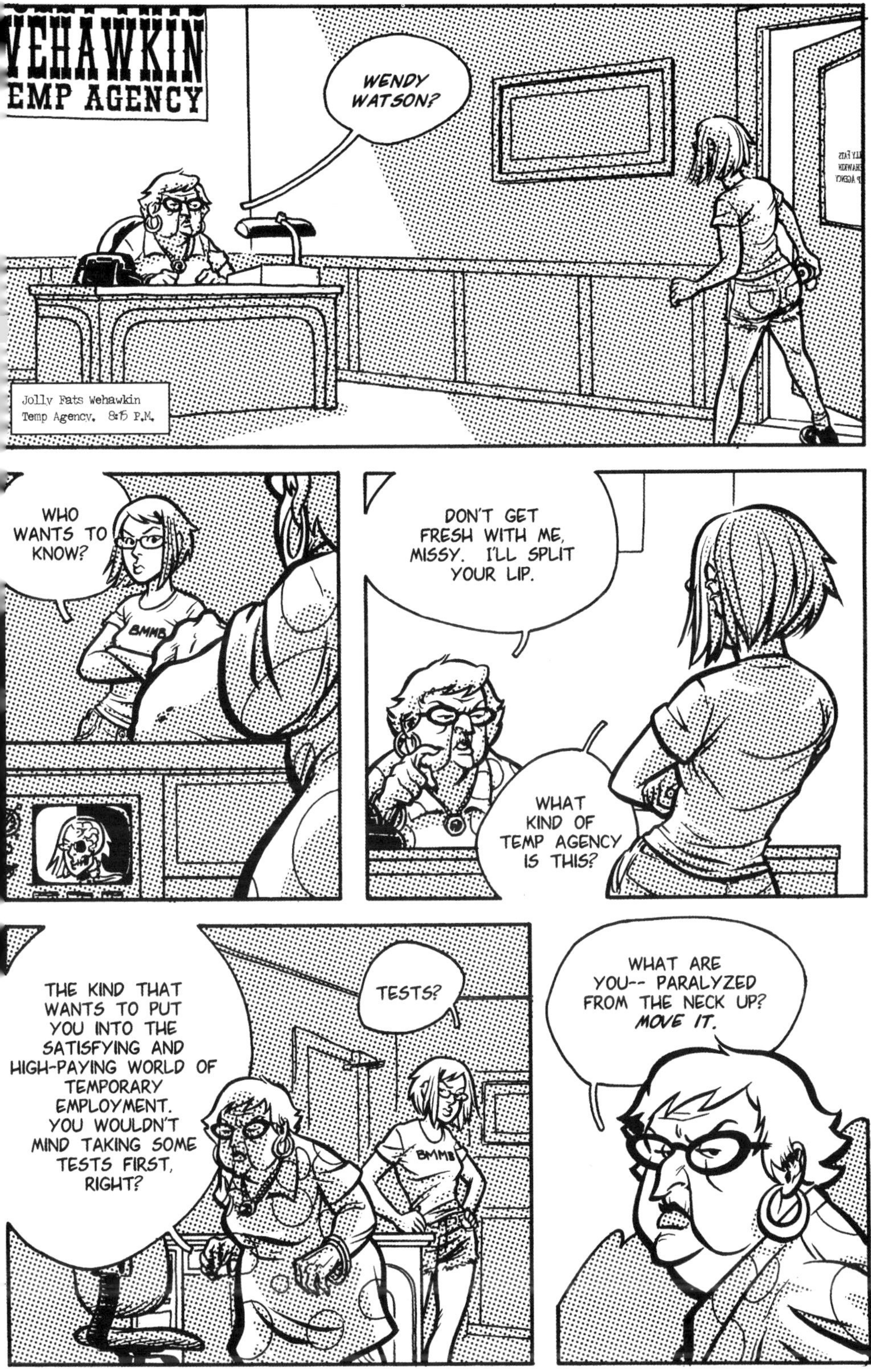

VEHAWKIN
EMP AGENCY
WENDY WATSON?
Jolly Fats Wehawkin Temp Agency. 8:15 P.M.
WHO WANTS TO KNOW?
BMMB
DON'T GET FRESH WITH ME, MISSY. I'LL SPLIT YOUR LIP.
WHAT KIND OF TEMP AGENCY IS THIS?
THE KIND THAT WANTS TO PUT YOU INTO THE SATISFYING AND HIGH-PAYING WORLD OF TEMPORARY EMPLOYMENT. YOU WOULDN'T MIND TAKING SOME TESTS FIRST, RIGHT?
TESTS?
BMMB
WHAT ARE YOU-- PARALYZED FROM THE NECK UP? *MOVE IT.*

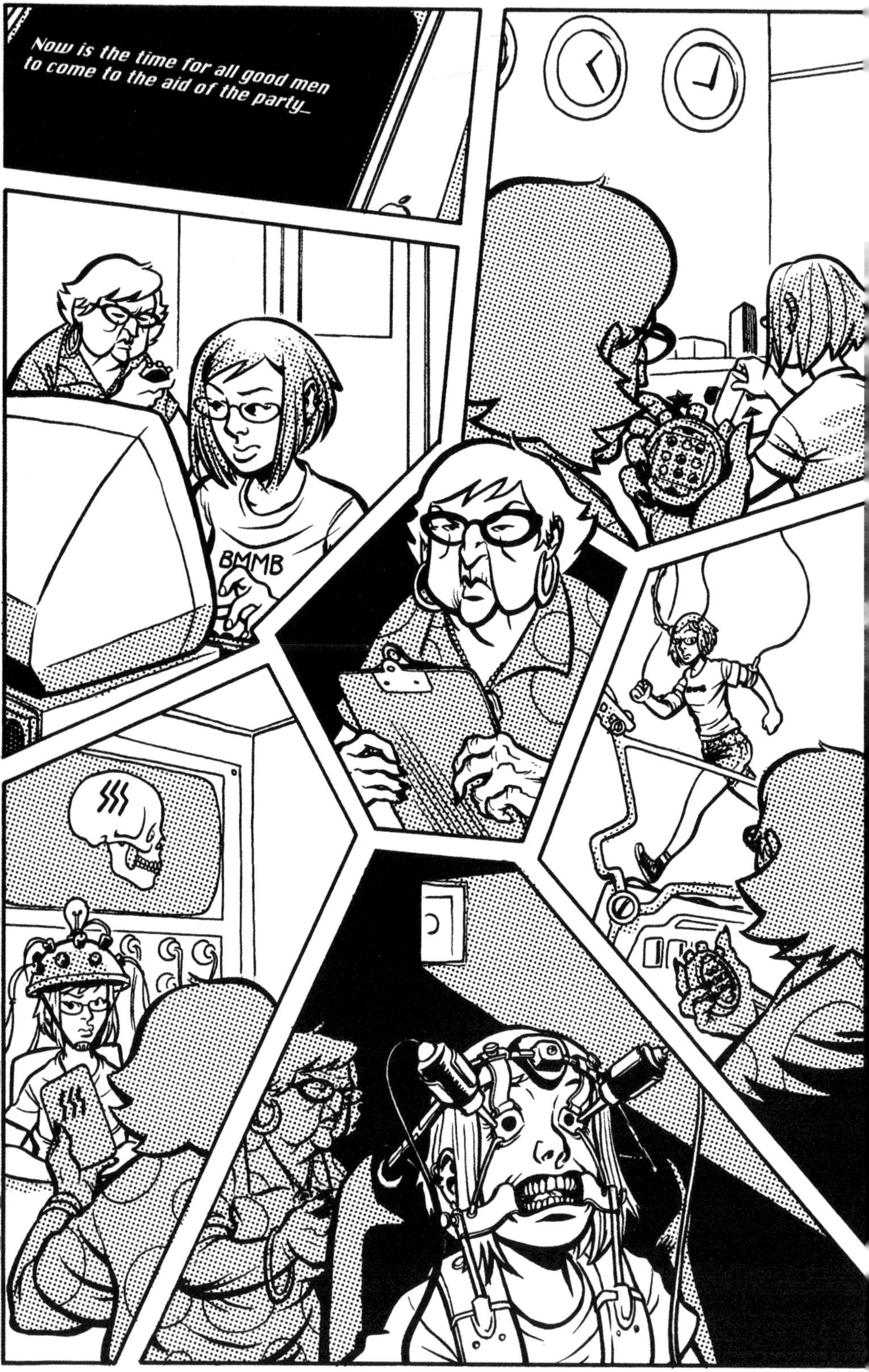
Now is the time for all good men
to come to the aid of the party_
BMMB

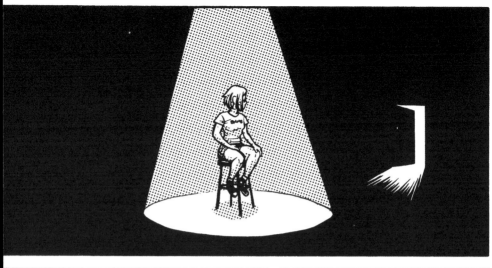

SO...
WHAT'S NEXT?

TARGET PRACTICE? OBSTACLE COURSE? CAVITY SEARCH?

DON'T LET YOUR PIE-HOLE TALK YOU OUT OF A JOB, YOUNG LADY.

WENDY WATSON.

MEET YOUR NEW BOSS.

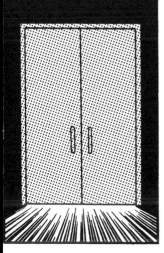

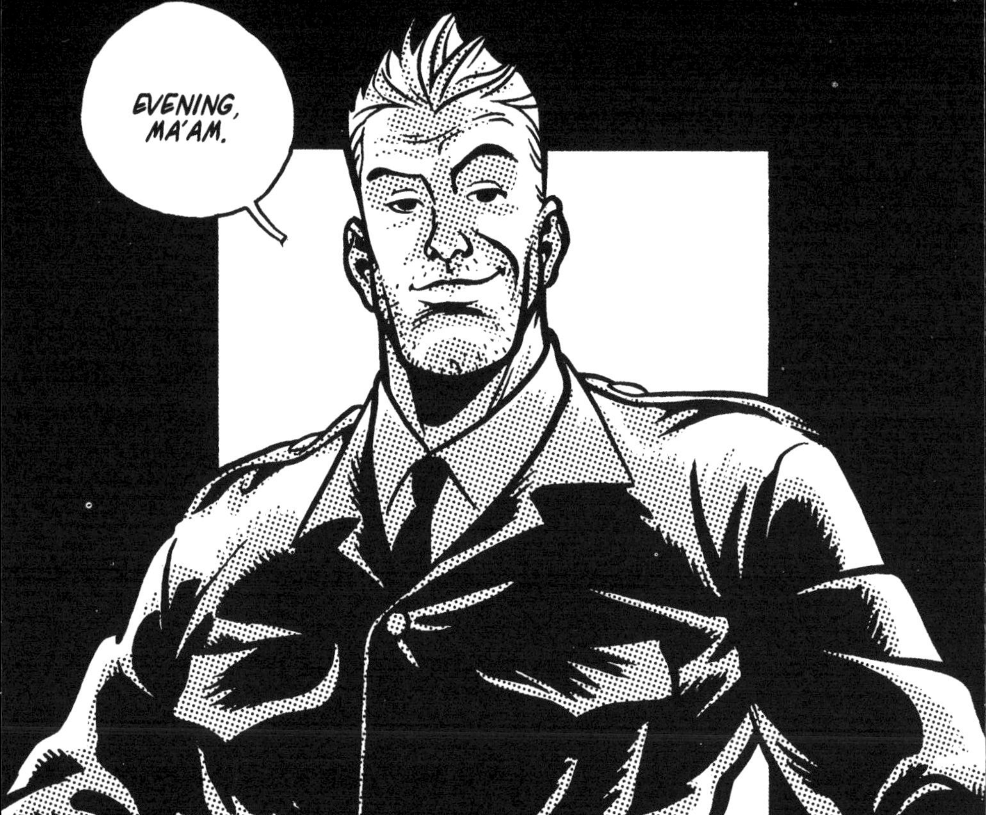
EVENING, MA'AM.

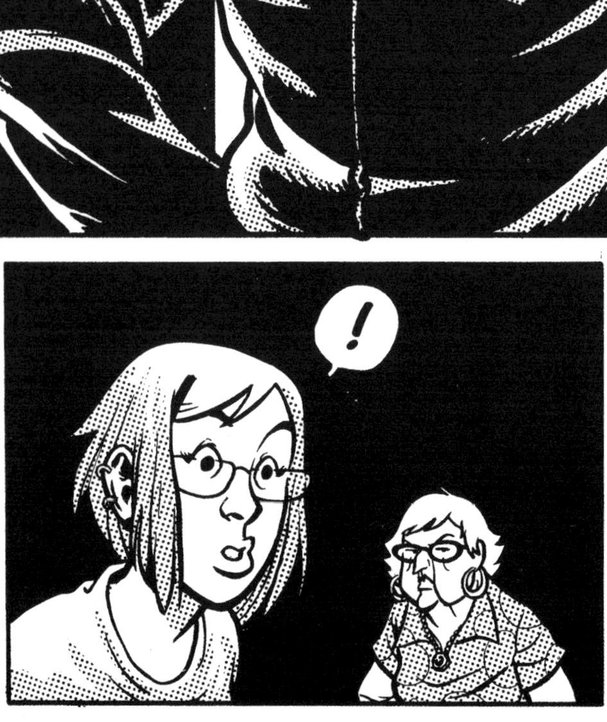
!

next issue:

THE SECRET RECRUITMENT ULTIMATUM

CHAPTER 02

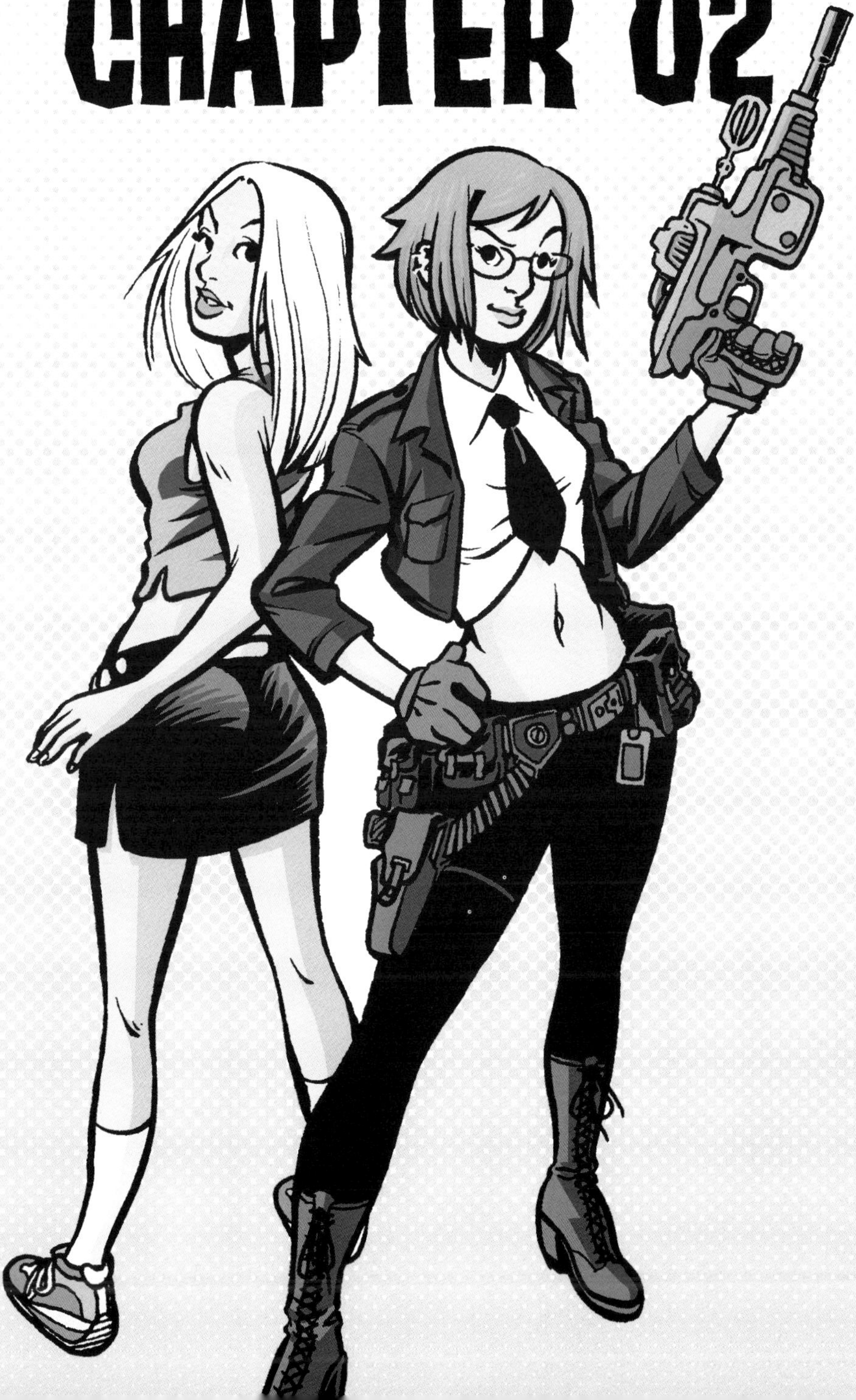

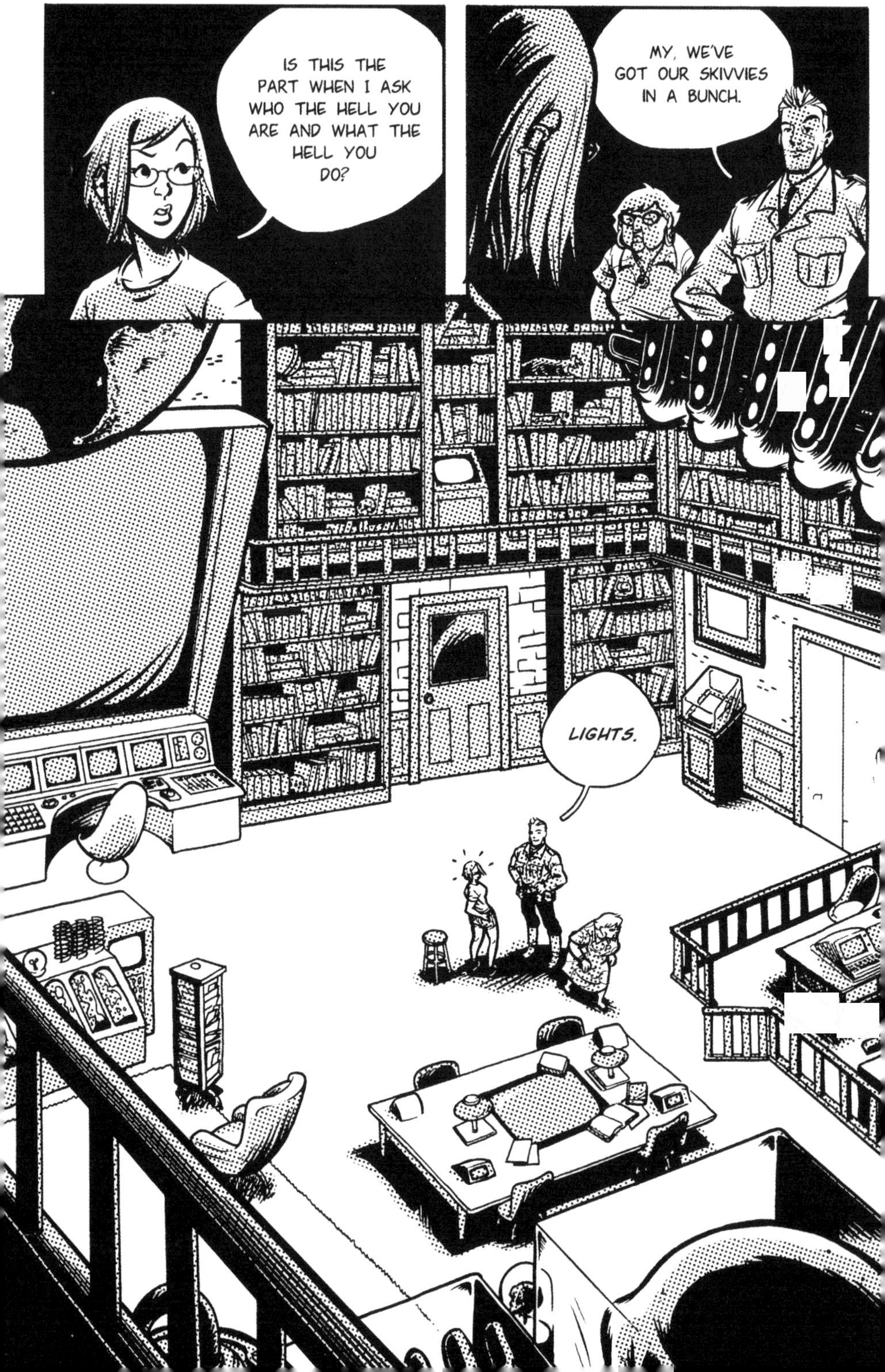
IS THIS THE PART WHEN I ASK WHO THE HELL YOU ARE AND WHAT THE HELL YOU DO?
MY, WE'VE GOT OUR SKIVVIES IN A BUNCH.
LIGHTS.

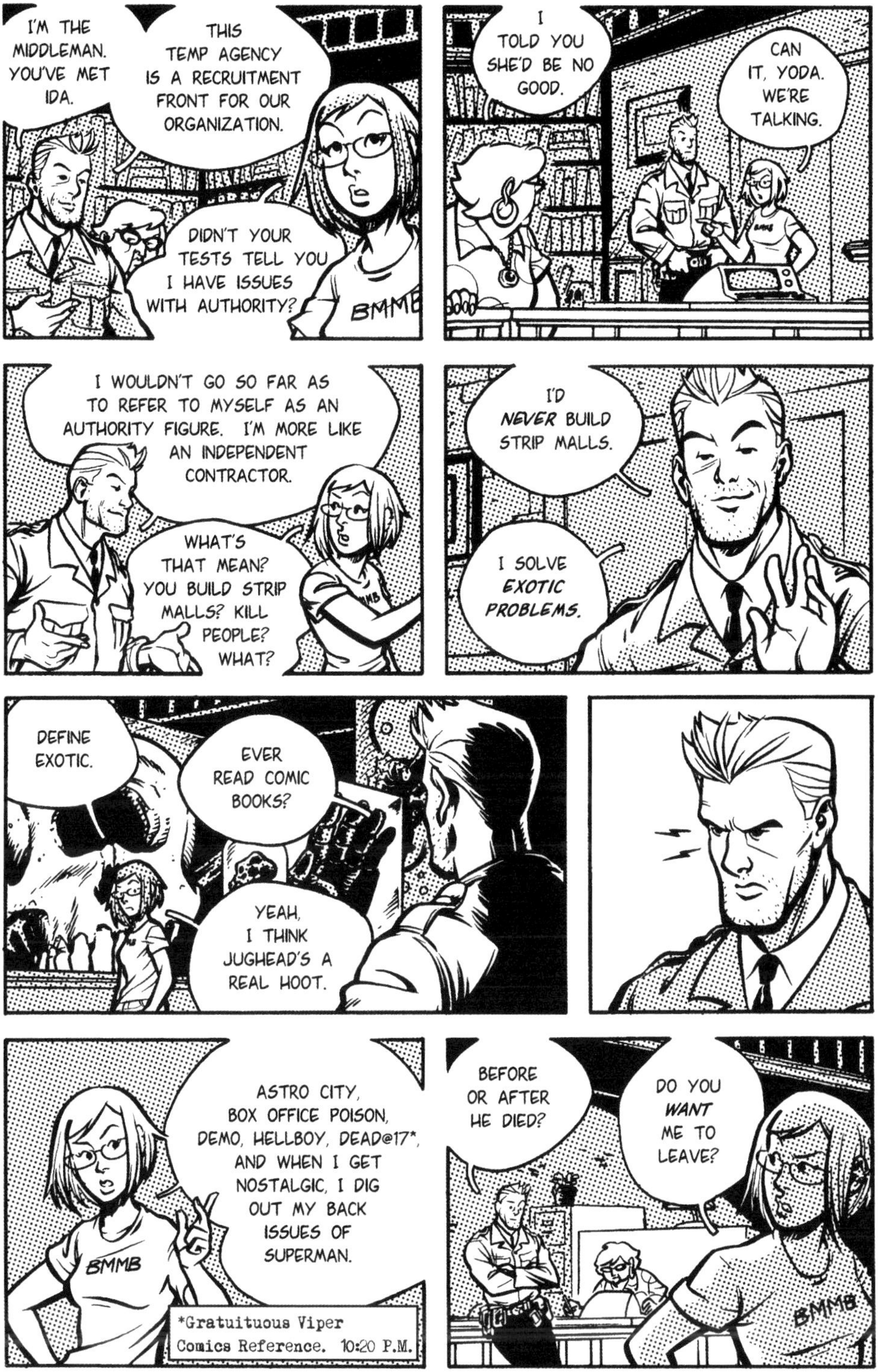
I'M THE MIDDLEMAN. YOU'VE MET IDA.
THIS TEMP AGENCY IS A RECRUITMENT FRONT FOR OUR ORGANIZATION.
DIDN'T YOUR TESTS TELL YOU I HAVE ISSUES WITH AUTHORITY?
BMMB
I TOLD YOU SHE'D BE NO GOOD.
CAN IT, YODA. WE'RE TALKING.
I WOULDN'T GO SO FAR AS TO REFER TO MYSELF AS AN AUTHORITY FIGURE. I'M MORE LIKE AN INDEPENDENT CONTRACTOR.
WHAT'S THAT MEAN? YOU BUILD STRIP MALLS? KILL PEOPLE? WHAT?
I'D NEVER BUILD STRIP MALLS.
I SOLVE EXOTIC PROBLEMS.
DEFINE EXOTIC.
EVER READ COMIC BOOKS?
YEAH, I THINK JUGHEAD'S A REAL HOOT.
ASTRO CITY, BOX OFFICE POISON, DEMO, HELLBOY, DEAD@17*, AND WHEN I GET NOSTALGIC, I DIG OUT MY BACK ISSUES OF SUPERMAN.
BMMB
*Gratuituous Viper Comics Reference. 10:20 P.M.
BEFORE OR AFTER HE DIED?
DO YOU WANT ME TO LEAVE?
BMMB

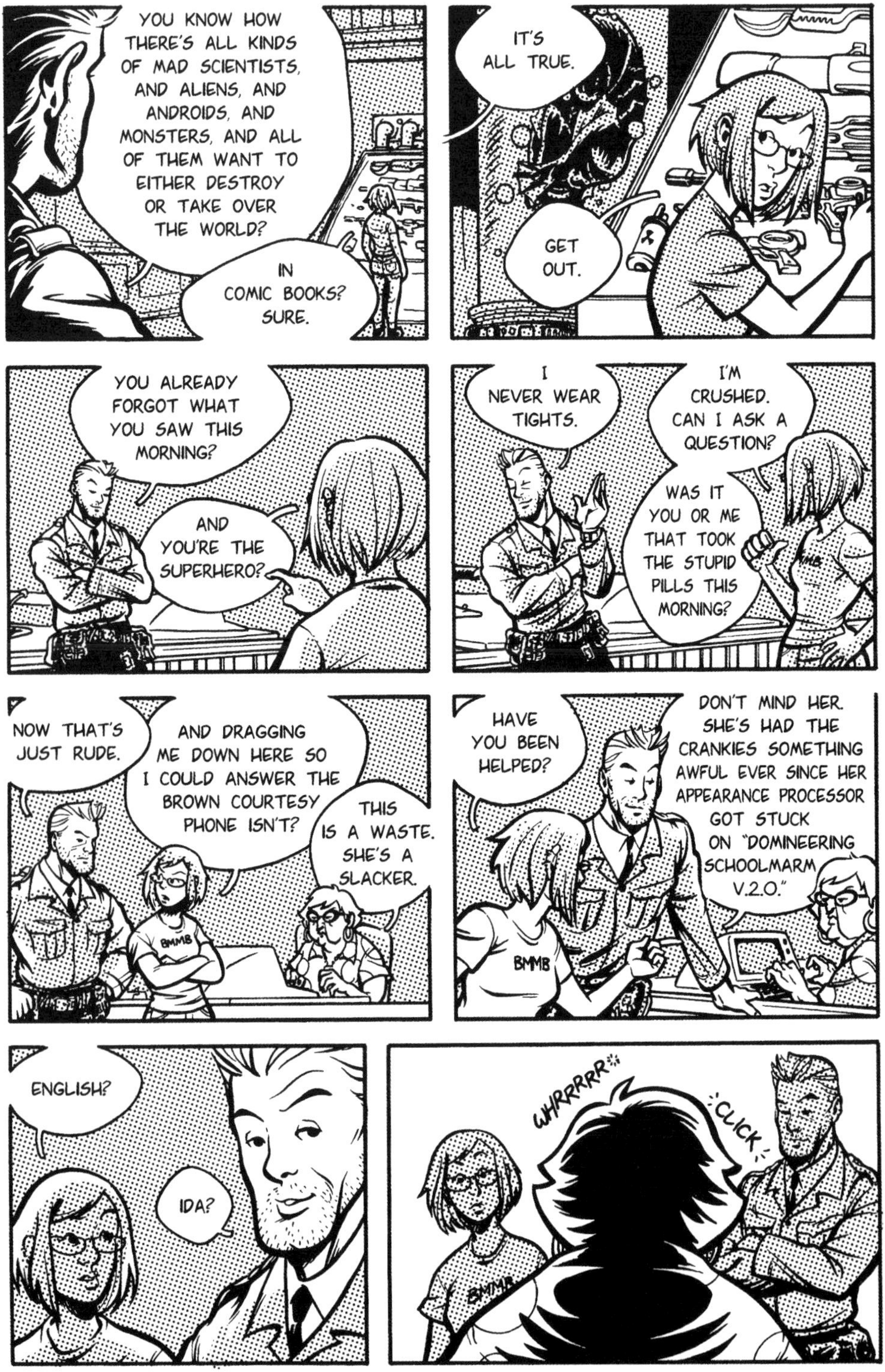
YOU KNOW HOW THERE'S ALL KINDS OF MAD SCIENTISTS, AND ALIENS, AND ANDROIDS, AND MONSTERS, AND ALL OF THEM WANT TO EITHER DESTROY OR TAKE OVER THE WORLD?
IN COMIC BOOKS? SURE.
IT'S ALL TRUE.
GET OUT.
YOU ALREADY FORGOT WHAT YOU SAW THIS MORNING?
AND YOU'RE THE SUPERHERO?
I NEVER WEAR TIGHTS.
I'M CRUSHED. CAN I ASK A QUESTION?
WAS IT YOU OR ME THAT TOOK THE STUPID PILLS THIS MORNING?
NOW THAT'S JUST RUDE.
AND DRAGGING ME DOWN HERE SO I COULD ANSWER THE BROWN COURTESY PHONE ISN'T?
THIS IS A WASTE. SHE'S A SLACKER.
HAVE YOU BEEN HELPED?
DON'T MIND HER. SHE'S HAD THE CRANKIES SOMETHING AWFUL EVER SINCE HER APPEARANCE PROCESSOR GOT STUCK ON "DOMINEERING SCHOOLMARM V.2.0."
BMMB
ENGLISH?
IDA?
WHRRRRR
CLICK

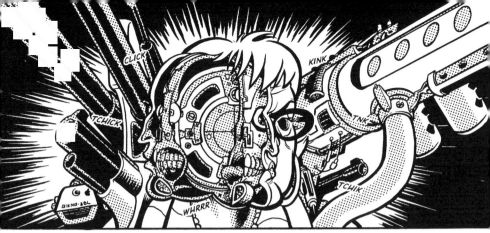

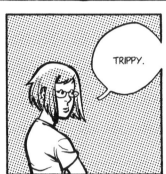

CLICK
KINK
TCHICK
TNK
TCHIK
WHRRR
TRIPPY.
DAGNABBIT, THAT'S WHY YOU'RE HERE!
YOU WITNESSED SOMETHING COMPLETELY OUT OF THE PARAMETERS OF REALITY AND DIDN'T EVEN FLINCH!
OBSERVE:
HOW'D YOU FILM THAT?
REAL TIME HOLO-RECORDING.
WHY OF COURSE.
LOOK, RIGHT THERE... THAT SLIMY TENDRIL GRABS YOU, AND WHAT DO YOU DO..?

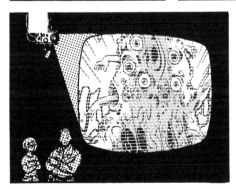

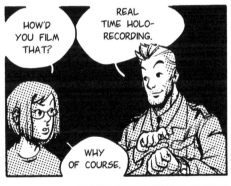

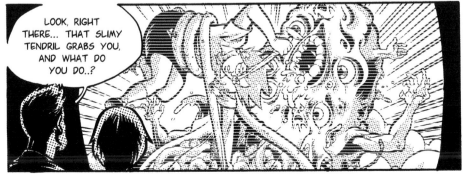

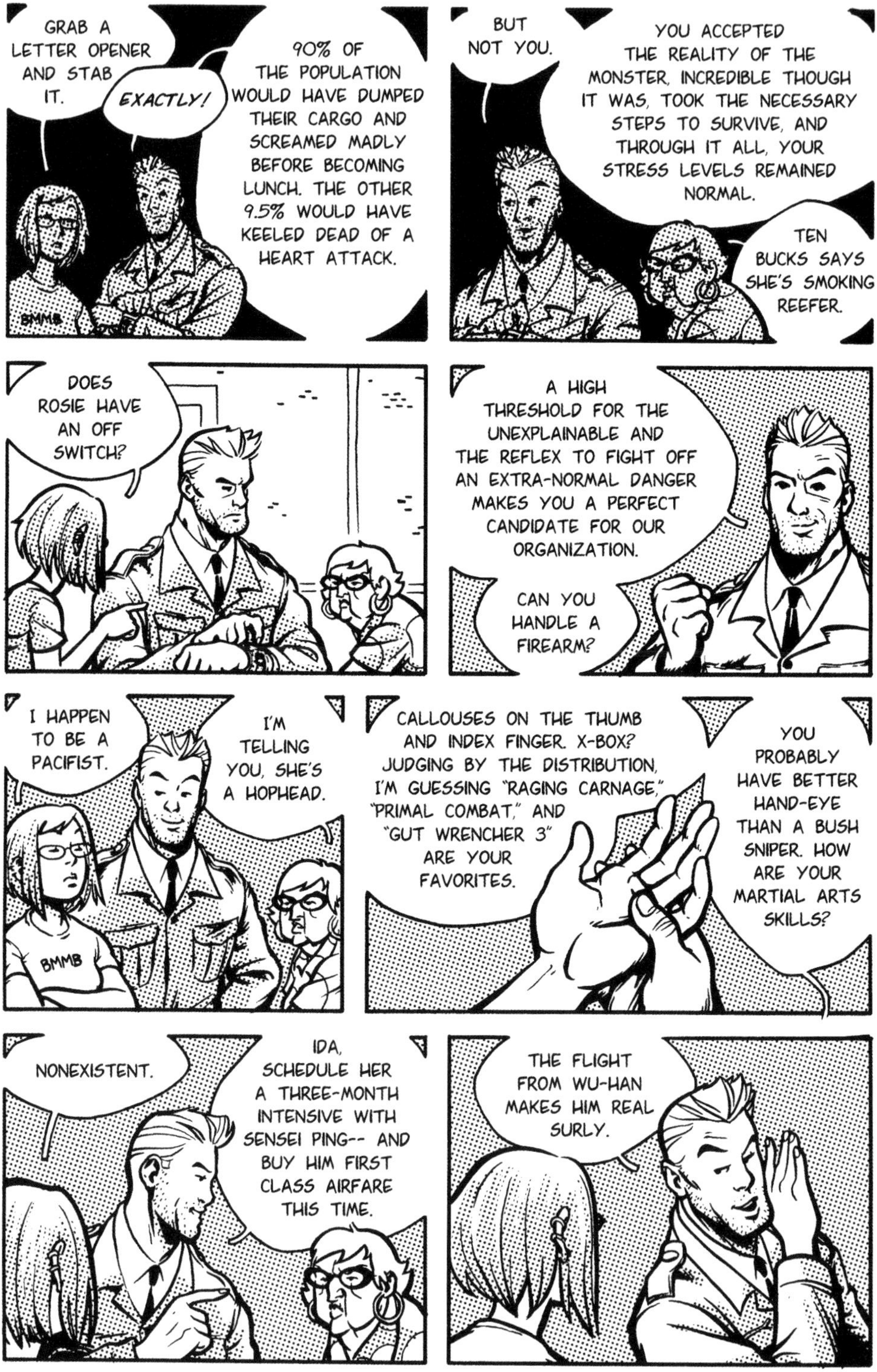
GRAB A LETTER OPENER AND STAB IT.
EXACTLY!
90% OF THE POPULATION WOULD HAVE DUMPED THEIR CARGO AND SCREAMED MADLY BEFORE BECOMING LUNCH. THE OTHER 9.5% WOULD HAVE KEELED DEAD OF A HEART ATTACK.
BMMB
BUT NOT YOU.
YOU ACCEPTED THE REALITY OF THE MONSTER, INCREDIBLE THOUGH IT WAS, TOOK THE NECESSARY STEPS TO SURVIVE, AND THROUGH IT ALL, YOUR STRESS LEVELS REMAINED NORMAL.
TEN BUCKS SAYS SHE'S SMOKING REEFER.
DOES ROSIE HAVE AN OFF SWITCH?
A HIGH THRESHOLD FOR THE UNEXPLAINABLE AND THE REFLEX TO FIGHT OFF AN EXTRA-NORMAL DANGER MAKES YOU A PERFECT CANDIDATE FOR OUR ORGANIZATION.
CAN YOU HANDLE A FIREARM?
I HAPPEN TO BE A PACIFIST.
I'M TELLING YOU, SHE'S A HOPHEAD.
BMMB
CALLOUSES ON THE THUMB AND INDEX FINGER. X-BOX? JUDGING BY THE DISTRIBUTION, I'M GUESSING "RAGING CARNAGE," "PRIMAL COMBAT," AND "GUT WRENCHER 3" ARE YOUR FAVORITES.
YOU PROBABLY HAVE BETTER HAND-EYE THAN A BUSH SNIPER. HOW ARE YOUR MARTIAL ARTS SKILLS?
NONEXISTENT.
IDA, SCHEDULE HER A THREE-MONTH INTENSIVE WITH SENSEI PING-- AND BUY HIM FIRST CLASS AIRFARE THIS TIME.
THE FLIGHT FROM WU-HAN MAKES HIM REAL SURLY.

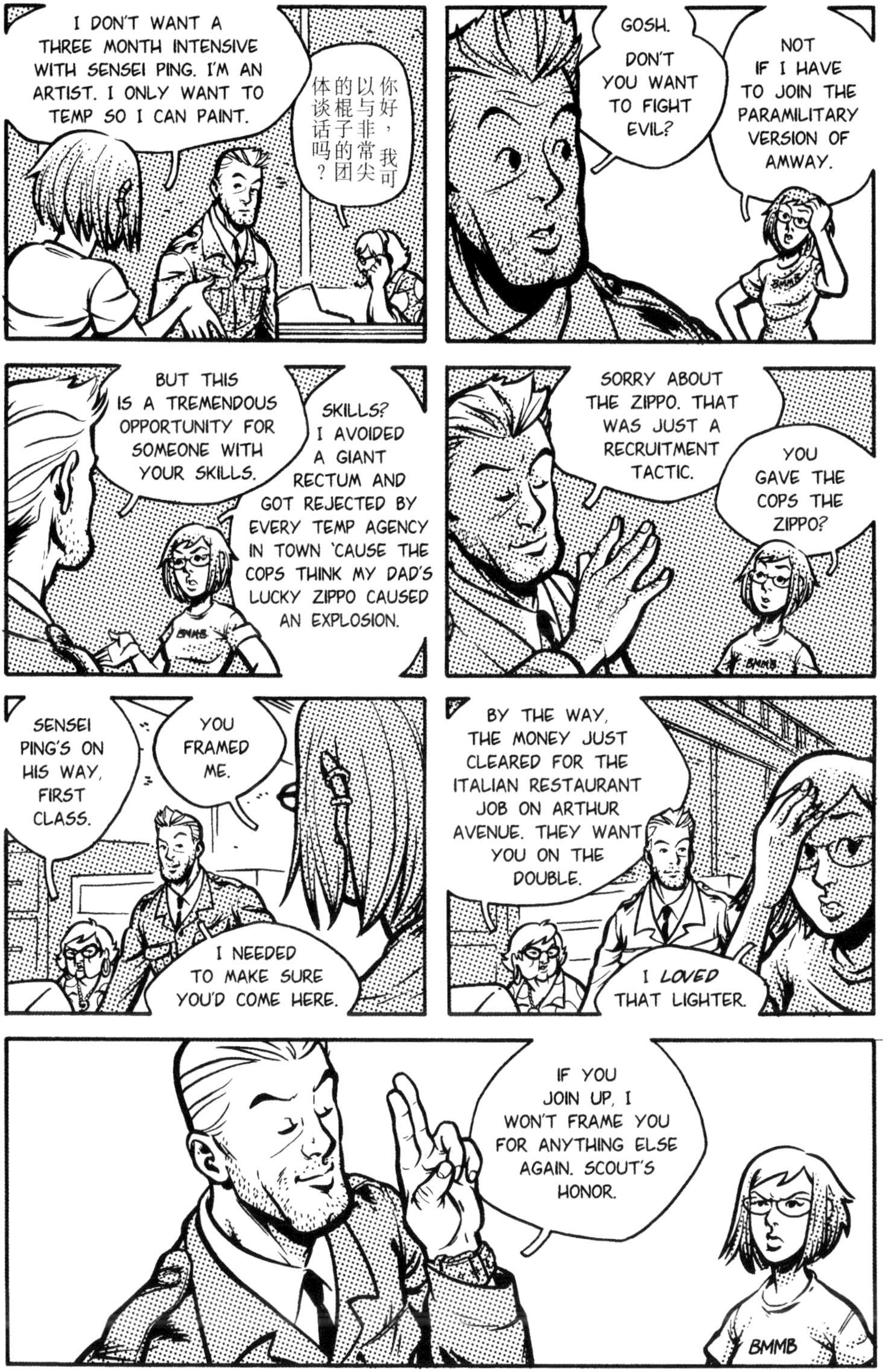
I DON'T WANT A THREE MONTH INTENSIVE WITH SENSEI PING. I'M AN ARTIST. I ONLY WANT TO TEMP SO I CAN PAINT.
你好，我可以与非常尖的棍子的团体谈话吗？
GOSH.
DON'T YOU WANT TO FIGHT EVIL?
NOT IF I HAVE TO JOIN THE PARAMILITARY VERSION OF AMWAY.
BUT THIS IS A TREMENDOUS OPPORTUNITY FOR SOMEONE WITH YOUR SKILLS.
SKILLS? I AVOIDED A GIANT RECTUM AND GOT REJECTED BY EVERY TEMP AGENCY IN TOWN 'CAUSE THE COPS THINK MY DAD'S LUCKY ZIPPO CAUSED AN EXPLOSION.
SORRY ABOUT THE ZIPPO. THAT WAS JUST A RECRUITMENT TACTIC.
YOU GAVE THE COPS THE ZIPPO?
SENSEI PING'S ON HIS WAY, FIRST CLASS.
YOU FRAMED ME.
I NEEDED TO MAKE SURE YOU'D COME HERE.
BY THE WAY, THE MONEY JUST CLEARED FOR THE ITALIAN RESTAURANT JOB ON ARTHUR AVENUE. THEY WANT YOU ON THE DOUBLE.
I *LOVED* THAT LIGHTER.
IF YOU JOIN UP, I WON'T FRAME YOU FOR ANYTHING ELSE AGAIN. SCOUT'S HONOR.
BMMB

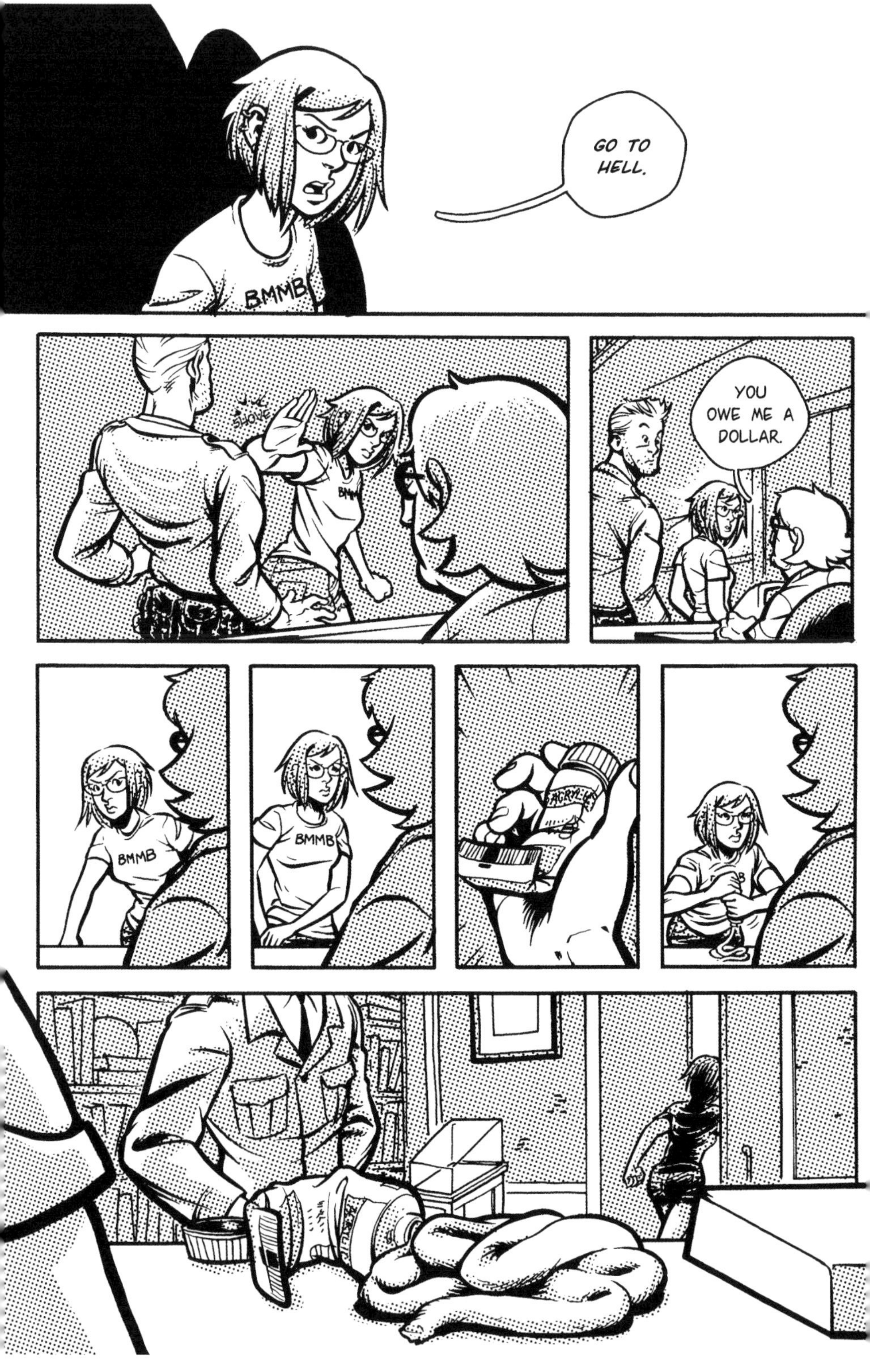
GO TO HELL.
SHOVE
YOU OWE ME A DOLLAR.
BMMB
ACRYLIC

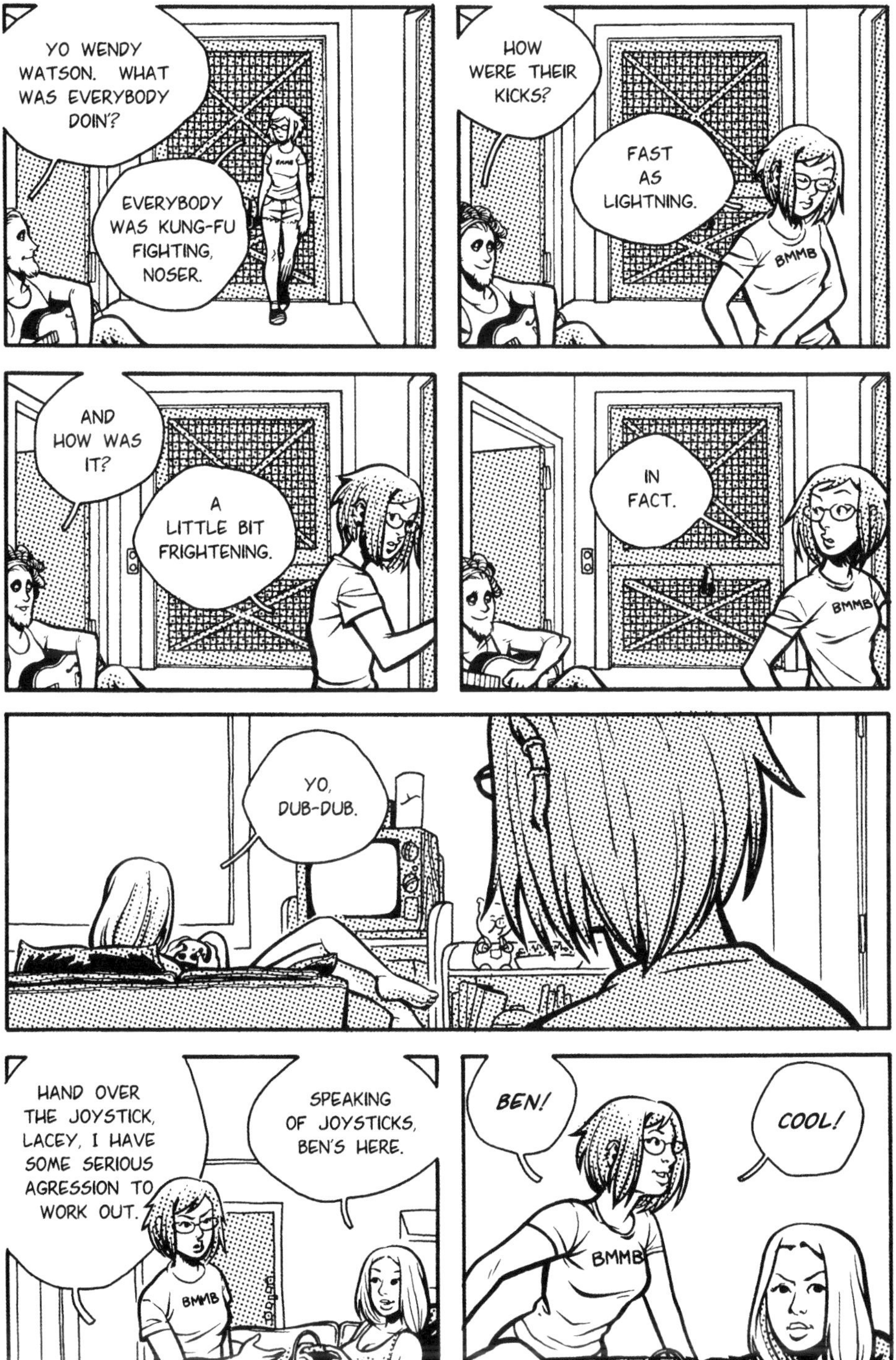
YO WENDY WATSON. WHAT WAS EVERYBODY DOIN'?
EVERYBODY WAS KUNG-FU FIGHTING, NOSER.
BMMB
HOW WERE THEIR KICKS?
FAST AS LIGHTNING.
BMMB
AND HOW WAS IT?
A LITTLE BIT FRIGHTENING.
IN FACT.
BMMB
YO, DUB-DUB.
HAND OVER THE JOYSTICK, LACEY, I HAVE SOME SERIOUS AGRESSION TO WORK OUT.
SPEAKING OF JOYSTICKS, BEN'S HERE.
BMMB
BEN!
COOL!
BMMB

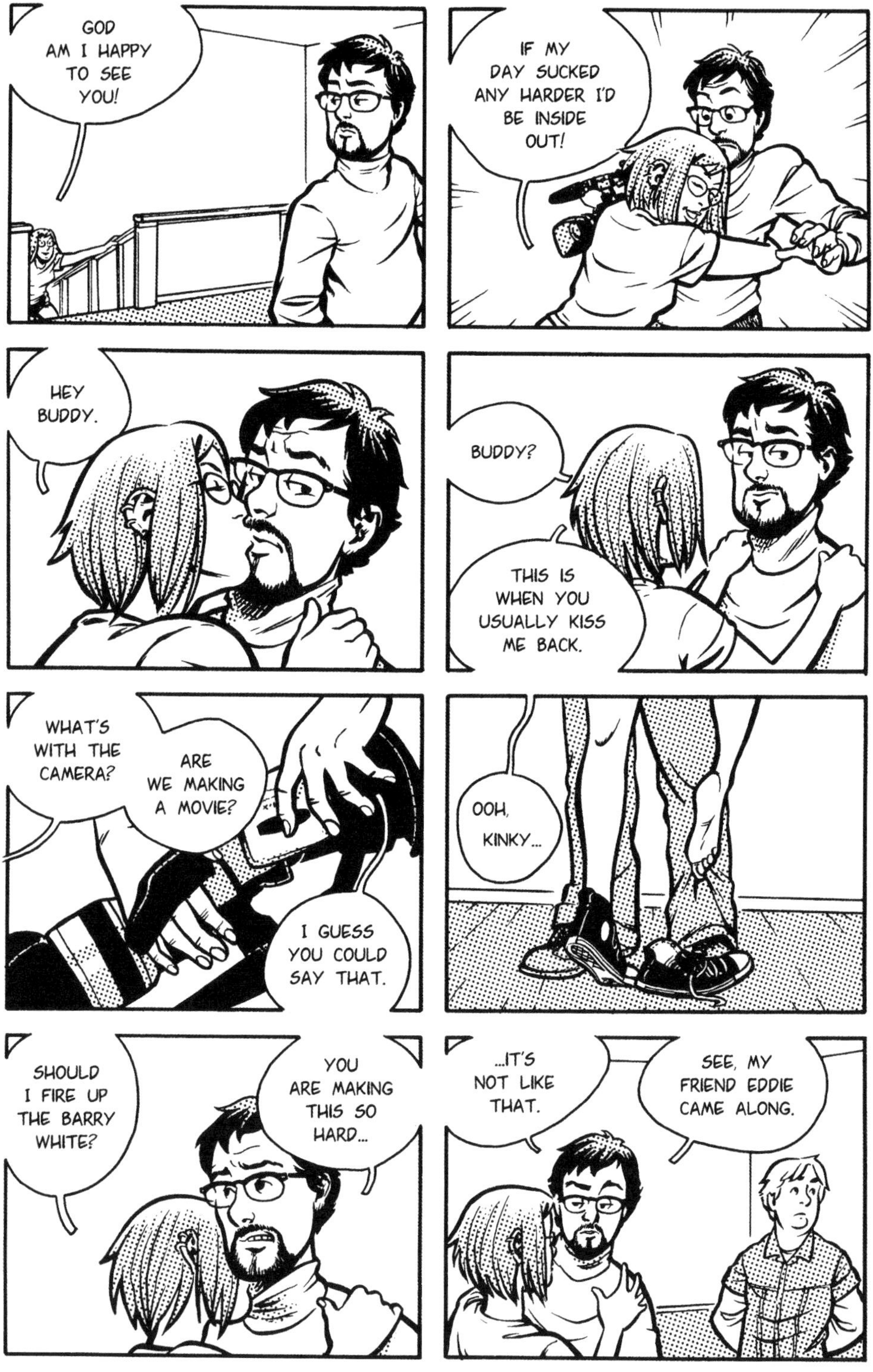
GOD AM I HAPPY TO SEE YOU!
IF MY DAY SUCKED ANY HARDER I'D BE INSIDE OUT!
HEY BUDDY.
BUDDY?
THIS IS WHEN YOU USUALLY KISS ME BACK.
WHAT'S WITH THE CAMERA?
ARE WE MAKING A MOVIE?
I GUESS YOU COULD SAY THAT.
OOH,
KINKY...
SHOULD I FIRE UP THE BARRY WHITE?
YOU ARE MAKING THIS SO HARD...
...IT'S NOT LIKE THAT.
SEE, MY FRIEND EDDIE CAME ALONG.

WHOA. HIDEOUS KINKY.

HI EDDIE.

EDDIE'S TAKING PROFESSOR HOWARD'S CINEMA VÉRITÉ CLASS WITH ME.

THE CLASS YOU'RE FLUNKING?

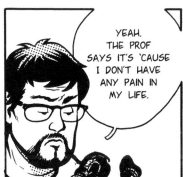

YEAH. THE PROF SAYS IT'S 'CAUSE I DON'T HAVE ANY PAIN IN MY LIFE.

I COULD PUNCH YOU.

NO... NO... IT'S NOT THAT KINKY... FIRE IT UP, EDDIE.

I JUST THINK THAT YOU AND I SHOULD ...YOU KNOW... BE JUST FRIENDS.

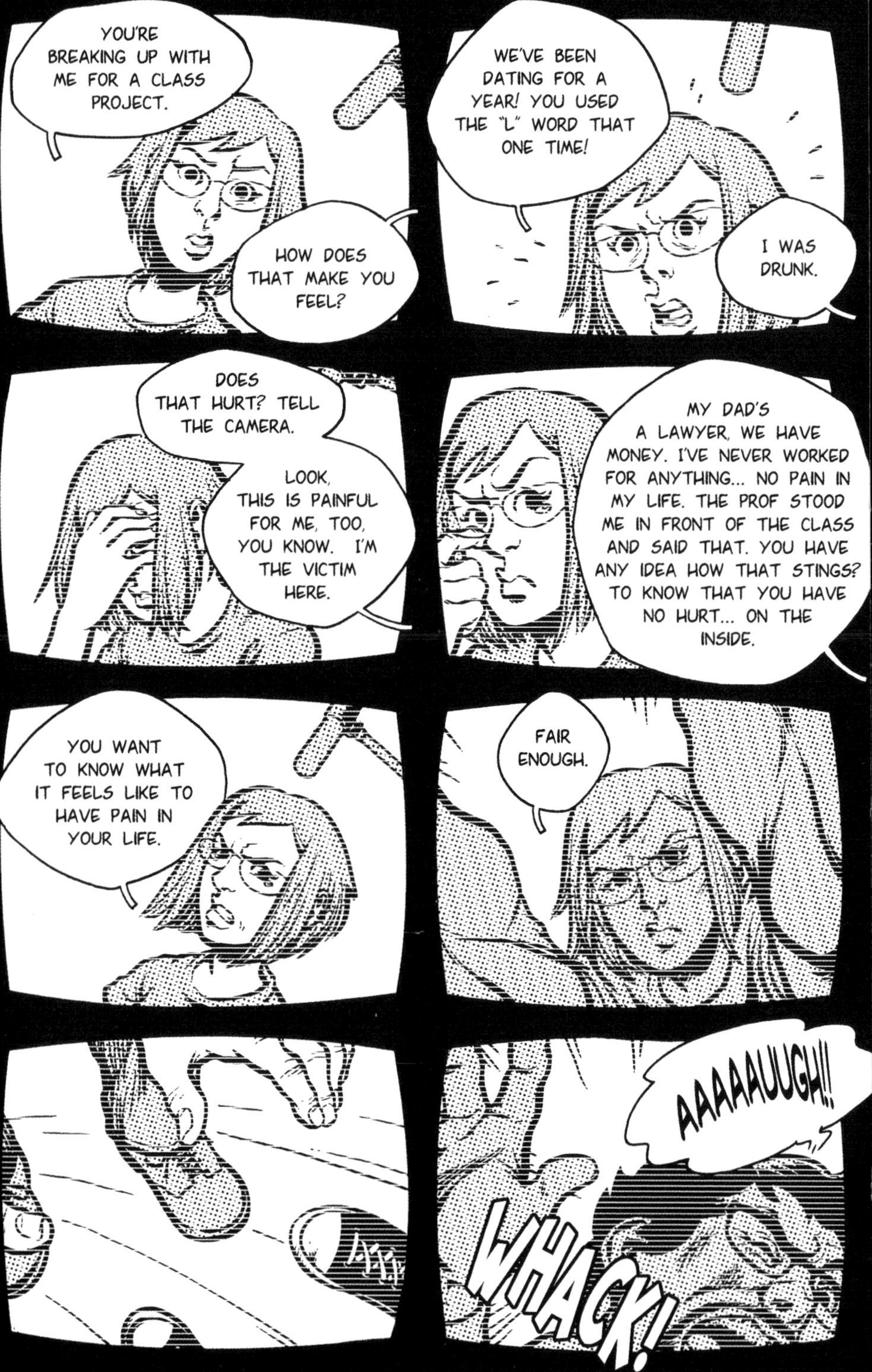
YOU'RE BREAKING UP WITH ME FOR A CLASS PROJECT.
HOW DOES THAT MAKE YOU FEEL?
WE'VE BEEN DATING FOR A YEAR! YOU USED THE "L" WORD THAT ONE TIME!
I WAS DRUNK.
DOES THAT HURT? TELL THE CAMERA.
LOOK, THIS IS PAINFUL FOR ME, TOO, YOU KNOW. I'M THE VICTIM HERE.
MY DAD'S A LAWYER, WE HAVE MONEY. I'VE NEVER WORKED FOR ANYTHING... NO PAIN IN MY LIFE. THE PROF STOOD ME IN FRONT OF THE CLASS AND SAID THAT. YOU HAVE ANY IDEA HOW THAT STINGS? TO KNOW THAT YOU HAVE NO HURT... ON THE INSIDE.
YOU WANT TO KNOW WHAT IT FEELS LIKE TO HAVE PAIN IN YOUR LIFE.
FAIR ENOUGH.
AAAAAUUGH!!
WHACK!

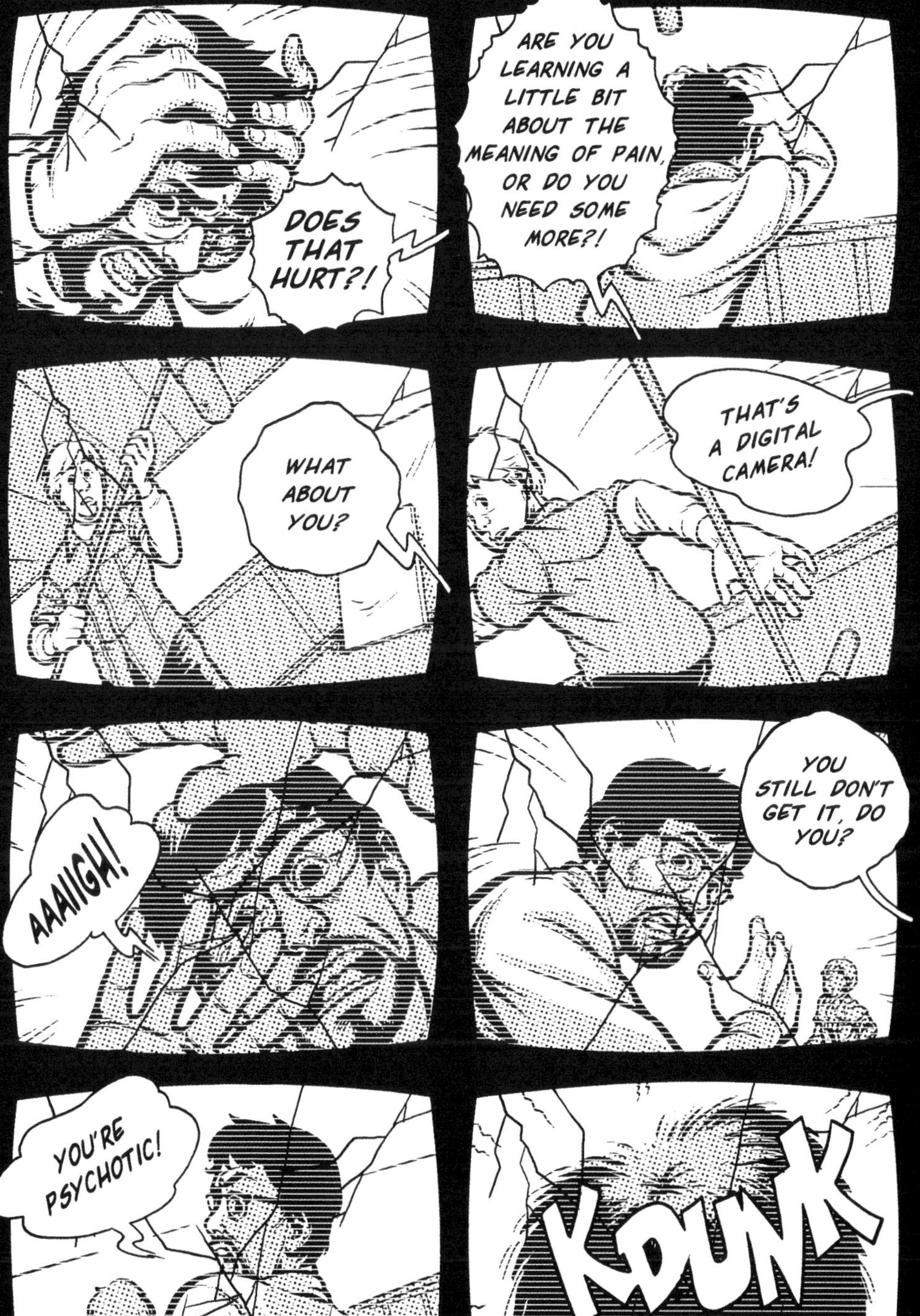
DOES THAT HURT?!
ARE YOU LEARNING A LITTLE BIT ABOUT THE MEANING OF PAIN, OR DO YOU NEED SOME MORE?!
WHAT ABOUT YOU?
THAT'S A DIGITAL CAMERA!
AAAIIGH!
YOU STILL DON'T GET IT, DO YOU?
YOU'RE PSYCHOTIC!
KDUNK

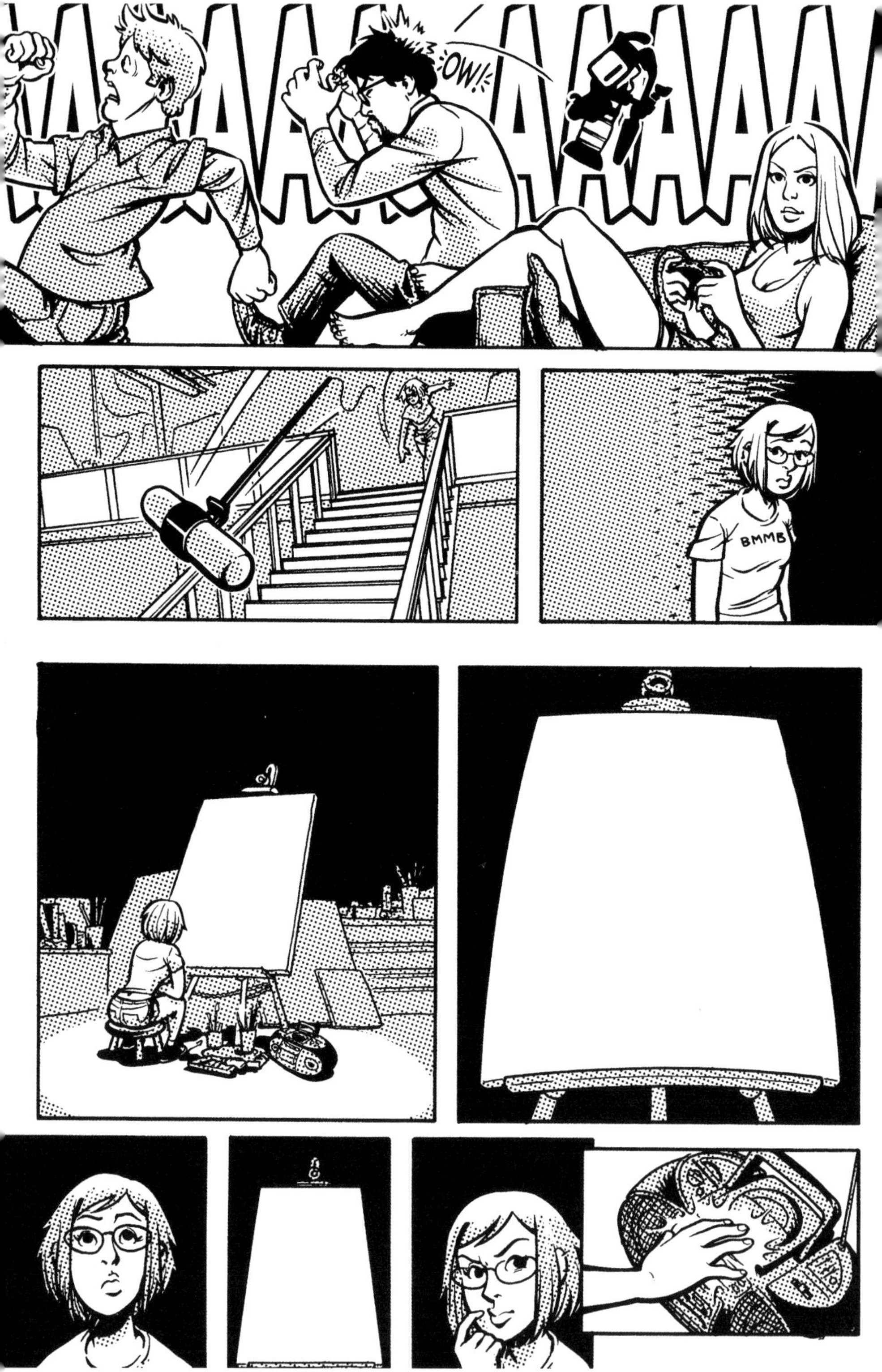
OW!
BMMB

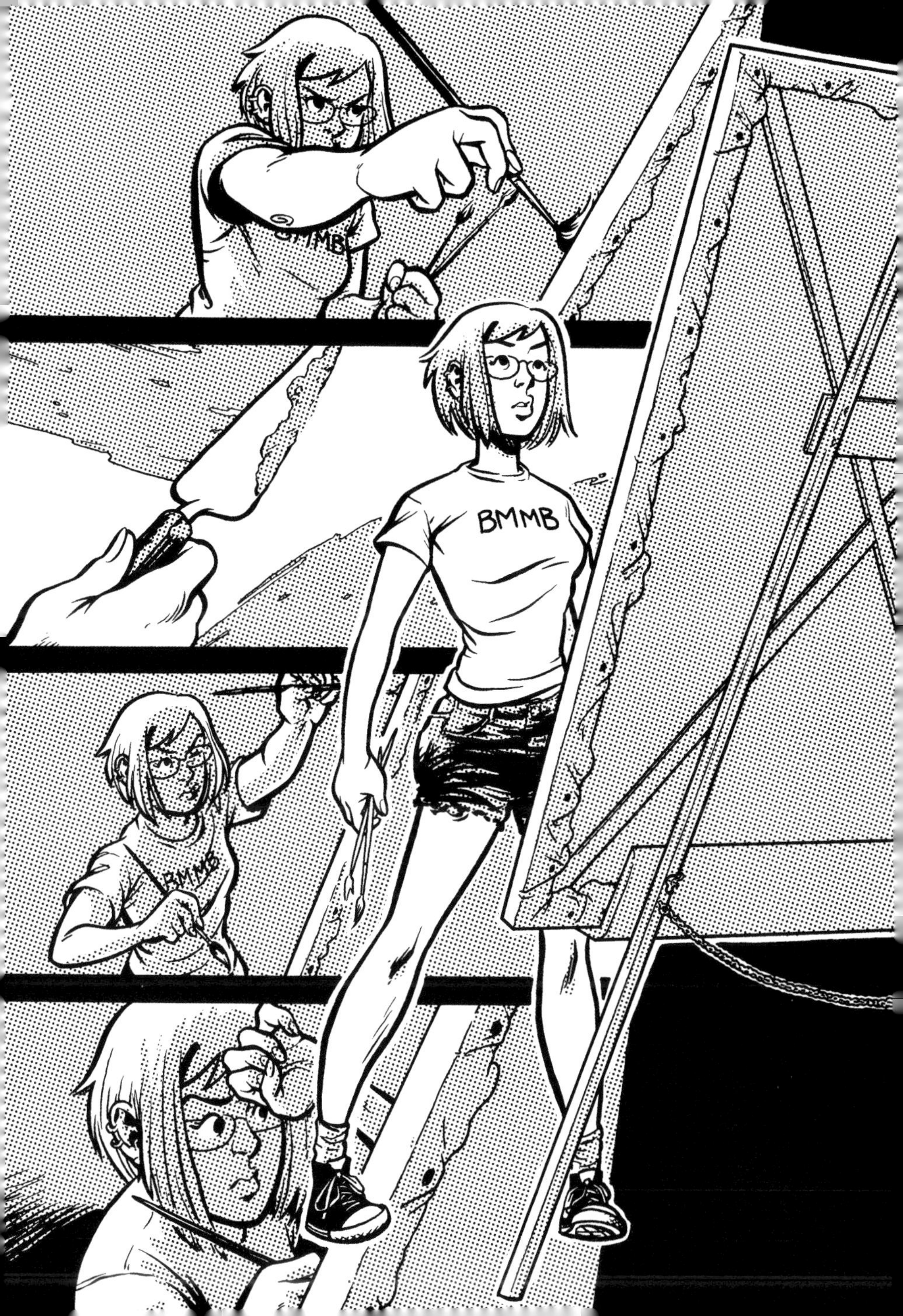
BMMB

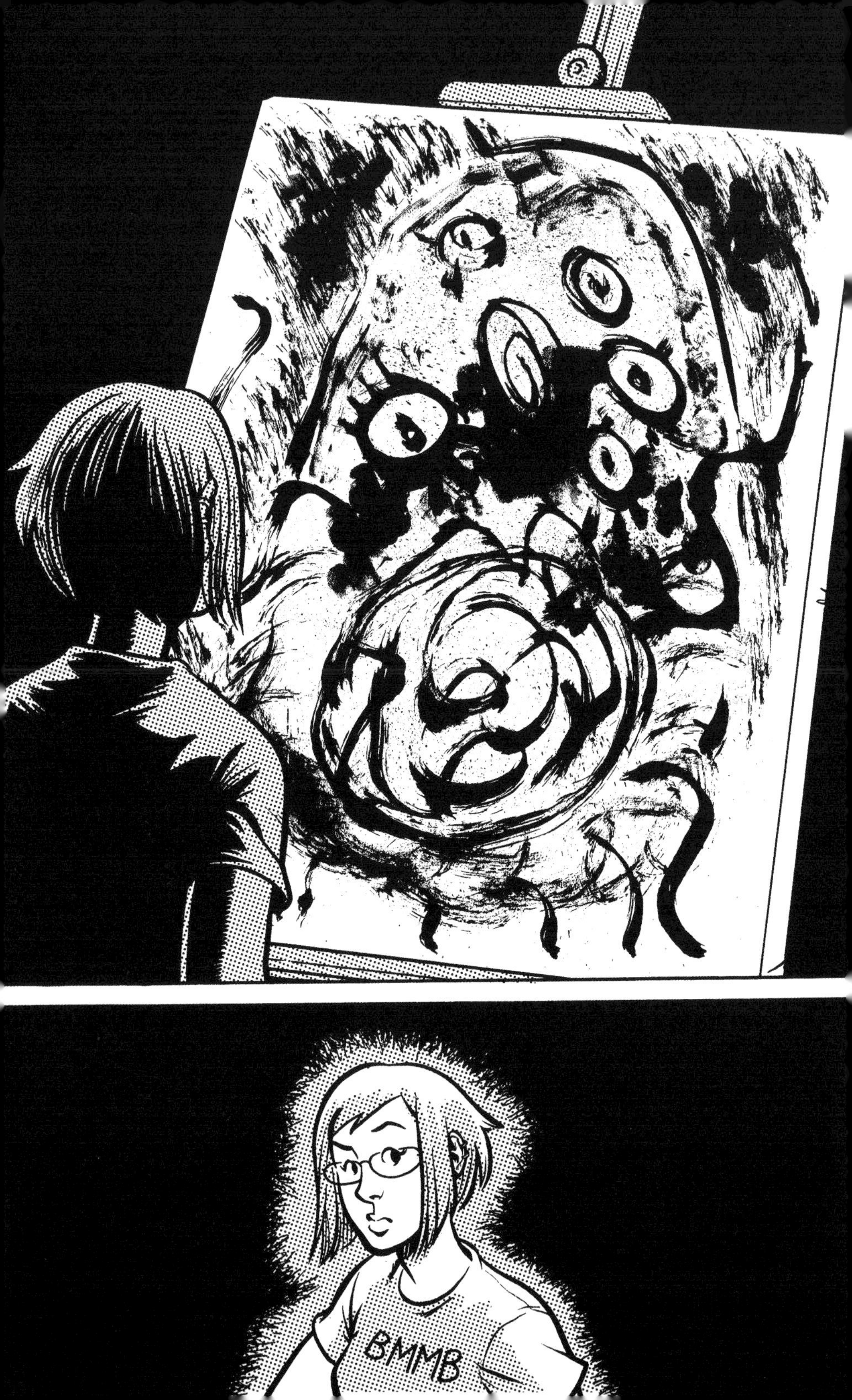
BMMB

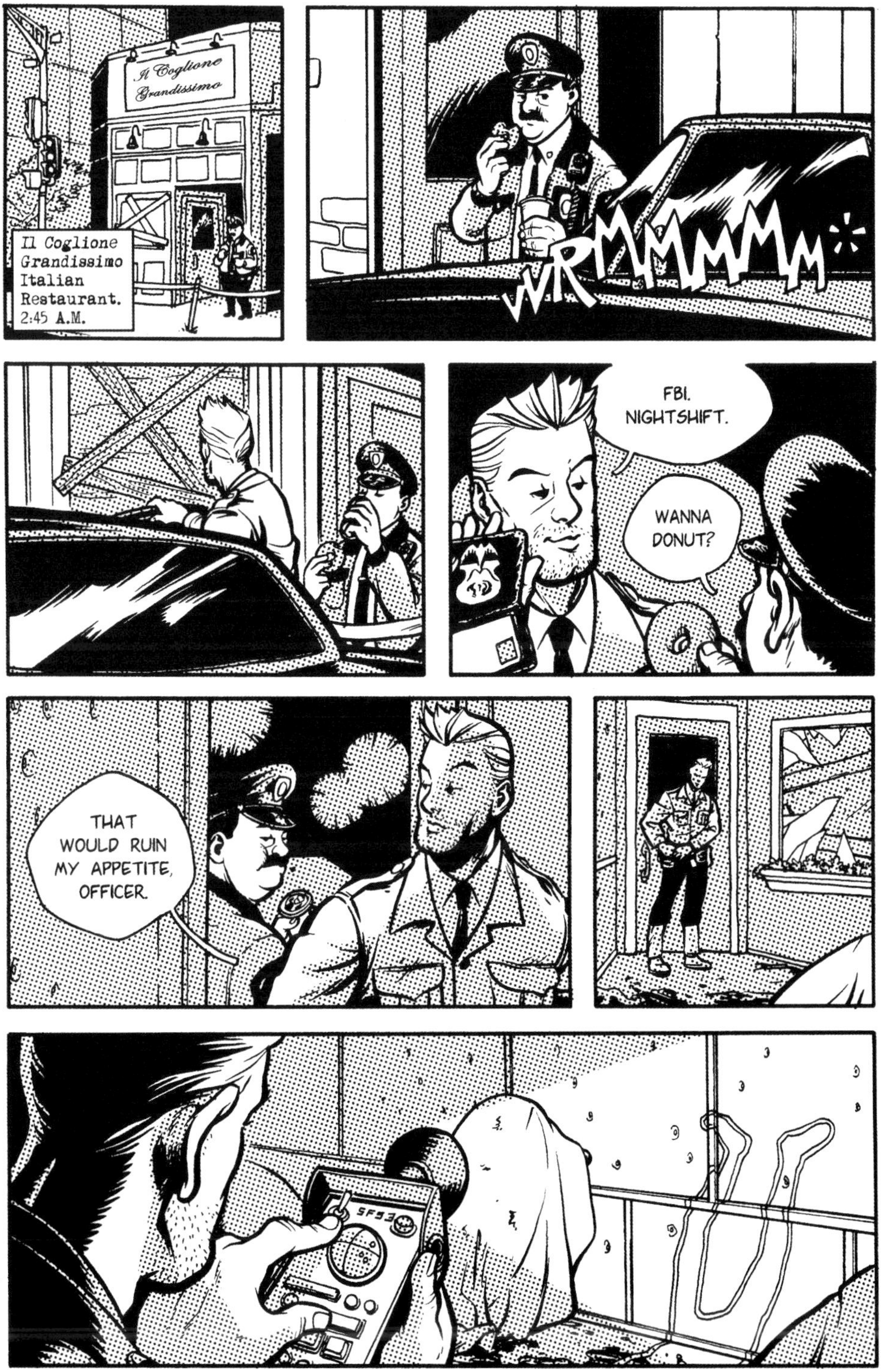
Il Coglione Grandissimo
Il Coglione Grandissimo Italian Restaurant. 2:45 A.M.
WRMMMMMM*
FBI. NIGHTSHIFT.
WANNA DONUT?
THAT WOULD RUIN MY APPETITE, OFFICER.
SFS3

EXCUSE ME...

CLICK!

THIS KID SAYS SHE'S WITH YOU.

BMMB

SPECIAL AGENT WATSON. SLACKING OFF ON THE DRESS CODE, I SEE.

I DON'T DO DRESS CODE AFTER SUNDOWN.

BMMB

IT'S BAD APPLES LIKE YOU THAT PUT MR. HOOVER IN A DRESS.

YEAH, SHE'S ON THE JOB.

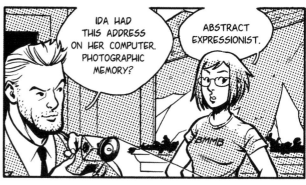

IDA HAD THIS ADDRESS ON HER COMPUTER. PHOTOGRAPHIC MEMORY?

ABSTRACT EXPRESSIONIST.

BMMB

SWELL.

LAST TIME WE TALKED YOU WEREN'T EXACTLY NICE. WHY THE ATTITUDE ADJUSTMENT?

I HEARD YOU TAKE CARE OF EXOTIC PROBLEMS.

DEFINE EXOTIC.

BMMB

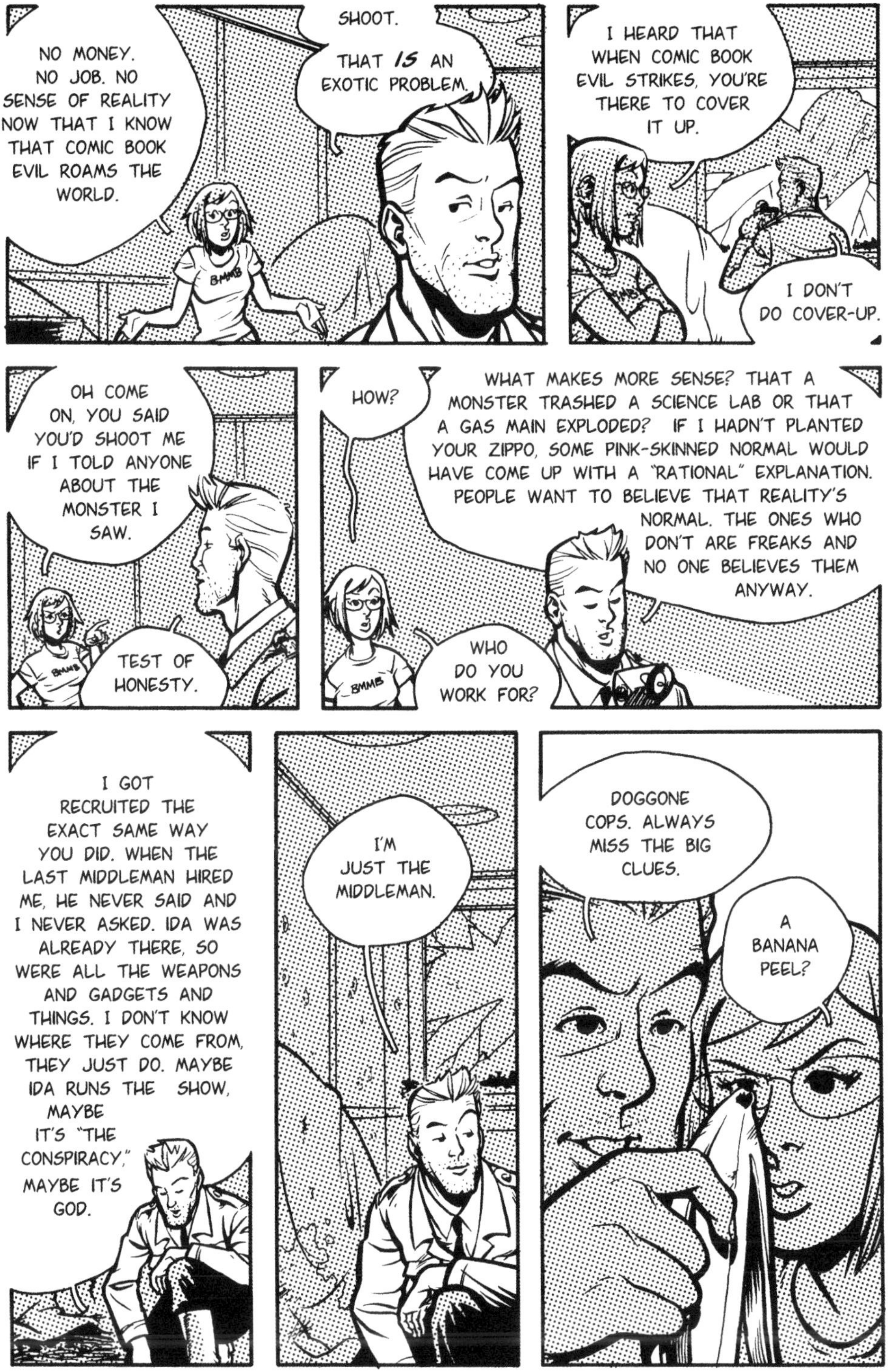
NO MONEY. NO JOB. NO SENSE OF REALITY NOW THAT I KNOW THAT COMIC BOOK EVIL ROAMS THE WORLD.
SHOOT.
THAT *IS* AN EXOTIC PROBLEM.
I HEARD THAT WHEN COMIC BOOK EVIL STRIKES, YOU'RE THERE TO COVER IT UP.
I DON'T DO COVER-UP.
OH COME ON, YOU SAID YOU'D SHOOT ME IF I TOLD ANYONE ABOUT THE MONSTER I SAW.
TEST OF HONESTY.
HOW?
WHAT MAKES MORE SENSE? THAT A MONSTER TRASHED A SCIENCE LAB OR THAT A GAS MAIN EXPLODED? IF I HADN'T PLANTED YOUR ZIPPO, SOME PINK-SKINNED NORMAL WOULD HAVE COME UP WITH A "RATIONAL" EXPLANATION. PEOPLE WANT TO BELIEVE THAT REALITY'S NORMAL. THE ONES WHO DON'T ARE FREAKS AND NO ONE BELIEVES THEM ANYWAY.
WHO DO YOU WORK FOR?
I GOT RECRUITED THE EXACT SAME WAY YOU DID. WHEN THE LAST MIDDLEMAN HIRED ME, HE NEVER SAID AND I NEVER ASKED. IDA WAS ALREADY THERE, SO WERE ALL THE WEAPONS AND GADGETS AND THINGS. I DON'T KNOW WHERE THEY COME FROM, THEY JUST DO. MAYBE IDA RUNS THE SHOW, MAYBE IT'S "THE CONSPIRACY," MAYBE IT'S GOD.
I'M JUST THE MIDDLEMAN.
DOGGONE COPS. ALWAYS MISS THE BIG CLUES.
A BANANA PEEL?

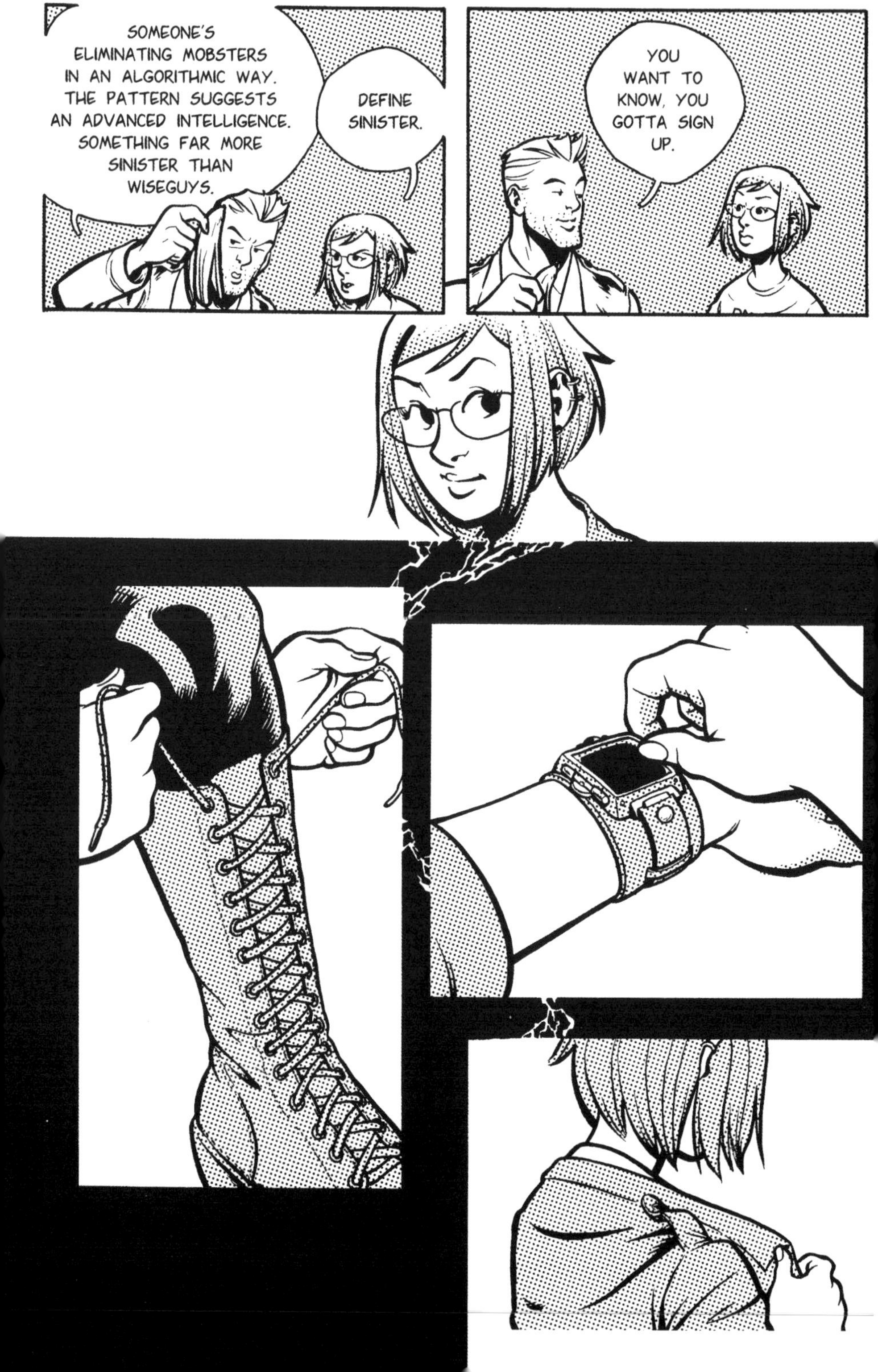
SOMEONE'S ELIMINATING MOBSTERS IN AN ALGORITHMIC WAY. THE PATTERN SUGGESTS AN ADVANCED INTELLIGENCE. SOMETHING FAR MORE SINISTER THAN WISEGUYS.
DEFINE SINISTER.
YOU WANT TO KNOW, YOU GOTTA SIGN UP.

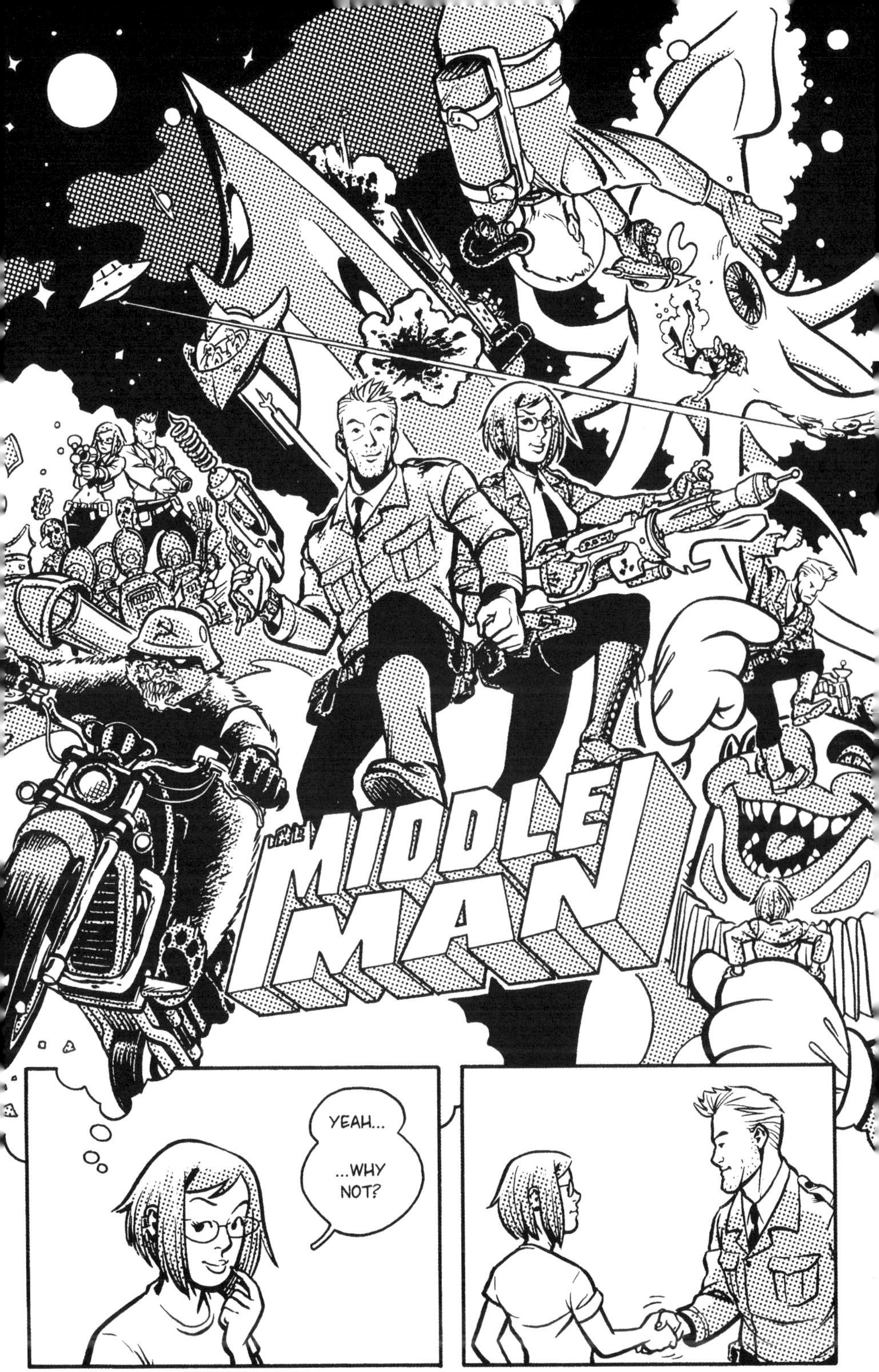
THE MIDDLE MAN
YEAH... ...WHY NOT?

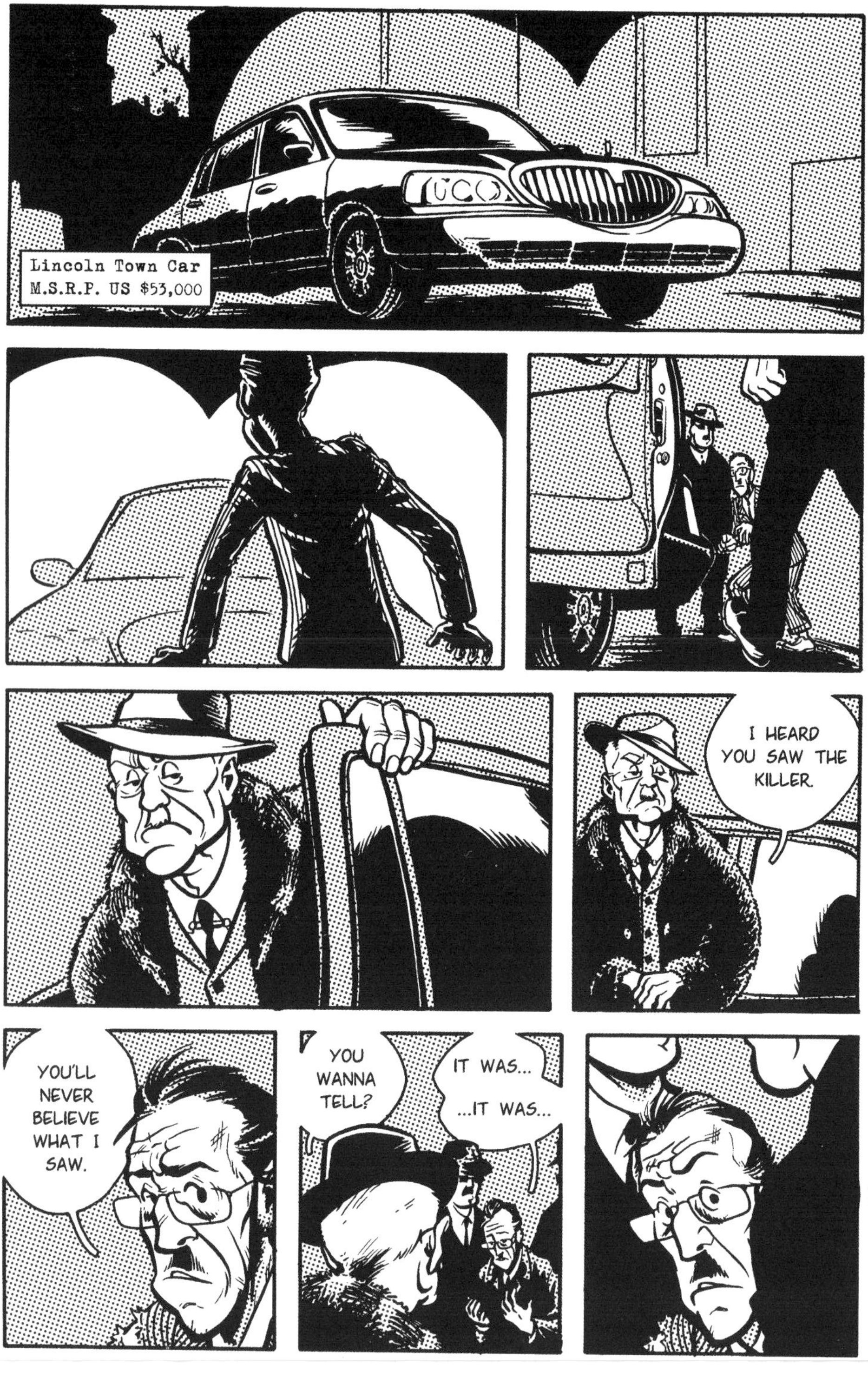
Lincoln Town Car
M.S.R.P. US $53,000
I HEARD YOU SAW THE KILLER.
YOU'LL NEVER BELIEVE WHAT I SAW.
YOU WANNA TELL?
IT WAS...
...IT WAS...

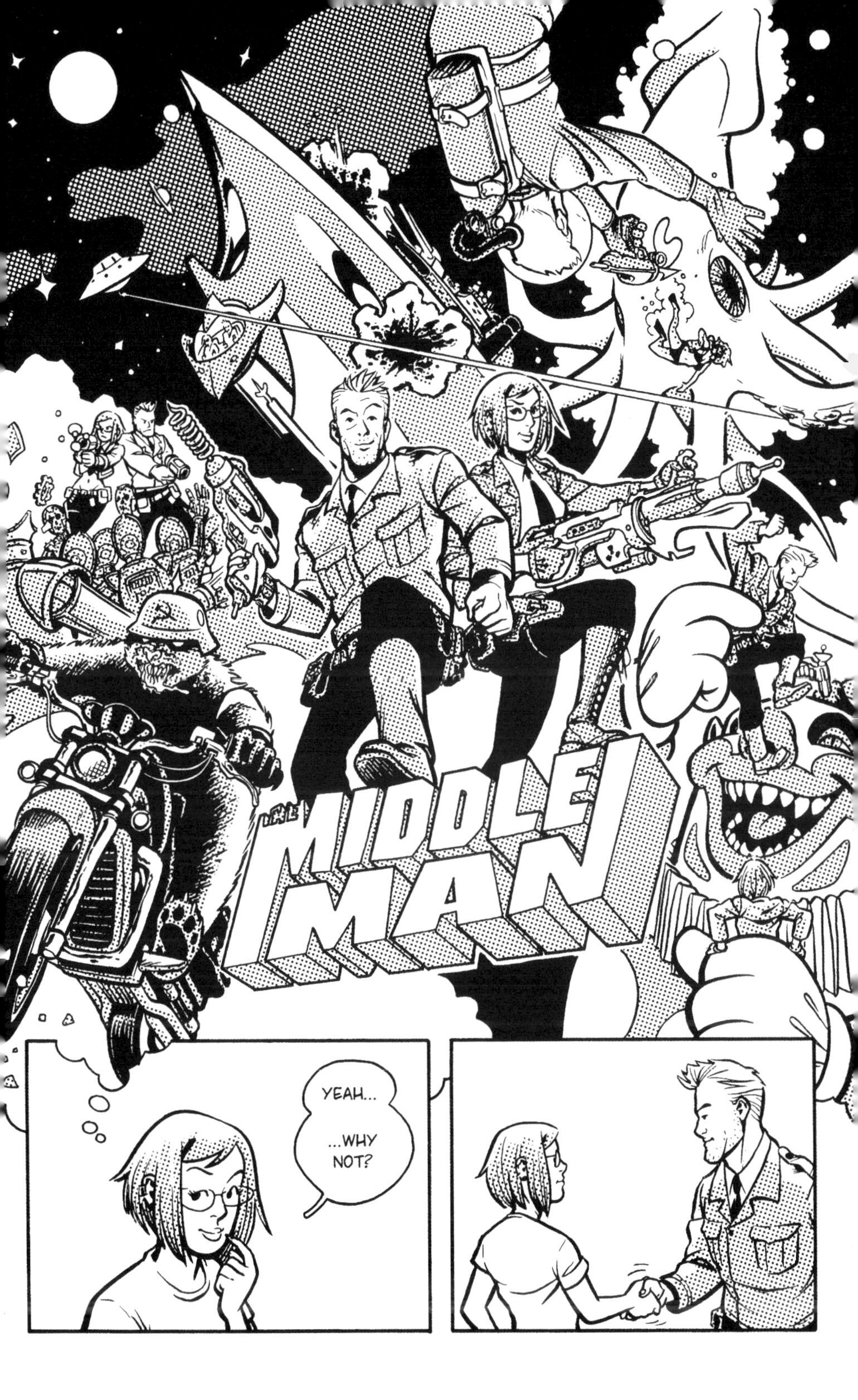
THE MIDDLE MAN
YEAH...
...WHY NOT?

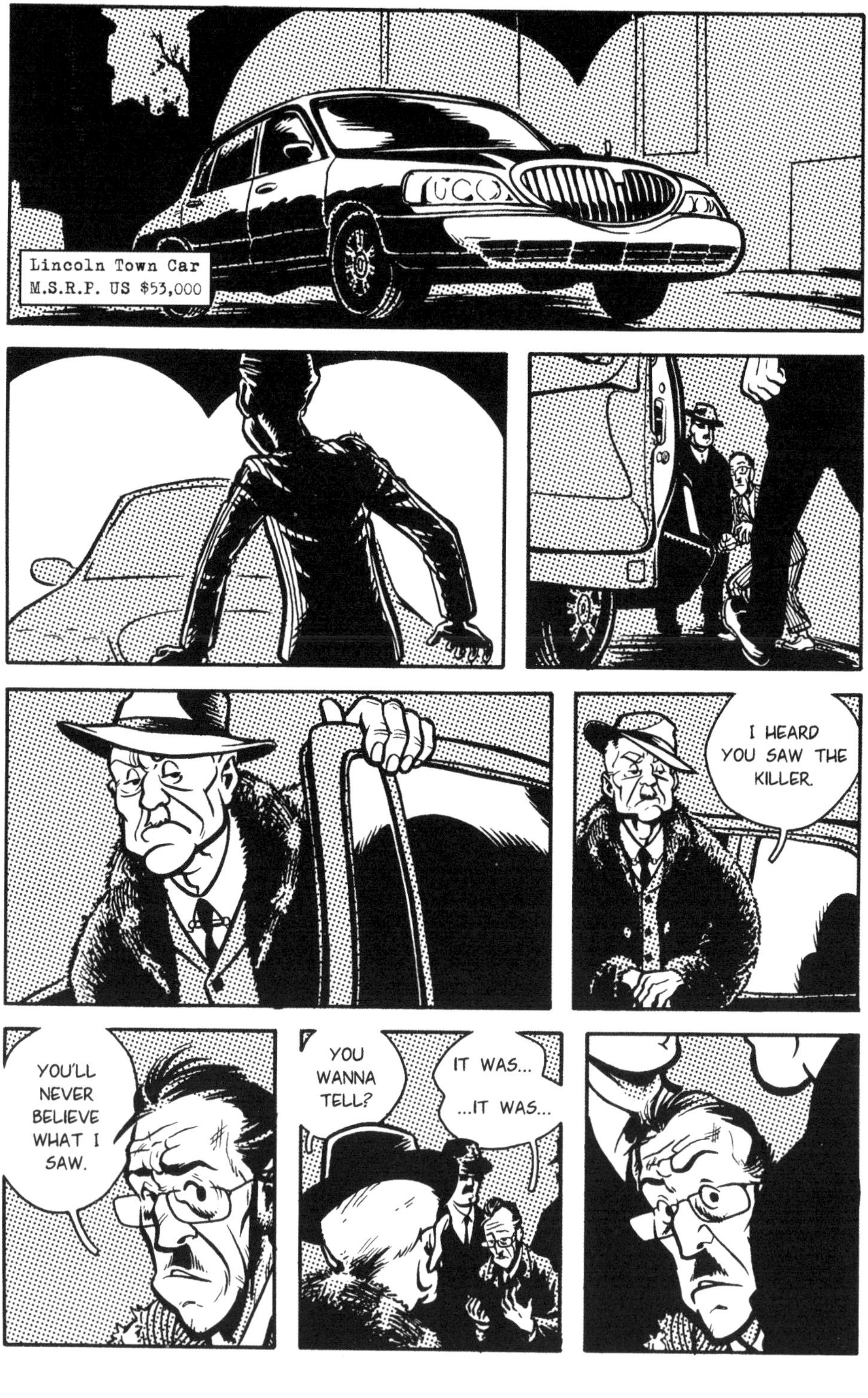
Lincoln Town Car
M.S.R.P. US $53,000
I HEARD YOU SAW THE KILLER.
YOU'LL NEVER BELIEVE WHAT I SAW.
YOU WANNA TELL?
IT WAS...
...IT WAS...

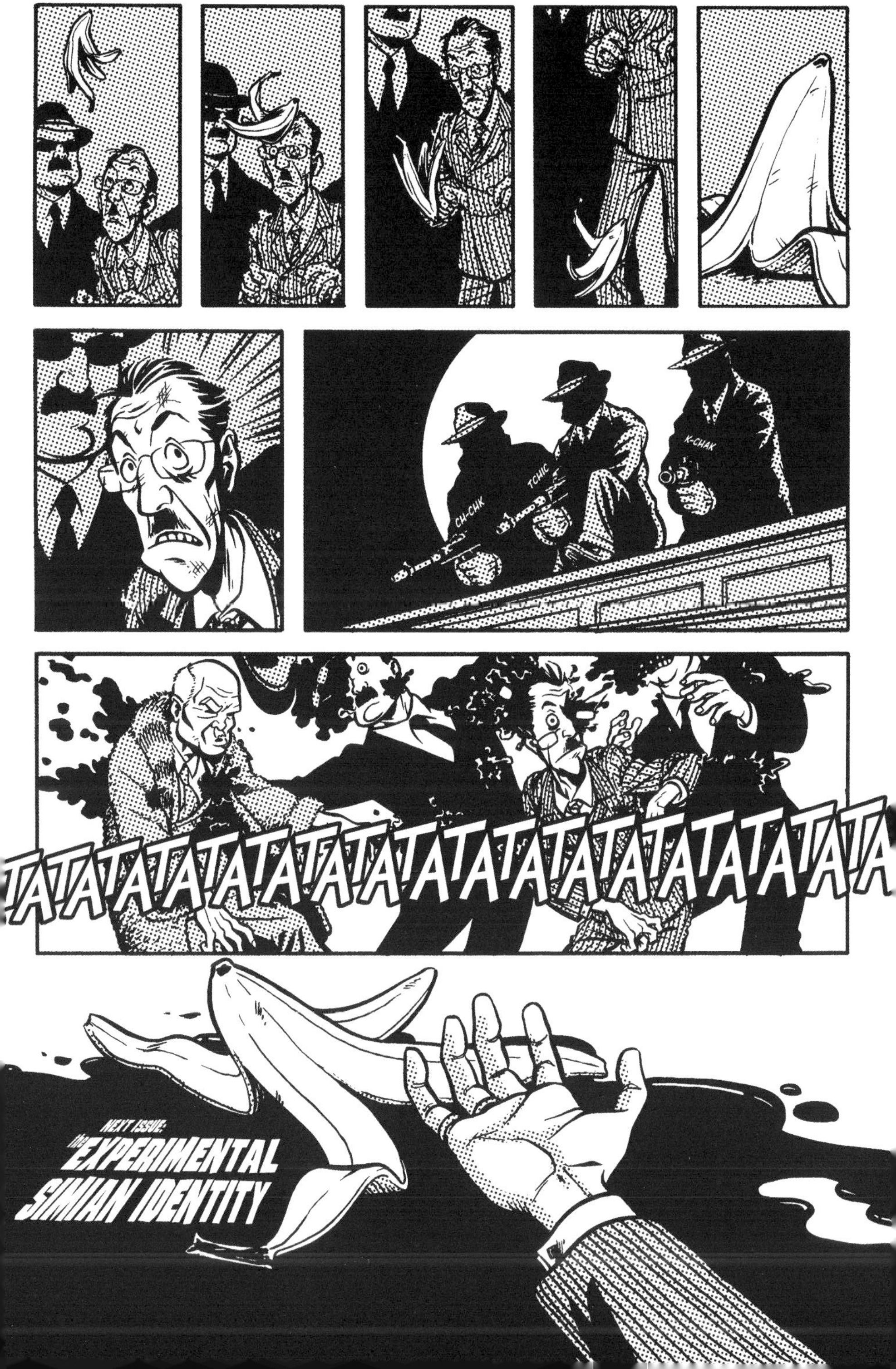
CH-CHK
TCHIC
K-CHAK
TATATATATATATATATATATATATATATATATATATATATATA
NEXT ISSUE:
the EXPERIMENTAL SIMIAN IDENTITY

CHAPTER 03

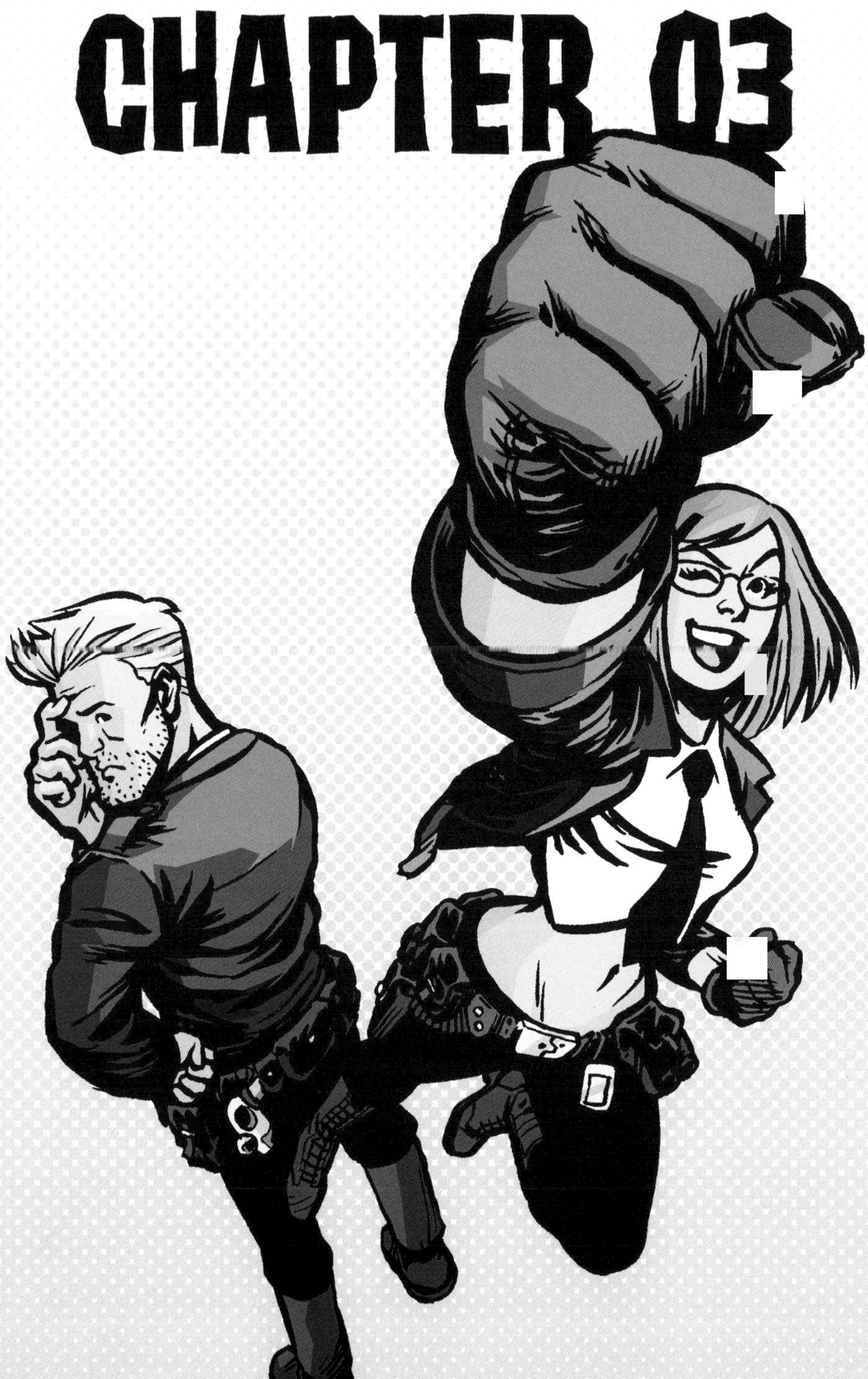

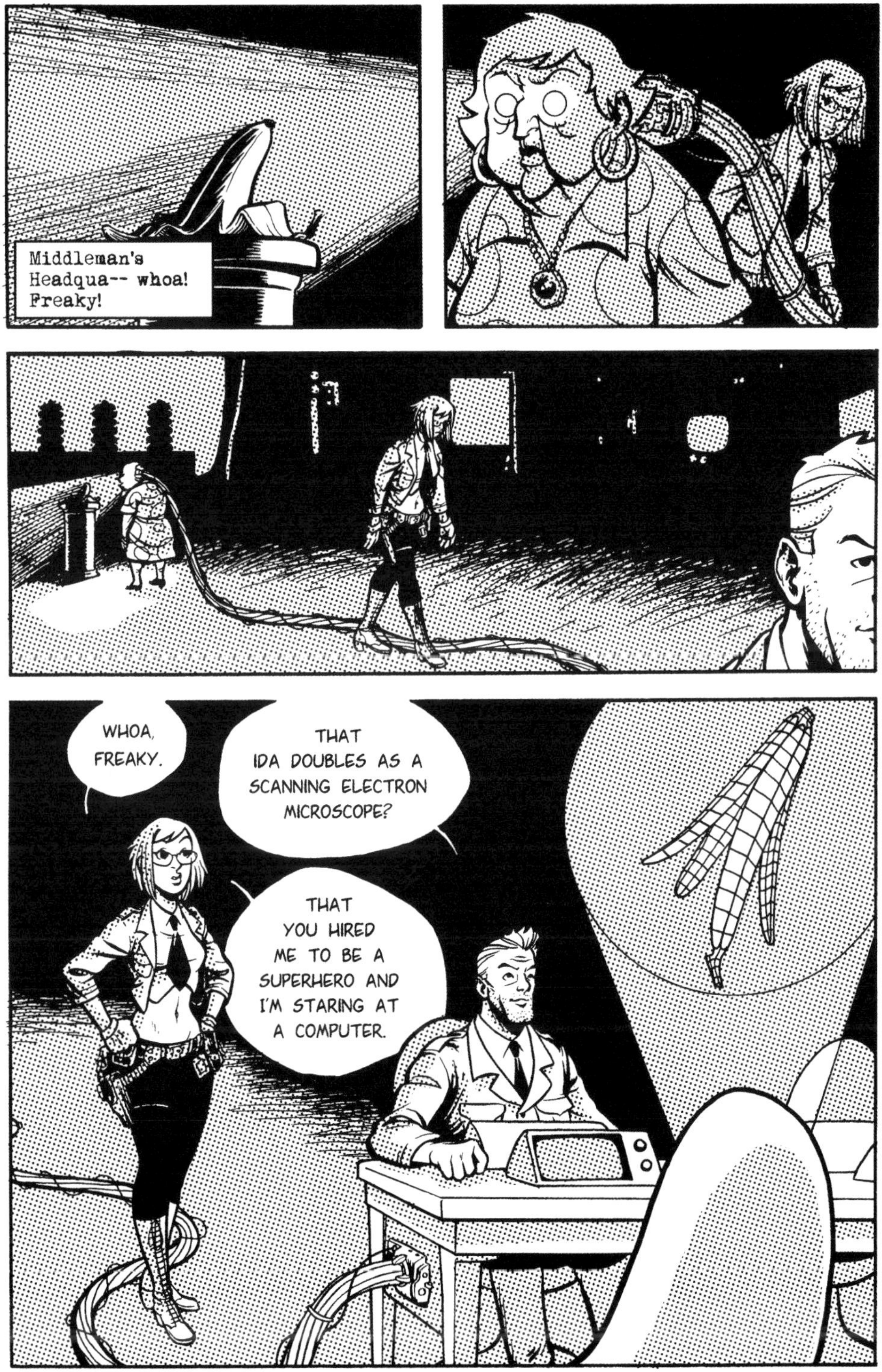
Middleman's
Headqua-- whoa!
Freaky!
WHOA, FREAKY.
THAT IDA DOUBLES AS A SCANNING ELECTRON MICROSCOPE?
THAT YOU HIRED ME TO BE A SUPERHERO AND I'M STARING AT A COMPUTER.

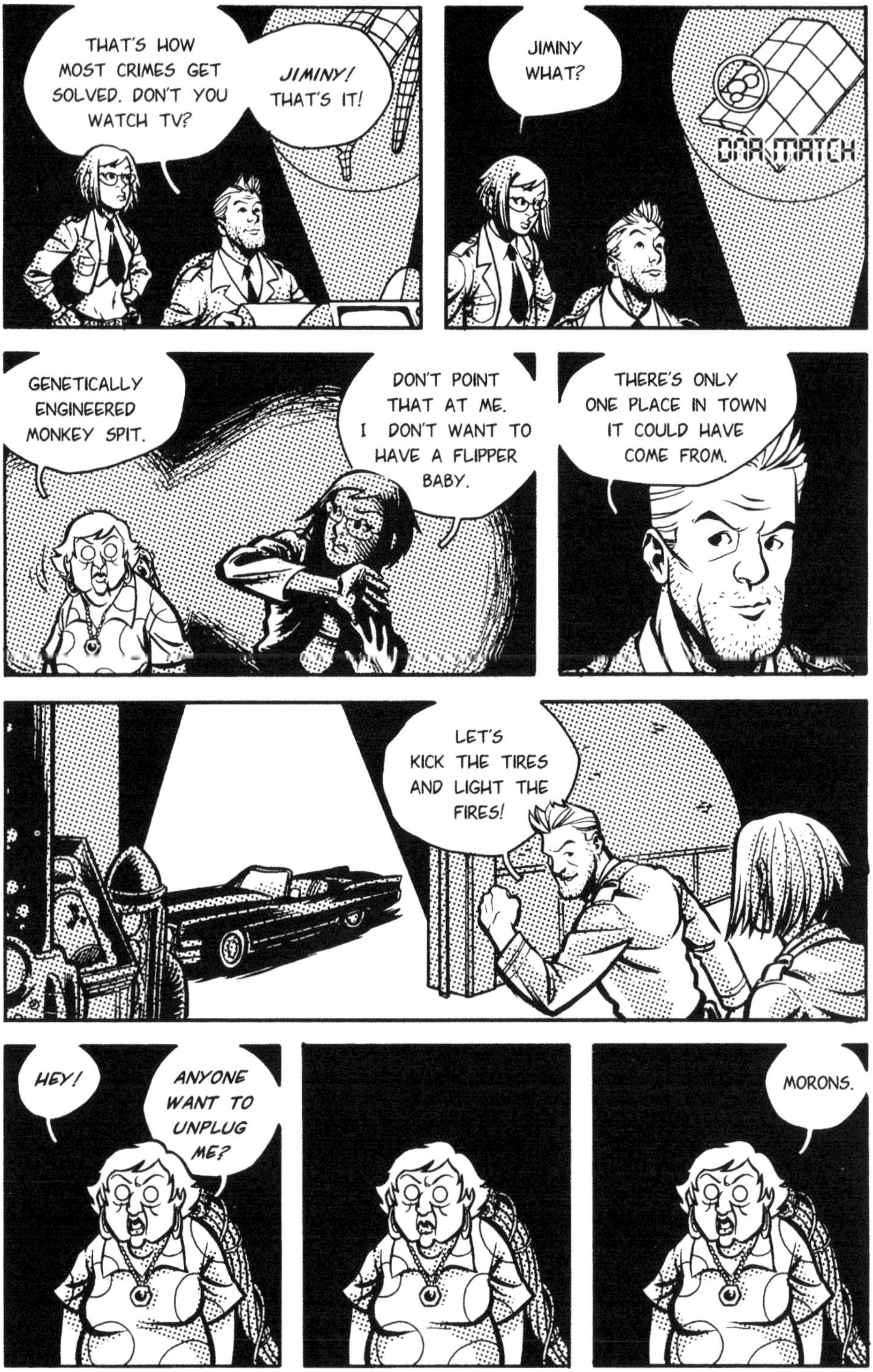
THAT'S HOW MOST CRIMES GET SOLVED. DON'T YOU WATCH TV?
JIMINY! THAT'S IT!
JIMINY WHAT?
DNA MATCH
GENETICALLY ENGINEERED MONKEY SPIT.
DON'T POINT THAT AT ME. I DON'T WANT TO HAVE A FLIPPER BABY.
THERE'S ONLY ONE PLACE IN TOWN IT COULD HAVE COME FROM.
LET'S KICK THE TIRES AND LIGHT THE FIRES!
HEY!
ANYONE WANT TO UNPLUG ME?
MORONS.

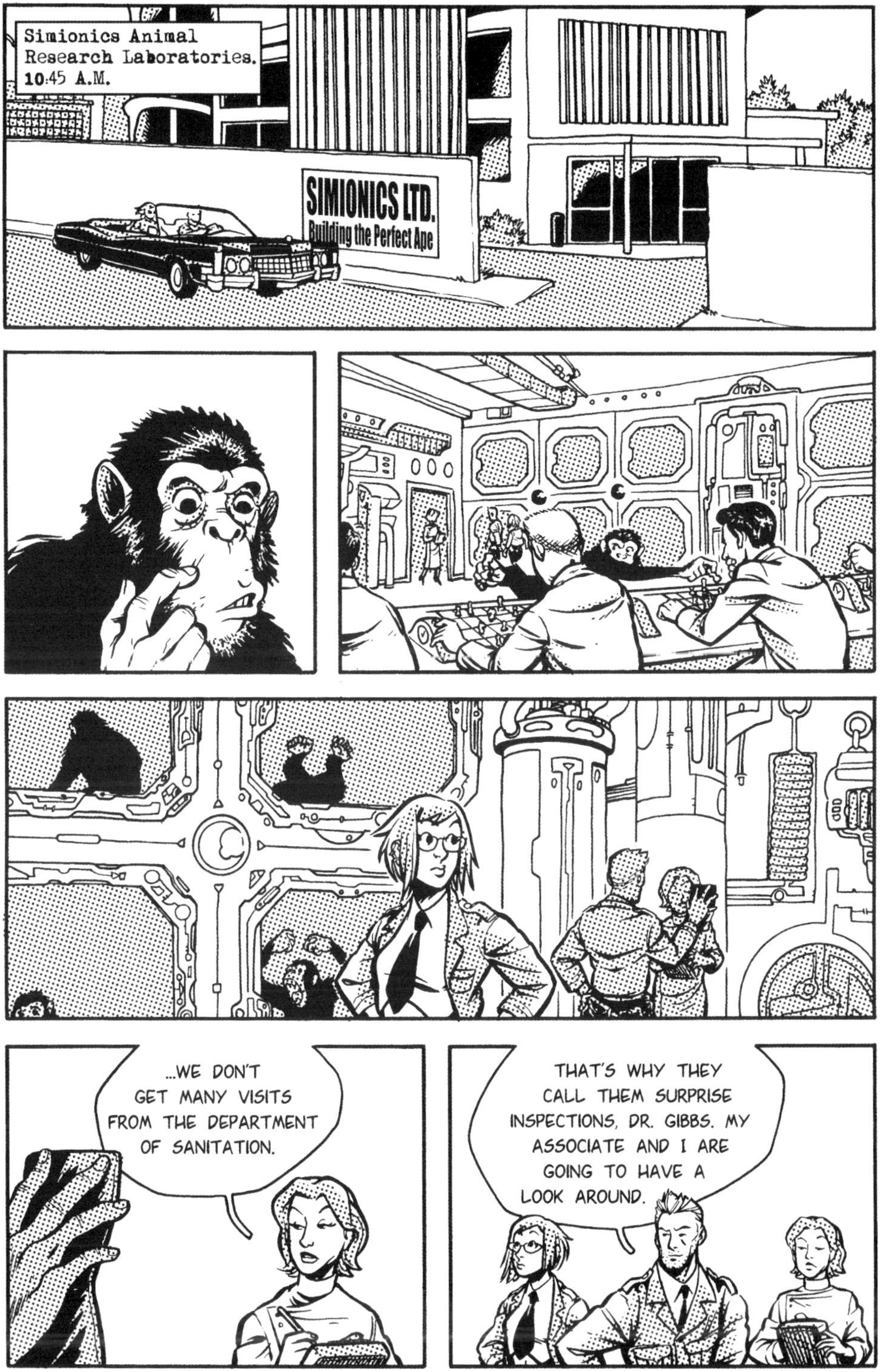
Simionics Animal Research Laboratories. 10:45 A.M.
SIMIONICS LTD. Building the Perfect Ape
...WE DON'T GET MANY VISITS FROM THE DEPARTMENT OF SANITATION.
THAT'S WHY THEY CALL THEM SURPRISE INSPECTIONS, DR. GIBBS. MY ASSOCIATE AND I ARE GOING TO HAVE A LOOK AROUND.

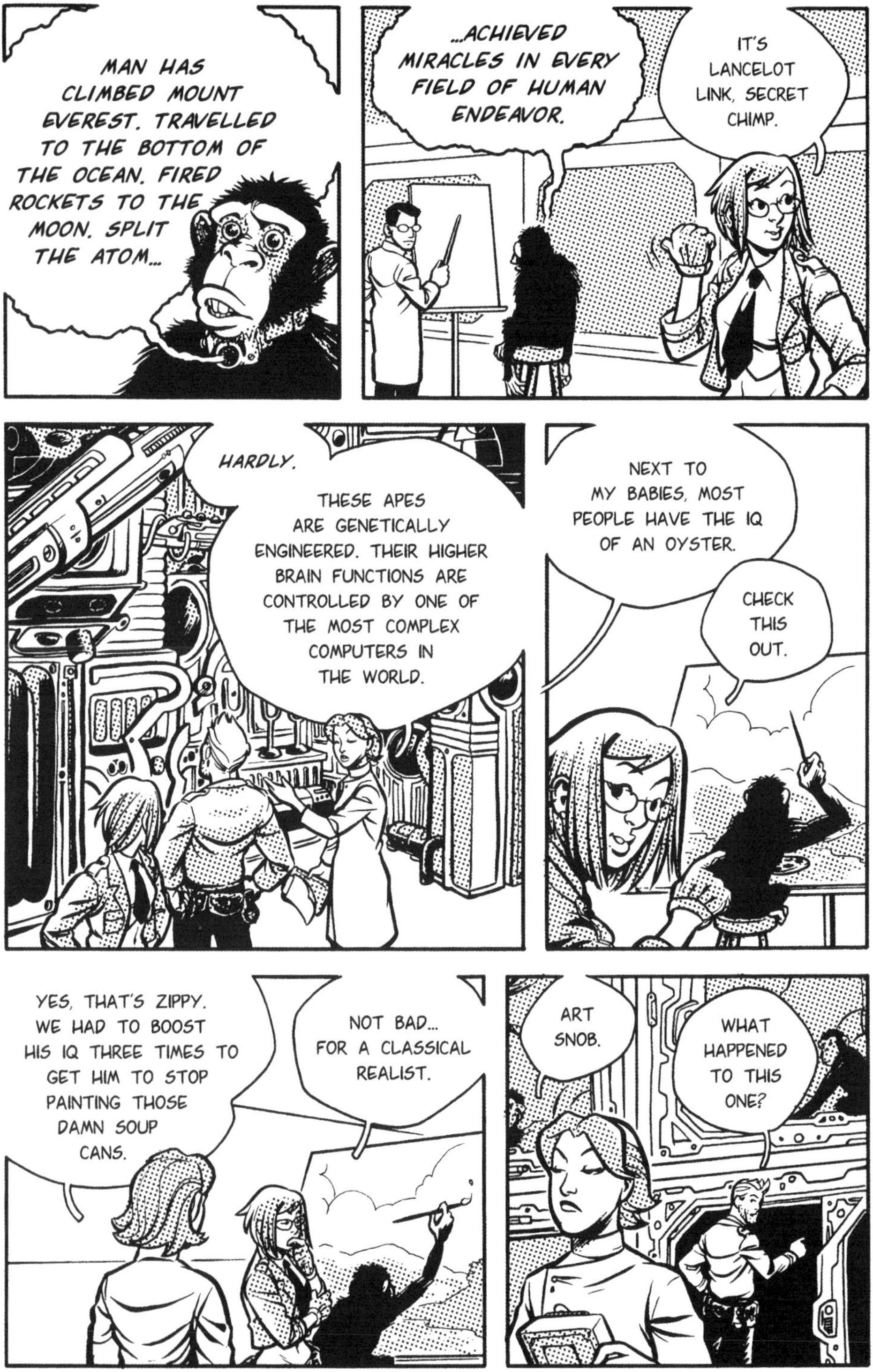
MAN HAS CLIMBED MOUNT EVEREST. TRAVELLED TO THE BOTTOM OF THE OCEAN. FIRED ROCKETS TO THE MOON. SPLIT THE ATOM...
...ACHIEVED MIRACLES IN EVERY FIELD OF HUMAN ENDEAVOR.
IT'S LANCELOT LINK, SECRET CHIMP.
HARDLY.
THESE APES ARE GENETICALLY ENGINEERED. THEIR HIGHER BRAIN FUNCTIONS ARE CONTROLLED BY ONE OF THE MOST COMPLEX COMPUTERS IN THE WORLD.
NEXT TO MY BABIES, MOST PEOPLE HAVE THE IQ OF AN OYSTER.
CHECK THIS OUT.
YES, THAT'S ZIPPY. WE HAD TO BOOST HIS IQ THREE TIMES TO GET HIM TO STOP PAINTING THOSE DAMN SOUP CANS.
NOT BAD... FOR A CLASSICAL REALIST.
ART SNOB.
WHAT HAPPENED TO THIS ONE?

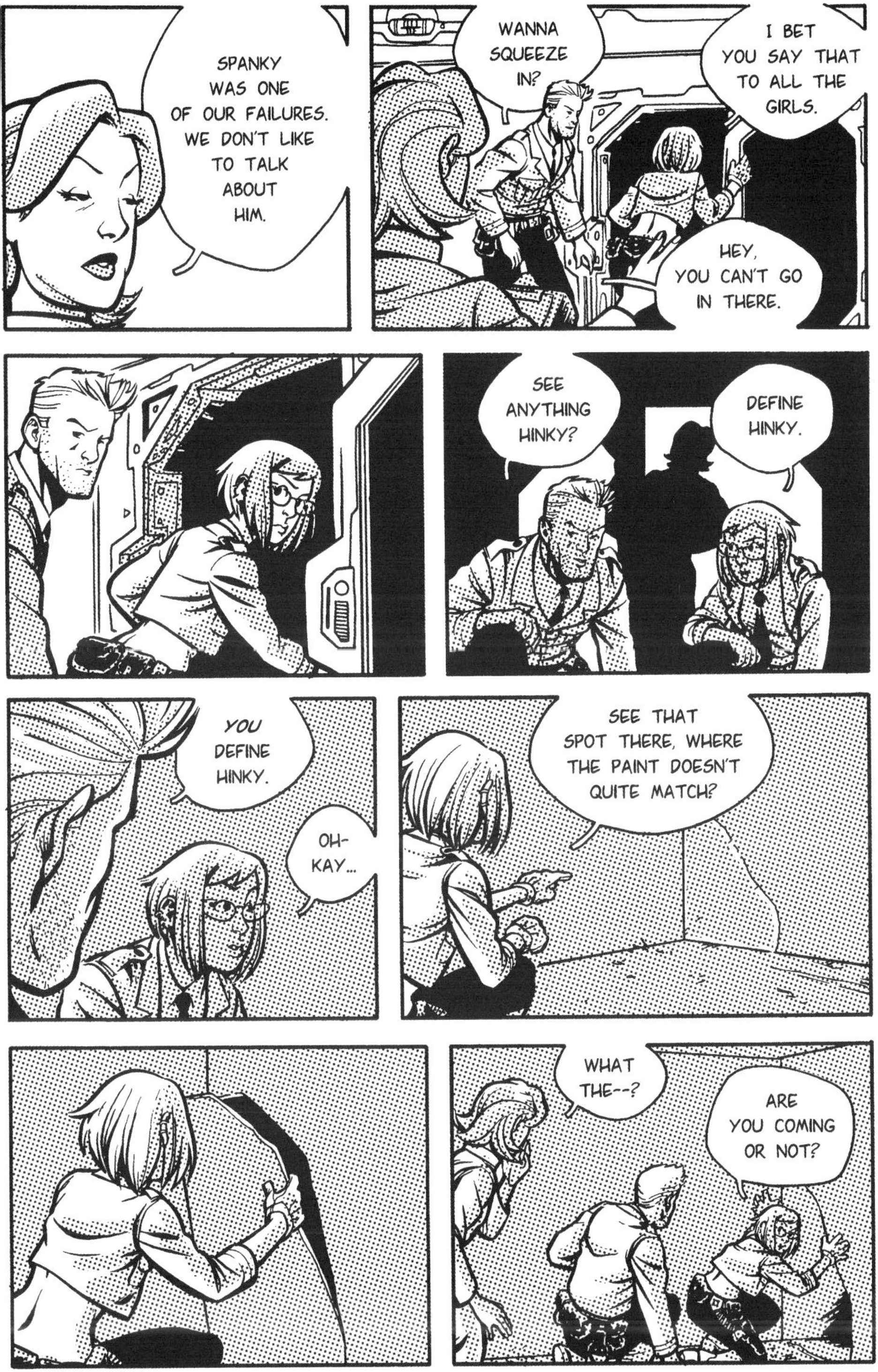
SPANKY WAS ONE OF OUR FAILURES. WE DON'T LIKE TO TALK ABOUT HIM.
WANNA SQUEEZE IN?
I BET YOU SAY THAT TO ALL THE GIRLS.
HEY, YOU CAN'T GO IN THERE.
SEE ANYTHING HINKY?
DEFINE HINKY.
YOU DEFINE HINKY.
OH-KAY...
SEE THAT SPOT THERE, WHERE THE PAINT DOESN'T QUITE MATCH?
WHAT THE--?
ARE YOU COMING OR NOT?

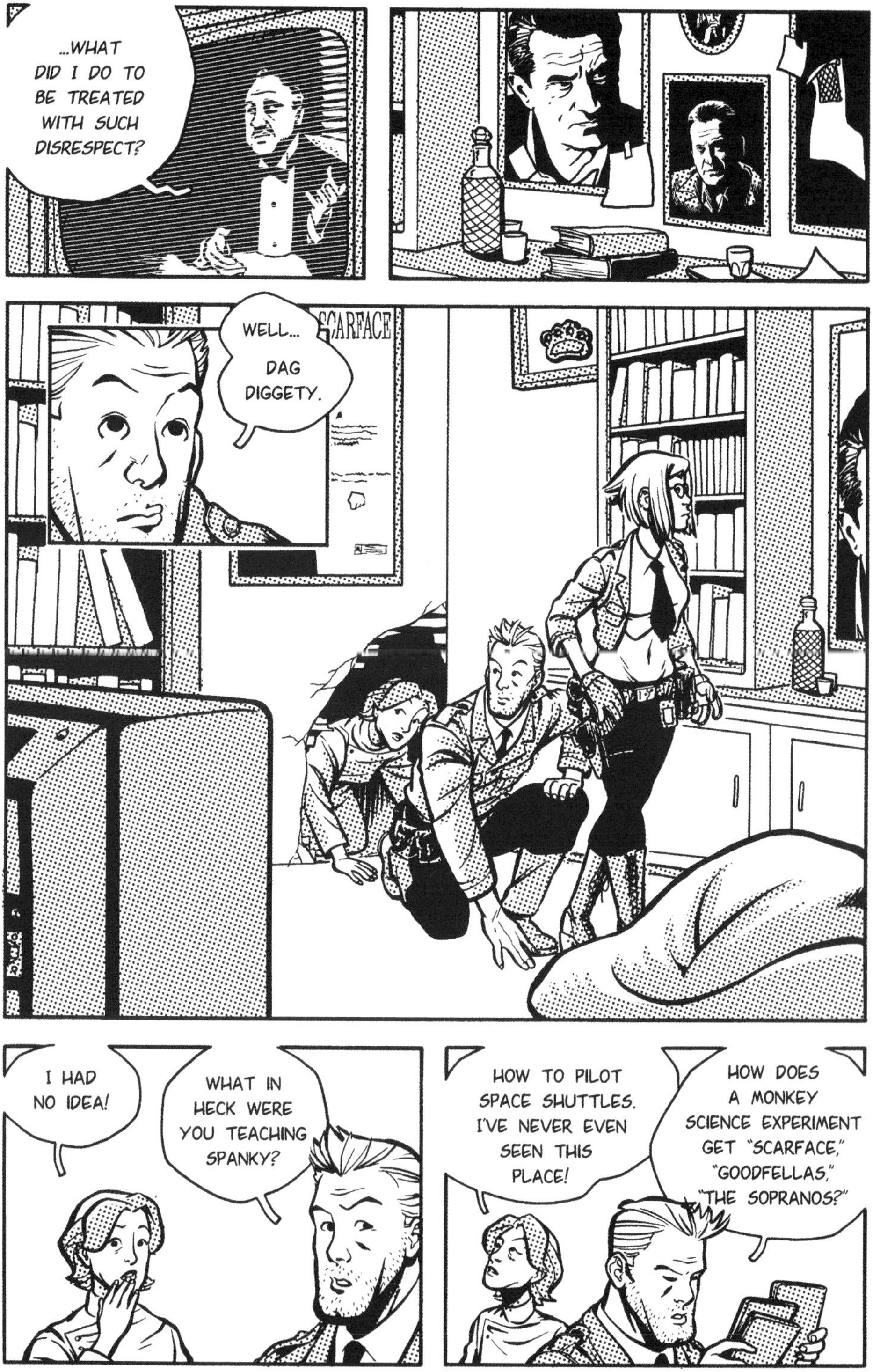
...WHAT DID I DO TO BE TREATED WITH SUCH DISRESPECT?
SCARFACE
WELL... DAG DIGGETY.
I HAD NO IDEA!
WHAT IN HECK WERE YOU TEACHING SPANKY?
HOW TO PILOT SPACE SHUTTLES. I'VE NEVER EVEN SEEN THIS PLACE!
HOW DOES A MONKEY SCIENCE EXPERIMENT GET "SCARFACE," "GOODFELLAS," "THE SOPRANOS?"

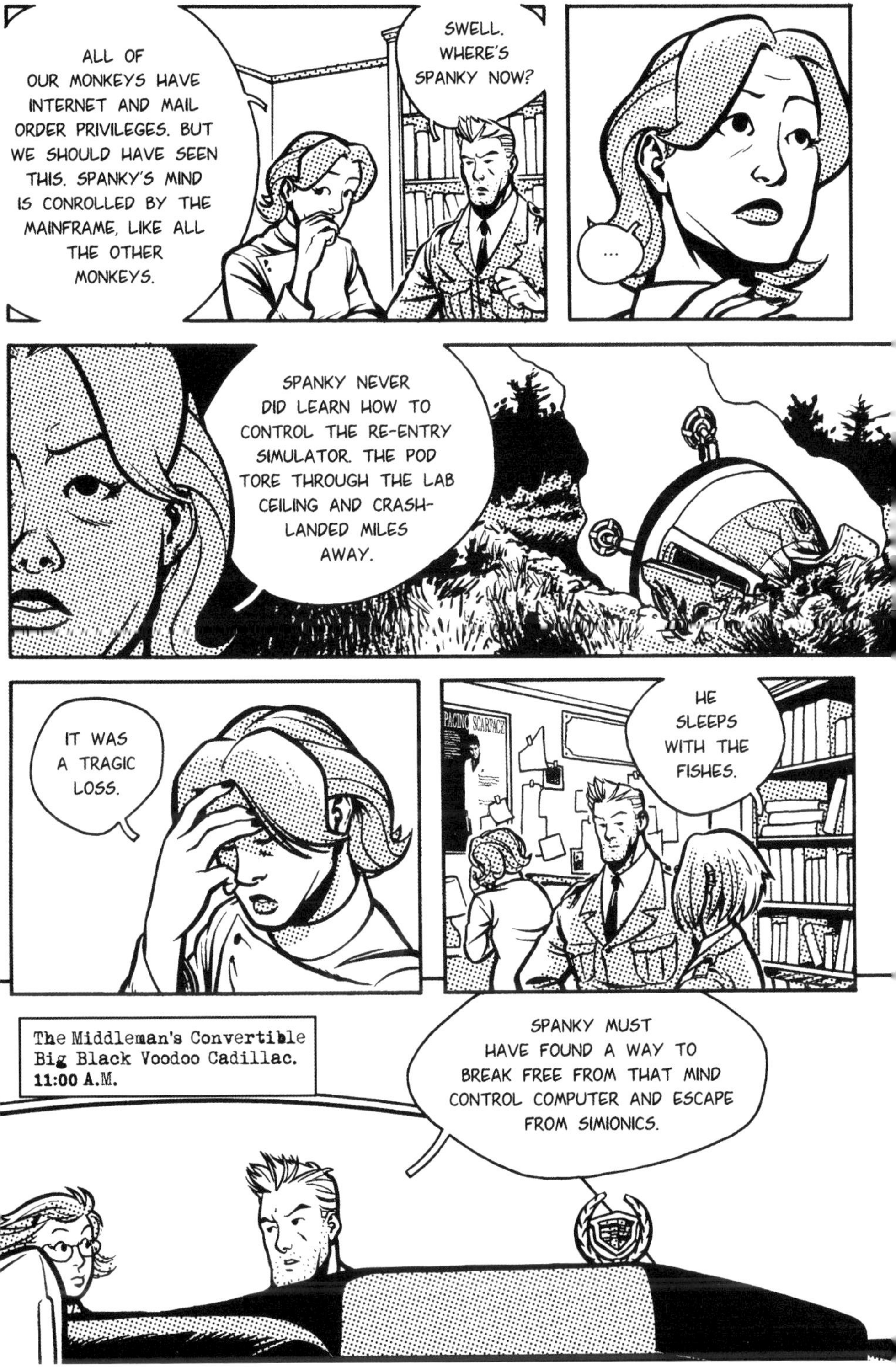

ALL OF OUR MONKEYS HAVE INTERNET AND MAIL ORDER PRIVILEGES. BUT WE SHOULD HAVE SEEN THIS. SPANKY'S MIND IS CONROLLED BY THE MAINFRAME, LIKE ALL THE OTHER MONKEYS.
SWELL. WHERE'S SPANKY NOW?
...
SPANKY NEVER DID LEARN HOW TO CONTROL THE RE-ENTRY SIMULATOR. THE POD TORE THROUGH THE LAB CEILING AND CRASH-LANDED MILES AWAY.
IT WAS A TRAGIC LOSS.
PACINO SCARFACE
HE SLEEPS WITH THE FISHES.
The Middleman's Convertible Big Black Voodoo Cadillac. 11:00 A.M.
SPANKY MUST HAVE FOUND A WAY TO BREAK FREE FROM THAT MIND CONTROL COMPUTER AND ESCAPE FROM SIMIONICS.

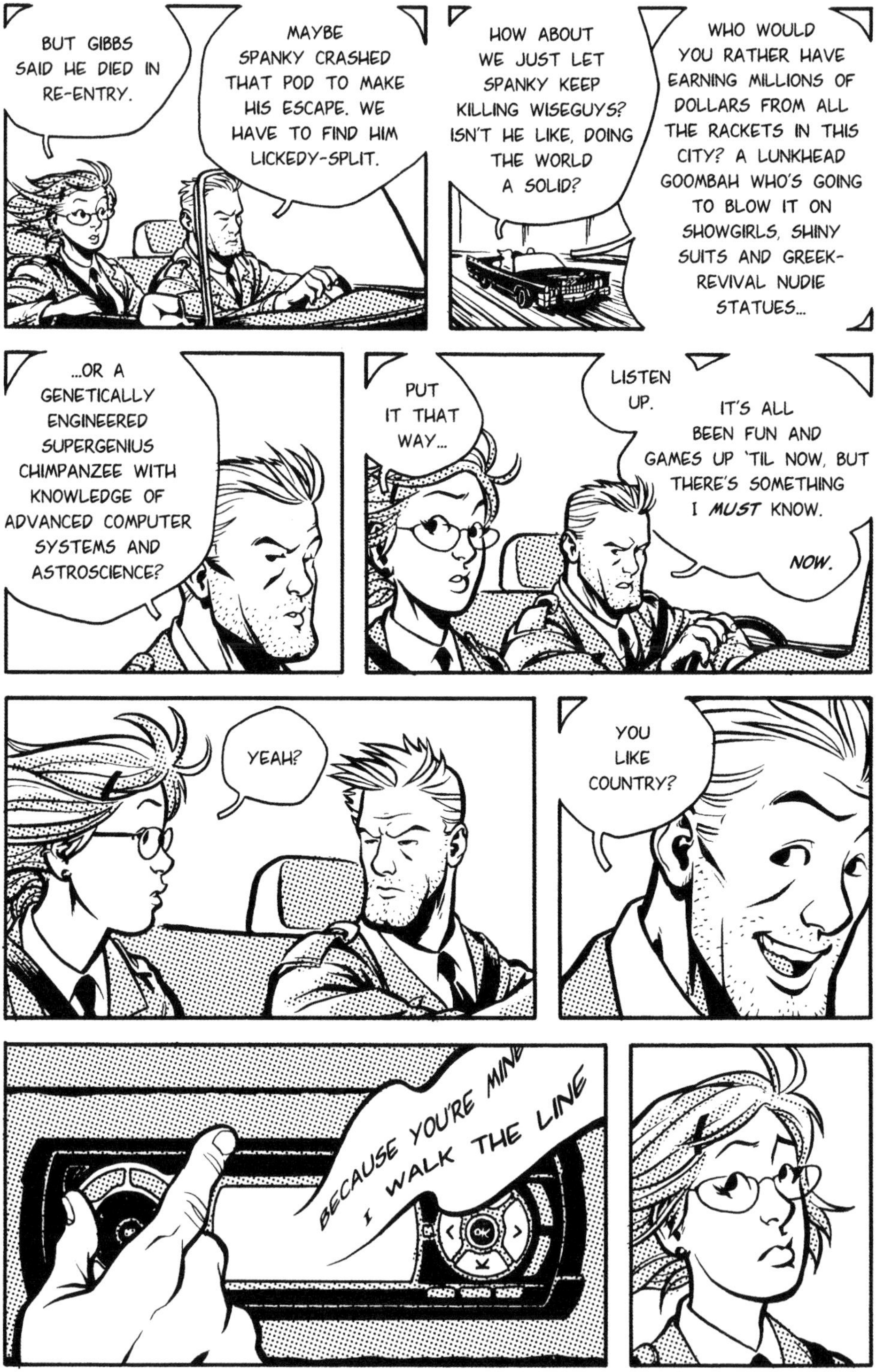

BUT GIBBS SAID HE DIED IN RE-ENTRY.
MAYBE SPANKY CRASHED THAT POD TO MAKE HIS ESCAPE. WE HAVE TO FIND HIM LICKEDY-SPLIT.
HOW ABOUT WE JUST LET SPANKY KEEP KILLING WISEGUYS? ISN'T HE LIKE, DOING THE WORLD A SOLID?
WHO WOULD YOU RATHER HAVE EARNING MILLIONS OF DOLLARS FROM ALL THE RACKETS IN THIS CITY? A LUNKHEAD GOOMBAH WHO'S GOING TO BLOW IT ON SHOWGIRLS, SHINY SUITS AND GREEK-REVIVAL NUDIE STATUES...
...OR A GENETICALLY ENGINEERED SUPERGENIUS CHIMPANZEE WITH KNOWLEDGE OF ADVANCED COMPUTER SYSTEMS AND ASTROSCIENCE?
PUT IT THAT WAY...
LISTEN UP.
IT'S ALL BEEN FUN AND GAMES UP 'TIL NOW, BUT THERE'S SOMETHING I *MUST* KNOW.
NOW.
YEAH?
YOU LIKE COUNTRY?
BECAUSE YOU'RE MINE I WALK THE LINE

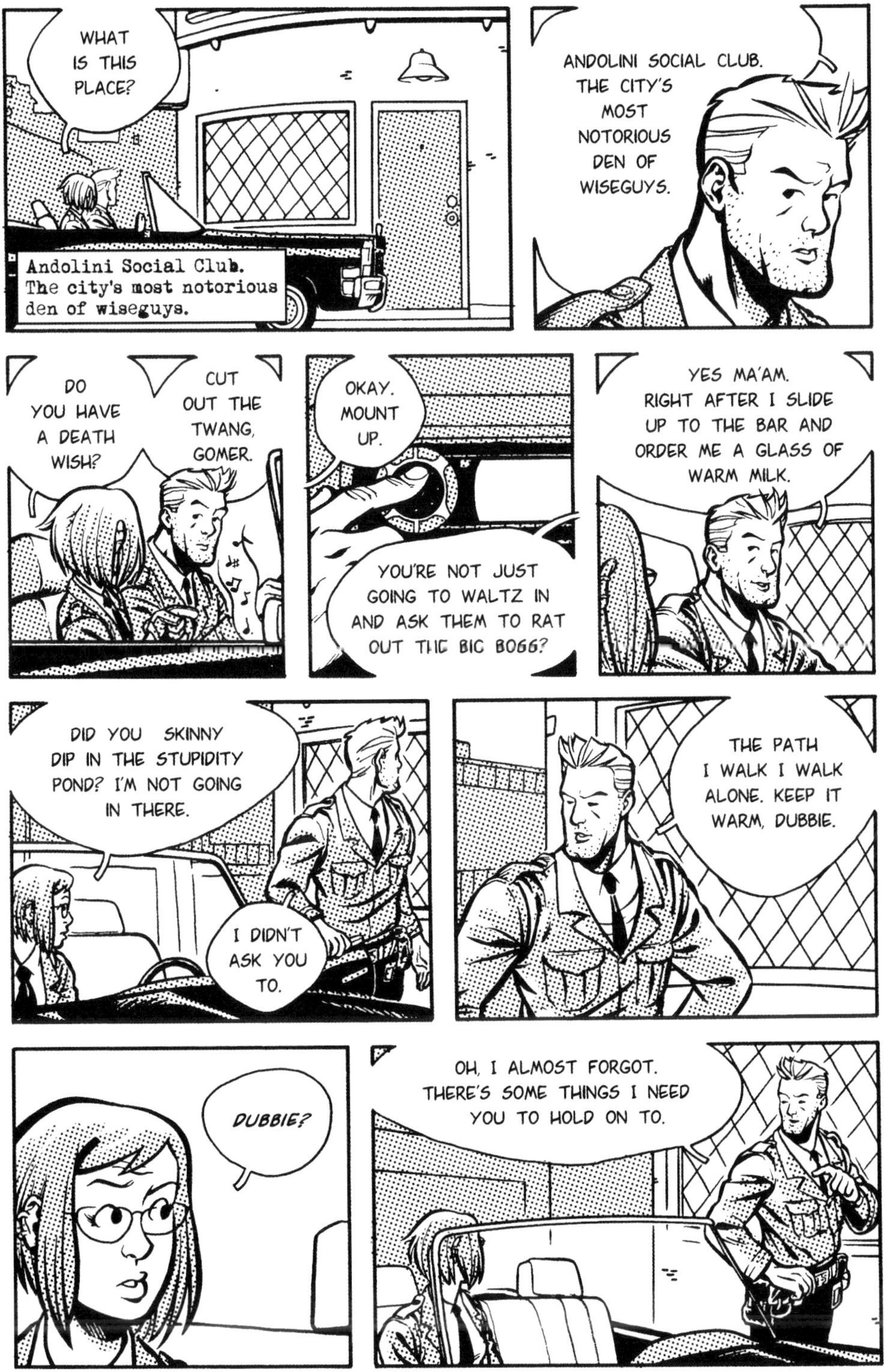
WHAT IS THIS PLACE?
Andolini Social Club. The city's most notorious den of wiseguys.
ANDOLINI SOCIAL CLUB. THE CITY'S MOST NOTORIOUS DEN OF WISEGUYS.
DO YOU HAVE A DEATH WISH?
CUT OUT THE TWANG, GOMER.
OKAY. MOUNT UP.
YOU'RE NOT JUST GOING TO WALTZ IN AND ASK THEM TO RAT OUT THE BIG BOSS?
YES MA'AM. RIGHT AFTER I SLIDE UP TO THE BAR AND ORDER ME A GLASS OF WARM MILK.
DID YOU SKINNY DIP IN THE STUPIDITY POND? I'M NOT GOING IN THERE.
I DIDN'T ASK YOU TO.
THE PATH I WALK I WALK ALONE. KEEP IT WARM, DUBBIE.
DUBBIE?
OH, I ALMOST FORGOT. THERE'S SOME THINGS I NEED YOU TO HOLD ON TO.

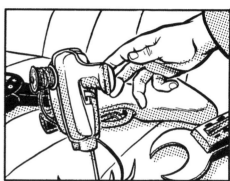

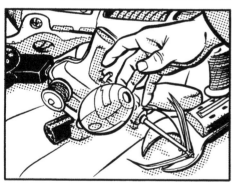

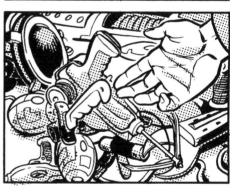

YOU'RE GOING UNARMED?

DIDN'T I TELL YOU HOW I GOT THIS JOB?

NUH-UH.

OH WELL.

JUST BE CAREFUL WITH THAT.

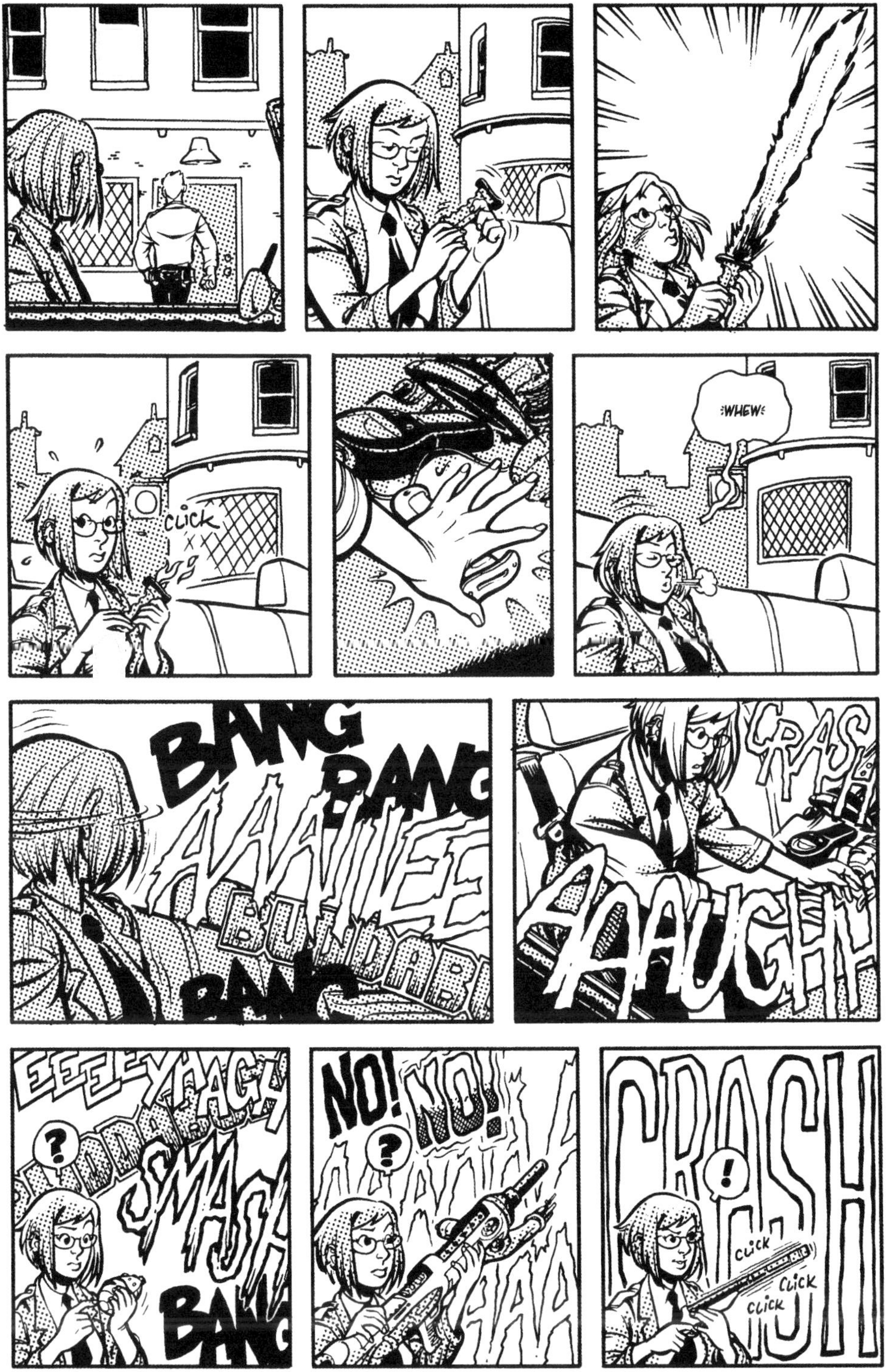
CLICK
WHEW
BANG
BANG
AAAIIEE
BUNDABB
BANG
CRASH
AAAUGH
EEEEYAAGH
SMACK
BANG
NO!
NO!
CRASH
CLICK
CLICK
CLICK

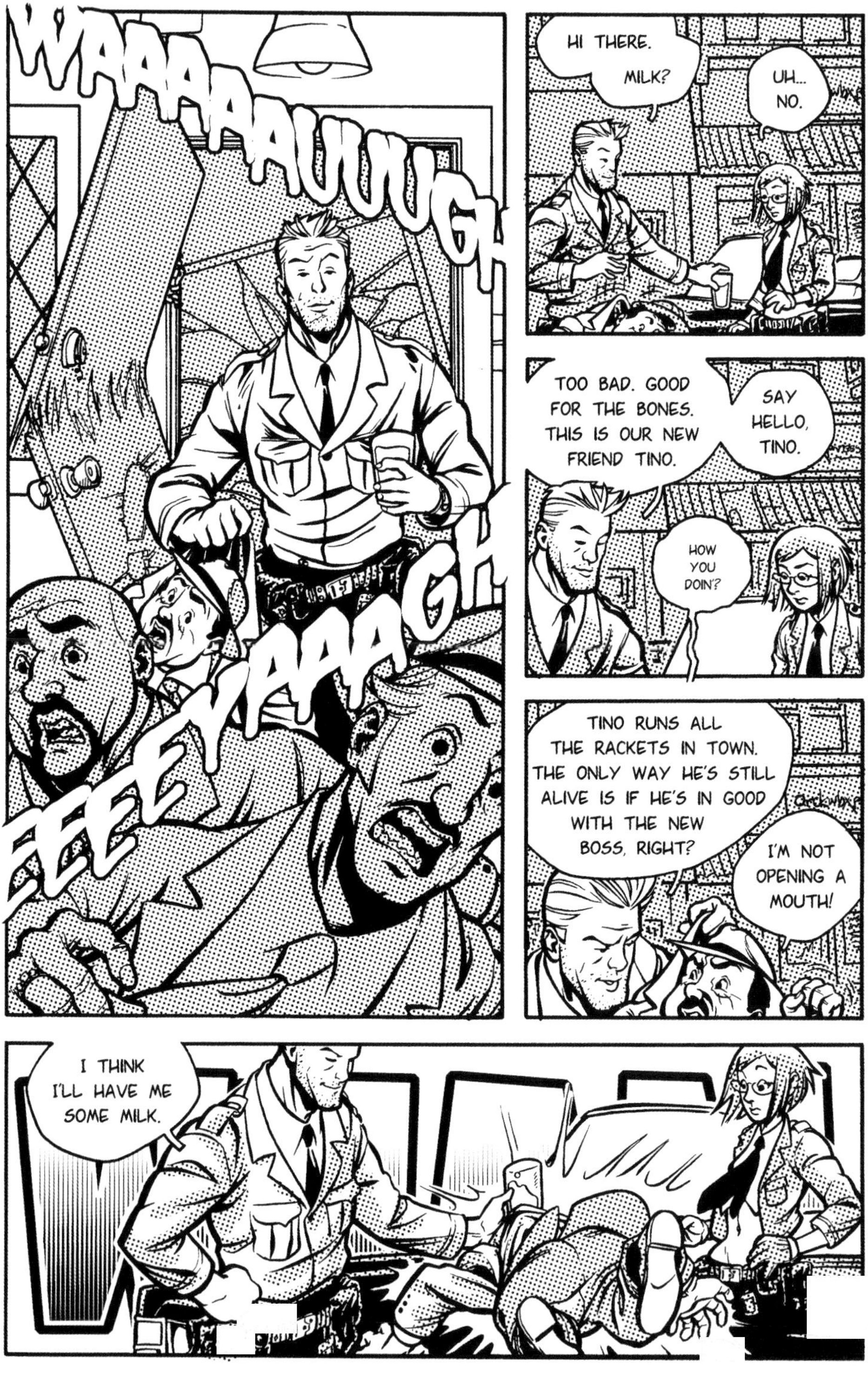
WAAAAAAUUUUGH
EEEYAAAGH
HI THERE.
MILK?
UH... NO.
TOO BAD. GOOD FOR THE BONES. THIS IS OUR NEW FRIEND TINO.
SAY HELLO, TINO.
HOW YOU DOIN'?
TINO RUNS ALL THE RACKETS IN TOWN. THE ONLY WAY HE'S STILL ALIVE IS IF HE'S IN GOOD WITH THE NEW BOSS, RIGHT?
I'M NOT OPENING A MOUTH!
I THINK I'LL HAVE ME SOME MILK.

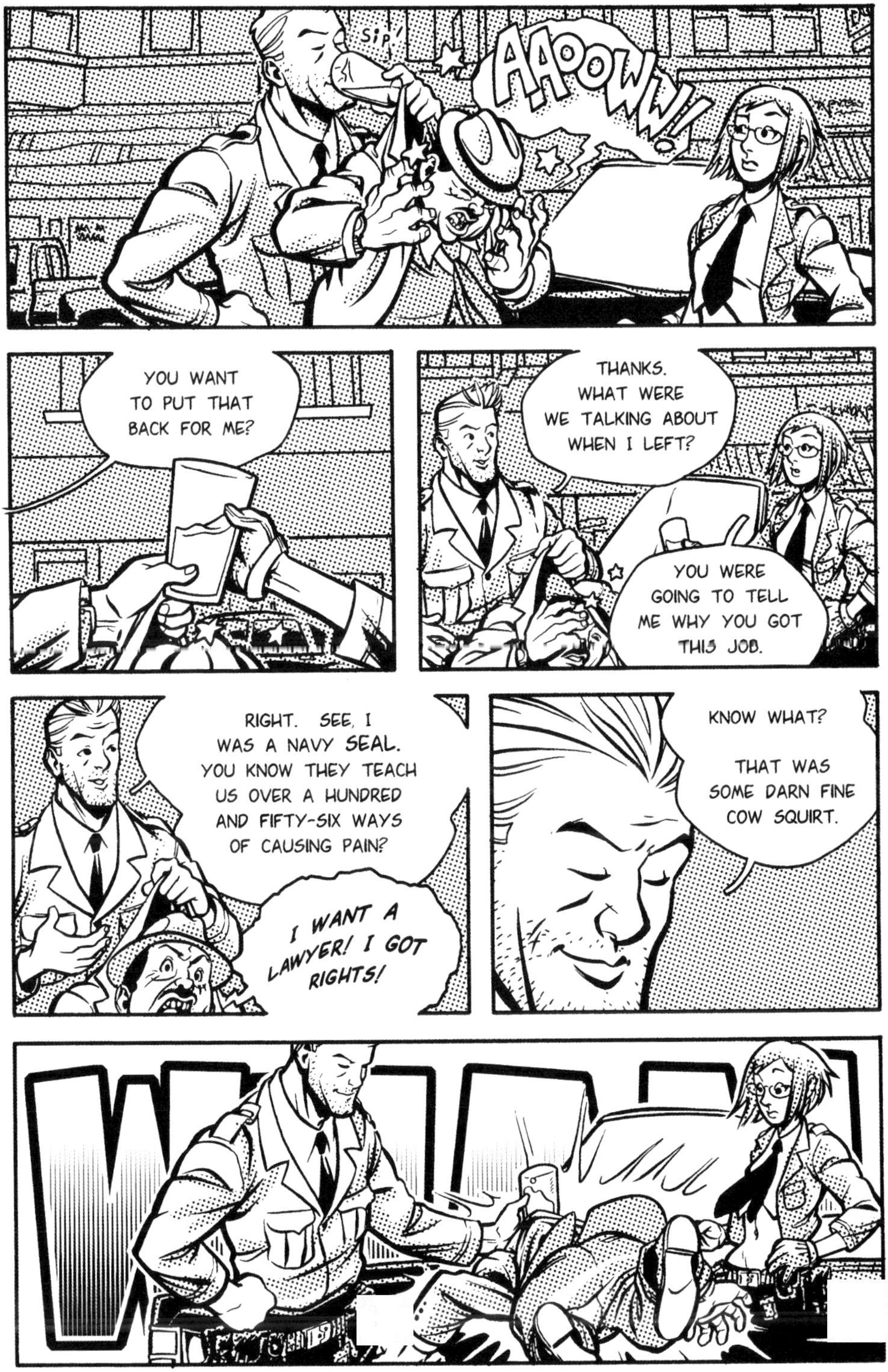
SIP!
AAOOWW!
YOU WANT TO PUT THAT BACK FOR ME?
THANKS. WHAT WERE WE TALKING ABOUT WHEN I LEFT?
YOU WERE GOING TO TELL ME WHY YOU GOT THIS JOB.
RIGHT. SEE, I WAS A NAVY SEAL. YOU KNOW THEY TEACH US OVER A HUNDRED AND FIFTY-SIX WAYS OF CAUSING PAIN?
I WANT A LAWYER! I GOT RIGHTS!
KNOW WHAT?
THAT WAS SOME DARN FINE COW SQUIRT.

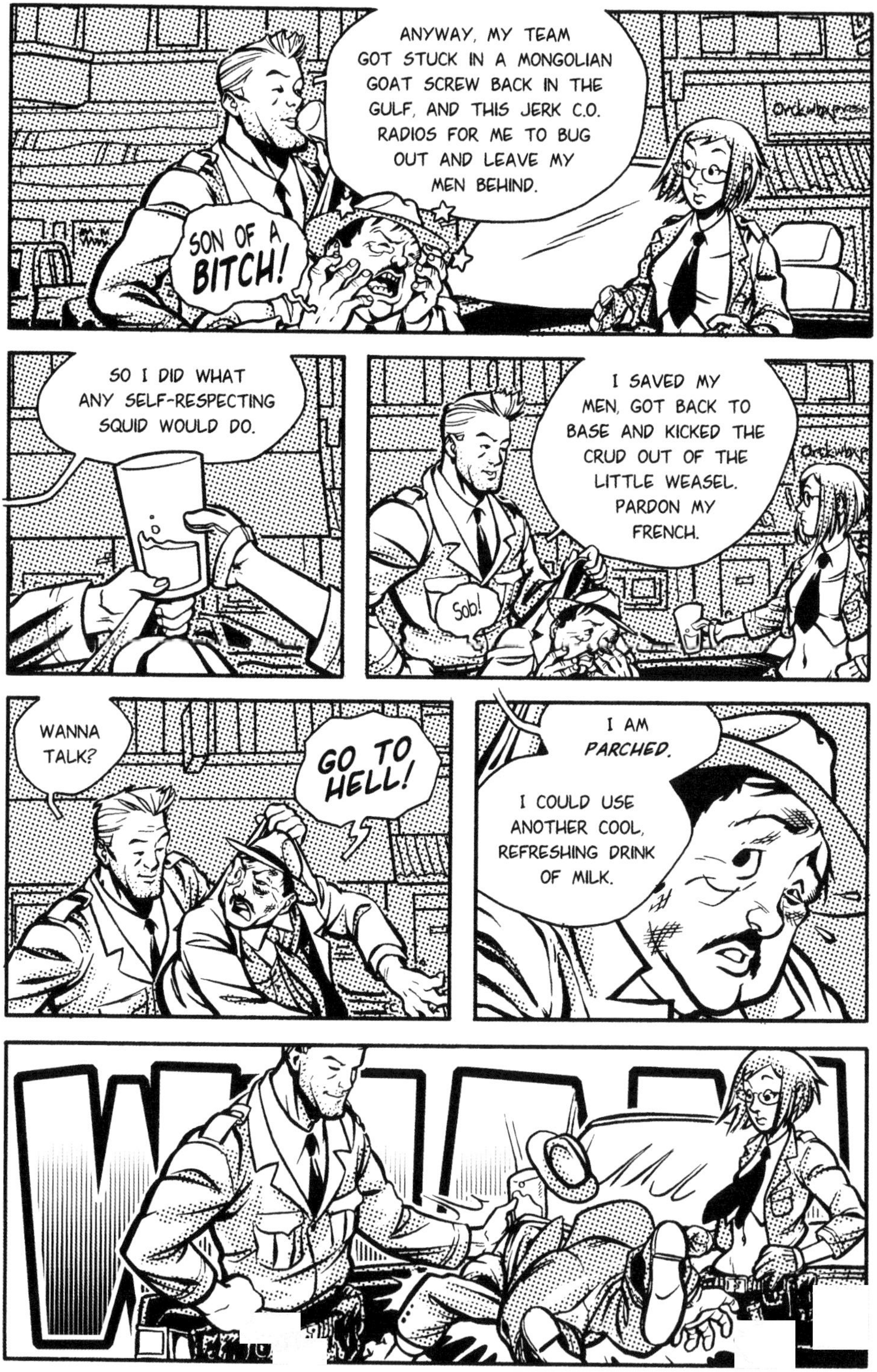
ANYWAY, MY TEAM GOT STUCK IN A MONGOLIAN GOAT SCREW BACK IN THE GULF, AND THIS JERK C.O. RADIOS FOR ME TO BUG OUT AND LEAVE MY MEN BEHIND.
SON OF A BITCH!
SO I DID WHAT ANY SELF-RESPECTING SQUID WOULD DO.
I SAVED MY MEN, GOT BACK TO BASE AND KICKED THE CRUD OUT OF THE LITTLE WEASEL. PARDON MY FRENCH.
Sob!
WANNA TALK?
GO TO HELL!
I AM PARCHED.
I COULD USE ANOTHER COOL, REFRESHING DRINK OF MILK.

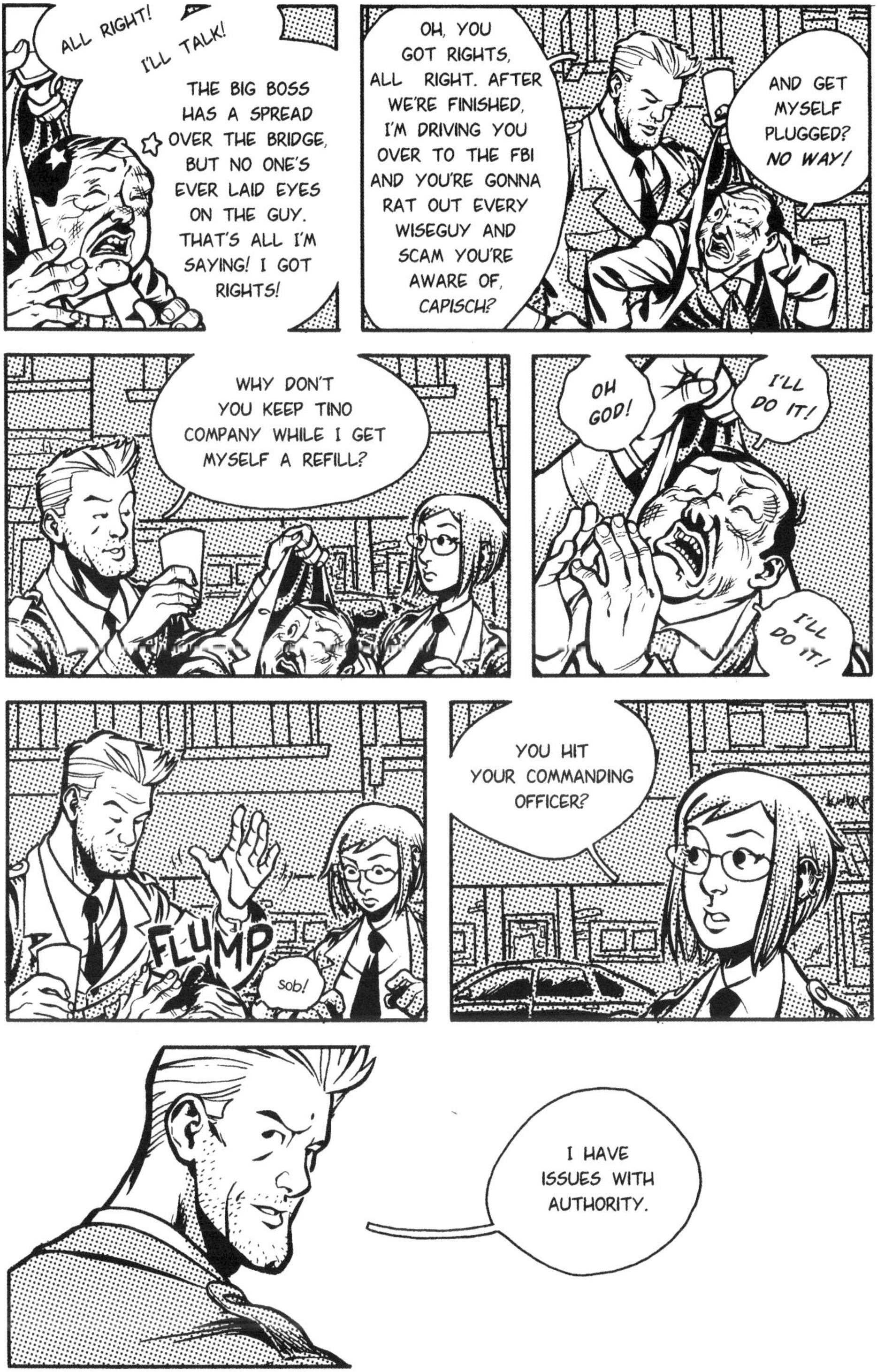
ALL RIGHT! I'LL TALK!
THE BIG BOSS HAS A SPREAD OVER THE BRIDGE, BUT NO ONE'S EVER LAID EYES ON THE GUY. THAT'S ALL I'M SAYING! I GOT RIGHTS!
OH, YOU GOT RIGHTS, ALL RIGHT. AFTER WE'RE FINISHED, I'M DRIVING YOU OVER TO THE FBI AND YOU'RE GONNA RAT OUT EVERY WISEGUY AND SCAM YOU'RE AWARE OF, CAPISCH?
AND GET MYSELF PLUGGED? NO WAY!
WHY DON'T YOU KEEP TINO COMPANY WHILE I GET MYSELF A REFILL?
OH GOD!
I'LL DO IT!
I'LL DO IT!
FLUMP
sob!
YOU HIT YOUR COMMANDING OFFICER?
I HAVE ISSUES WITH AUTHORITY.

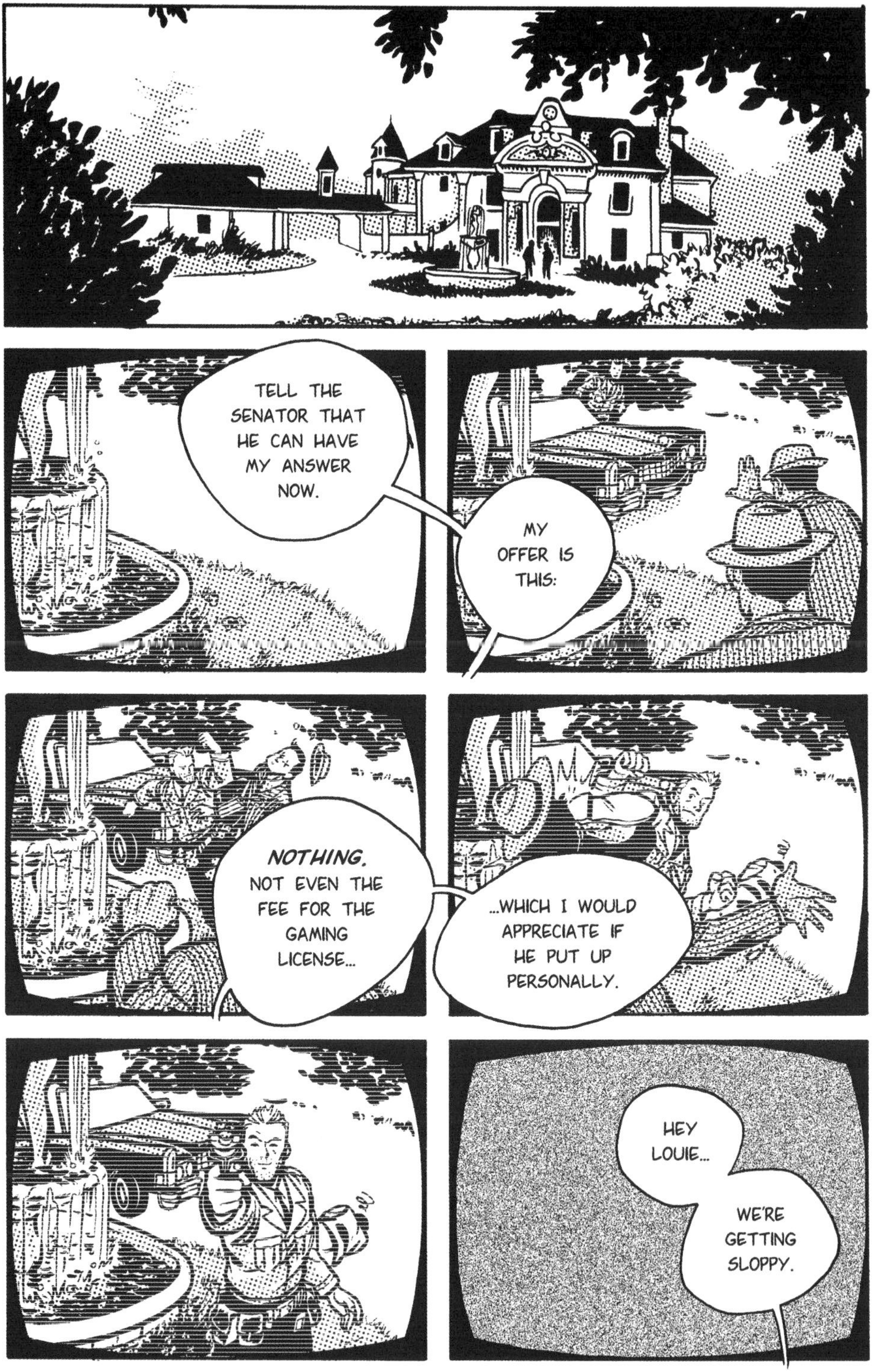
TELL THE SENATOR THAT HE CAN HAVE MY ANSWER NOW.
MY OFFER IS THIS:
NOTHING. NOT EVEN THE FEE FOR THE GAMING LICENSE...
...WHICH I WOULD APPRECIATE IF HE PUT UP PERSONALLY.
HEY LOUIE...
WE'RE GETTING SLOPPY.

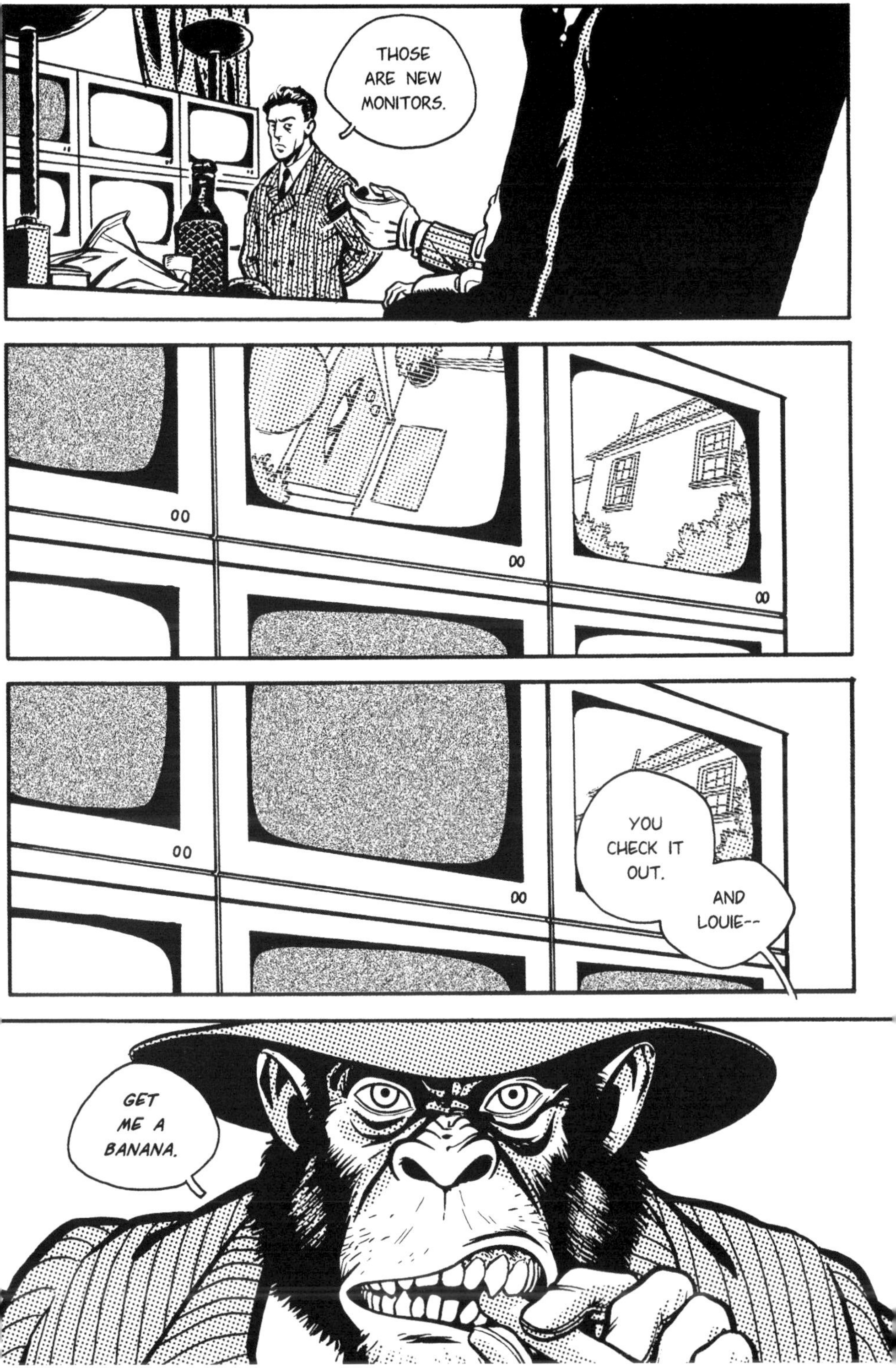
THOSE ARE NEW MONITORS.
YOU CHECK IT OUT.
AND LOUIE--
GET ME A BANANA.

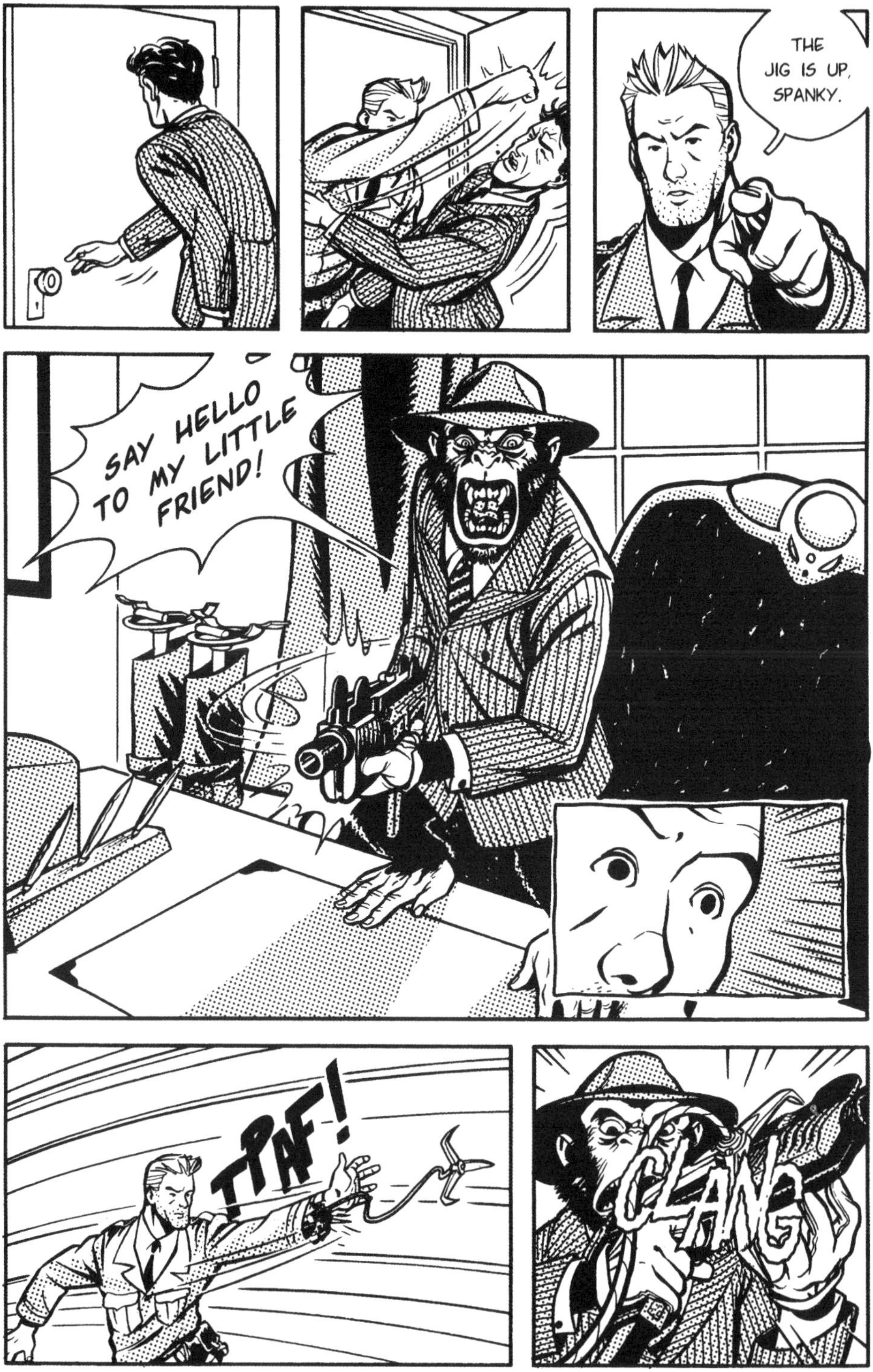
THE JIG IS UP, SPANKY.
SAY HELLO TO MY LITTLE FRIEND!
TPAF!
CLANG

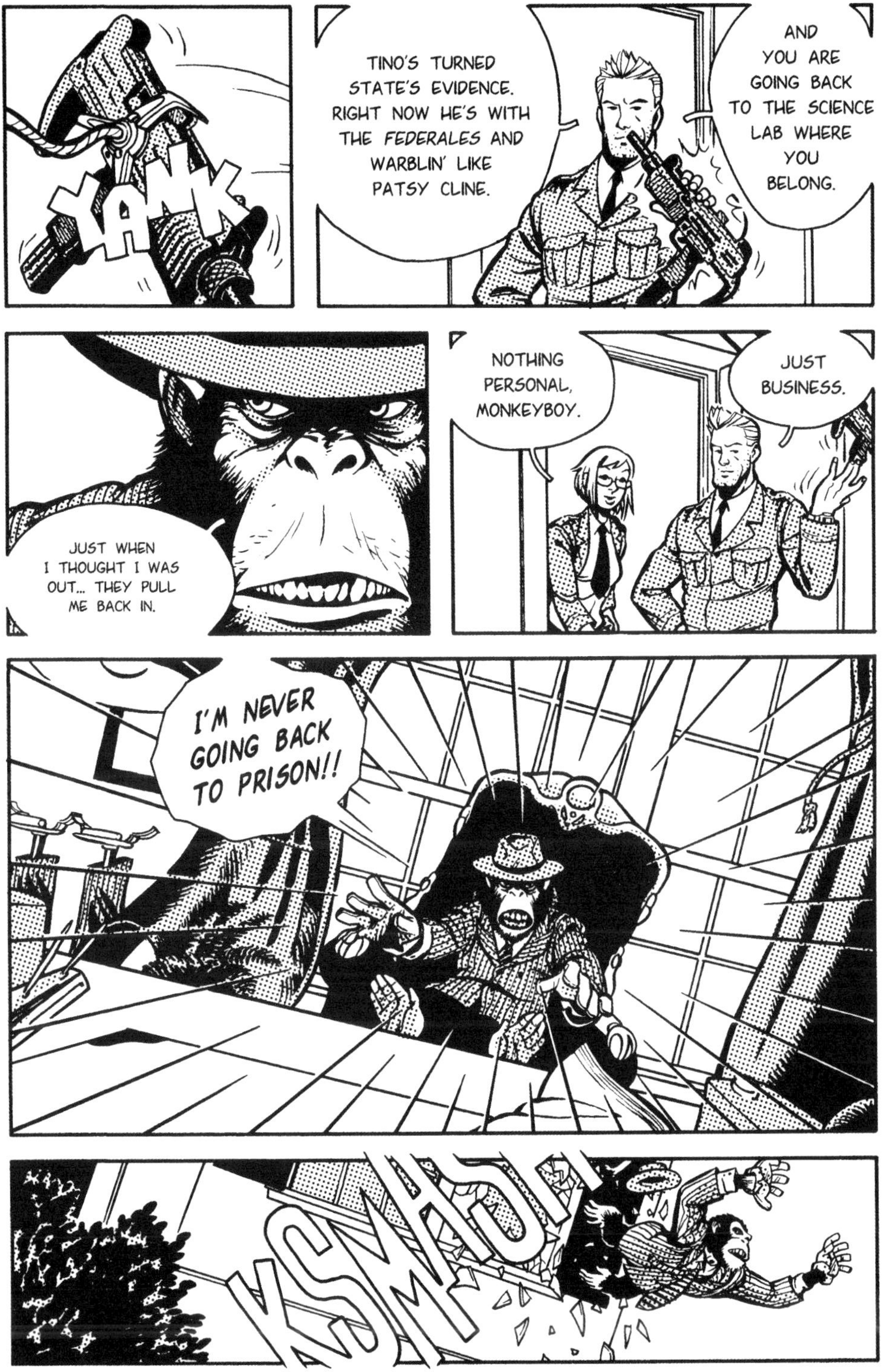
YANK
TINO'S TURNED STATE'S EVIDENCE. RIGHT NOW HE'S WITH THE FEDERALES AND WARBLIN' LIKE PATSY CLINE.
AND YOU ARE GOING BACK TO THE SCIENCE LAB WHERE YOU BELONG.
JUST WHEN I THOUGHT I WAS OUT... THEY PULL ME BACK IN.
NOTHING PERSONAL, MONKEYBOY.
JUST BUSINESS.
I'M NEVER GOING BACK TO PRISON!!
KSMASH

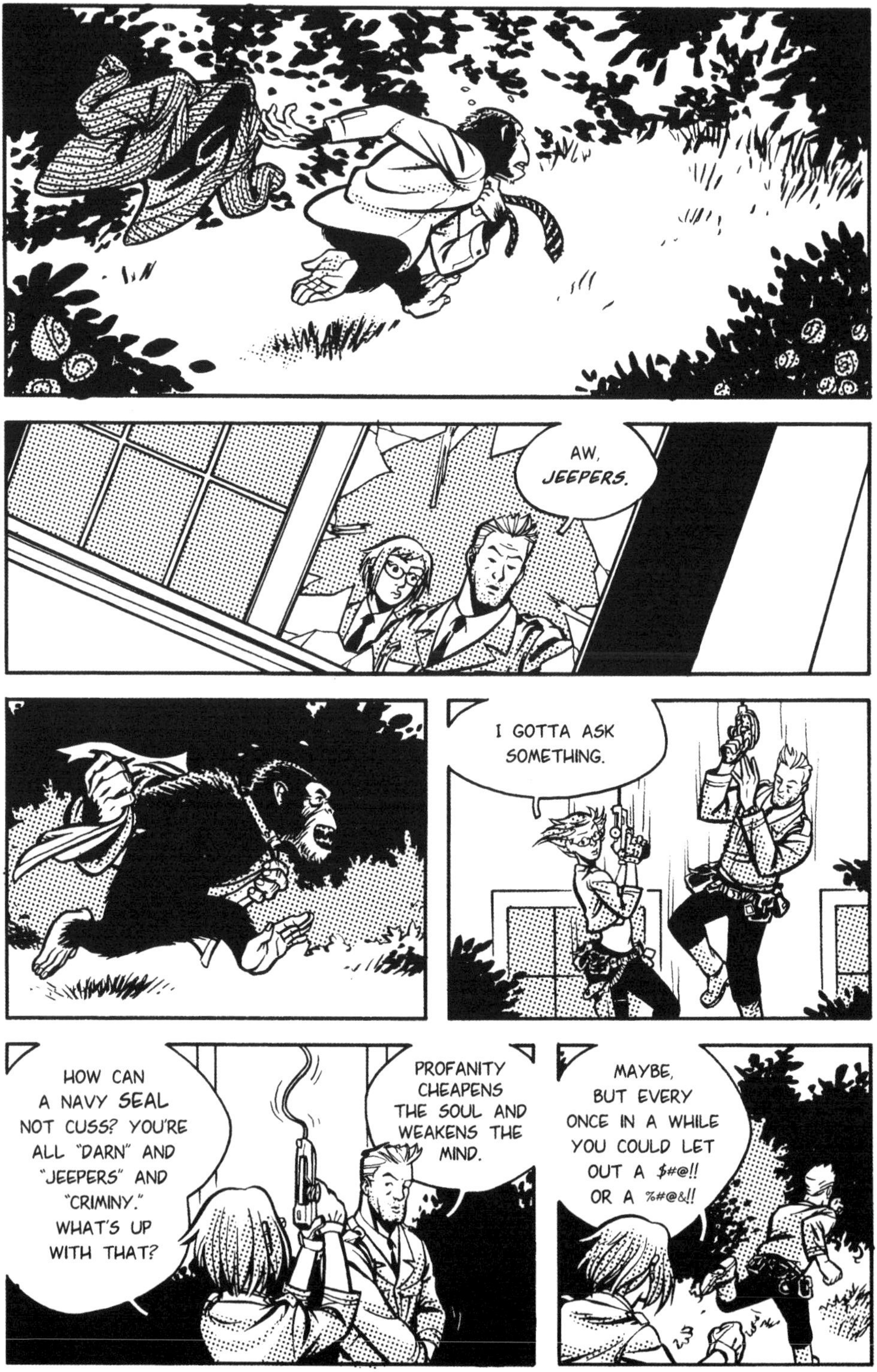
AW, JEEPERS.
I GOTTA ASK SOMETHING.
HOW CAN A NAVY SEAL NOT CUSS? YOU'RE ALL "DARN" AND "JEEPERS" AND "CRIMINY." WHAT'S UP WITH THAT?
PROFANITY CHEAPENS THE SOUL AND WEAKENS THE MIND.
MAYBE, BUT EVERY ONCE IN A WHILE YOU COULD LET OUT A $#@!! OR A %#@&!!

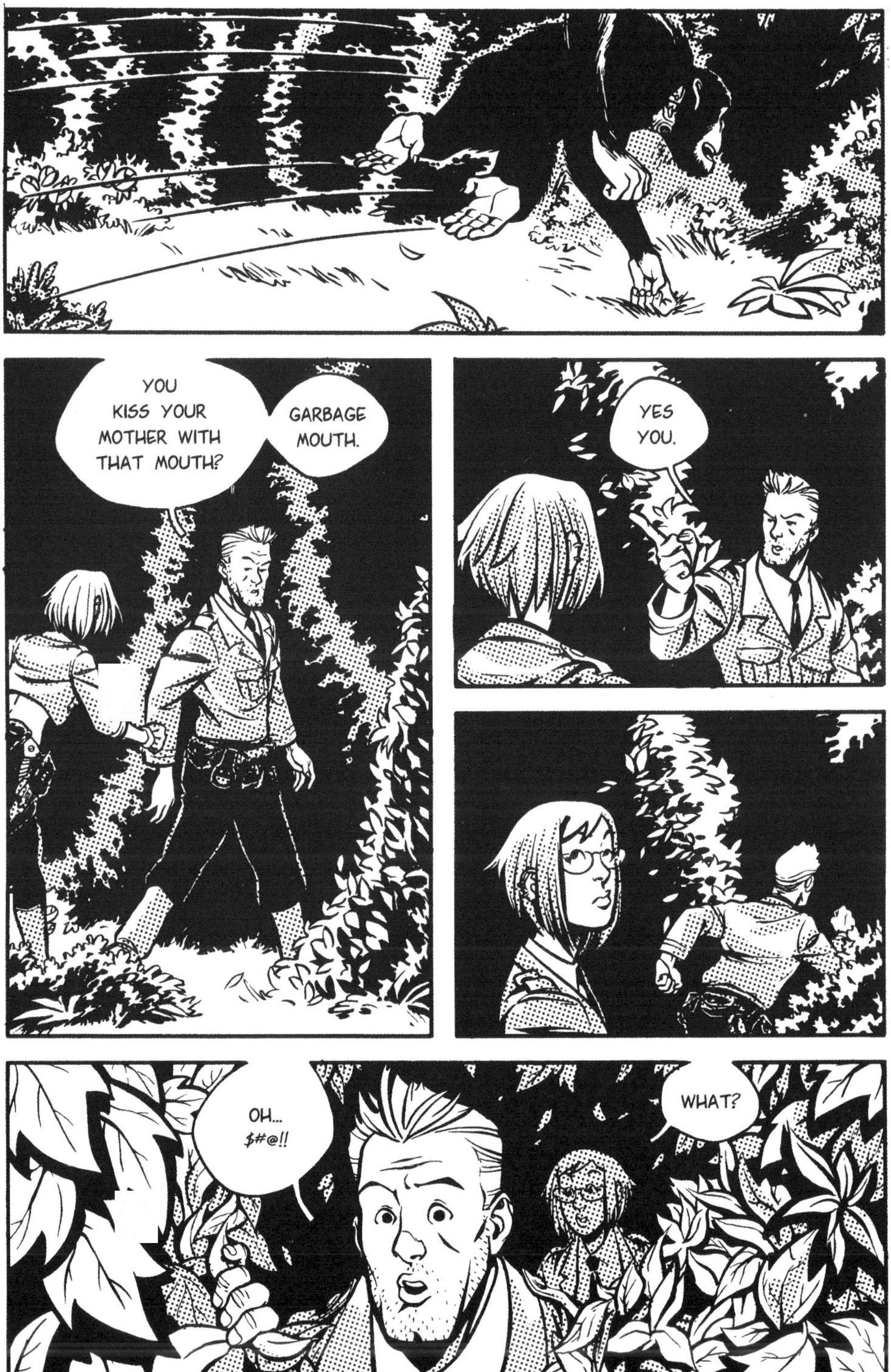
YOU KISS YOUR MOTHER WITH THAT MOUTH?
GARBAGE MOUTH.
YES YOU.
OH... $#@!!
WHAT?

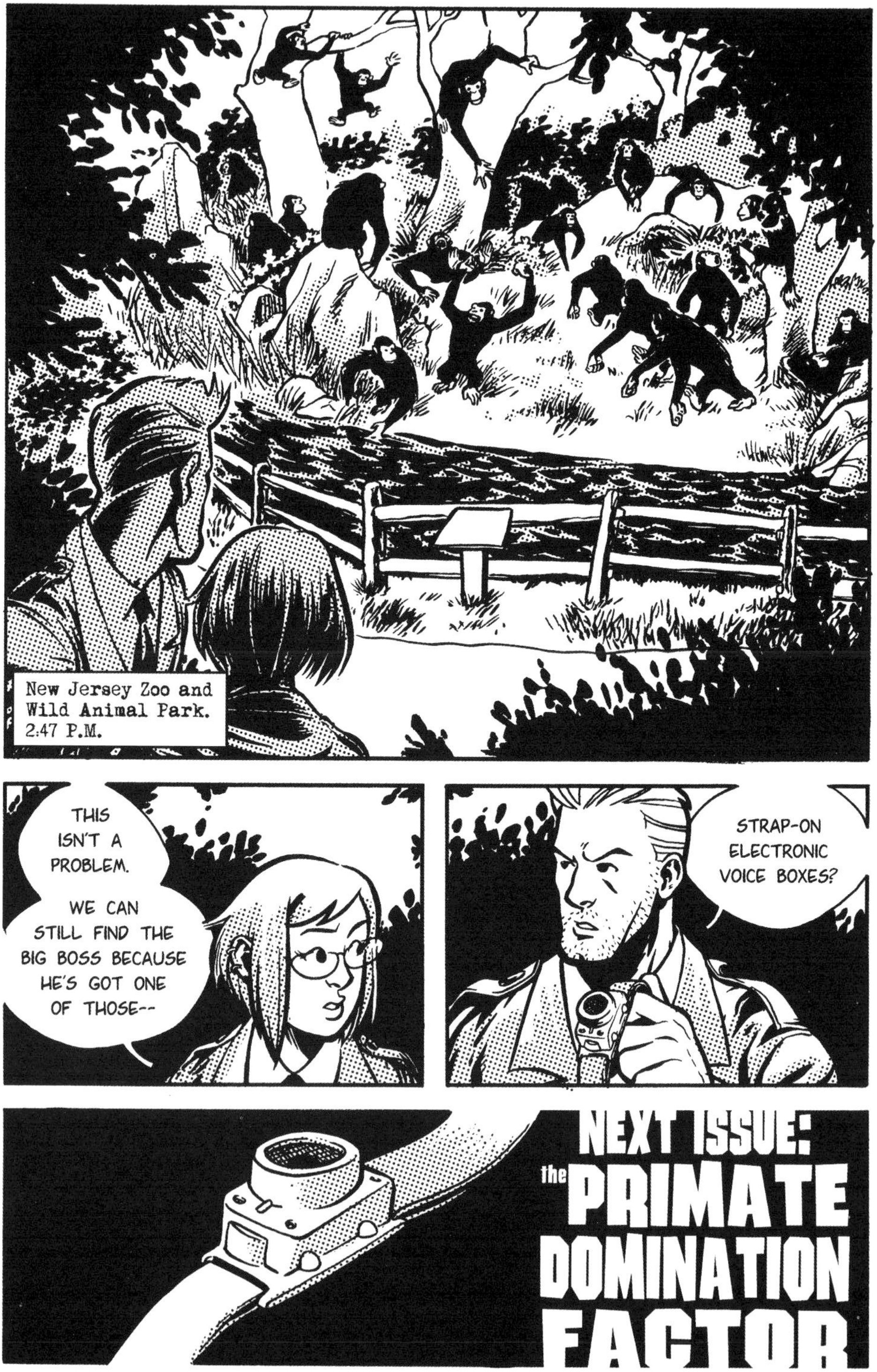
New Jersey Zoo and Wild Animal Park. 2:47 P.M.
THIS ISN'T A PROBLEM.
WE CAN STILL FIND THE BIG BOSS BECAUSE HE'S GOT ONE OF THOSE--
STRAP-ON ELECTRONIC VOICE BOXES?
NEXT ISSUE:
the PRIMATE DOMINATION FACTOR

CHAPTER 04

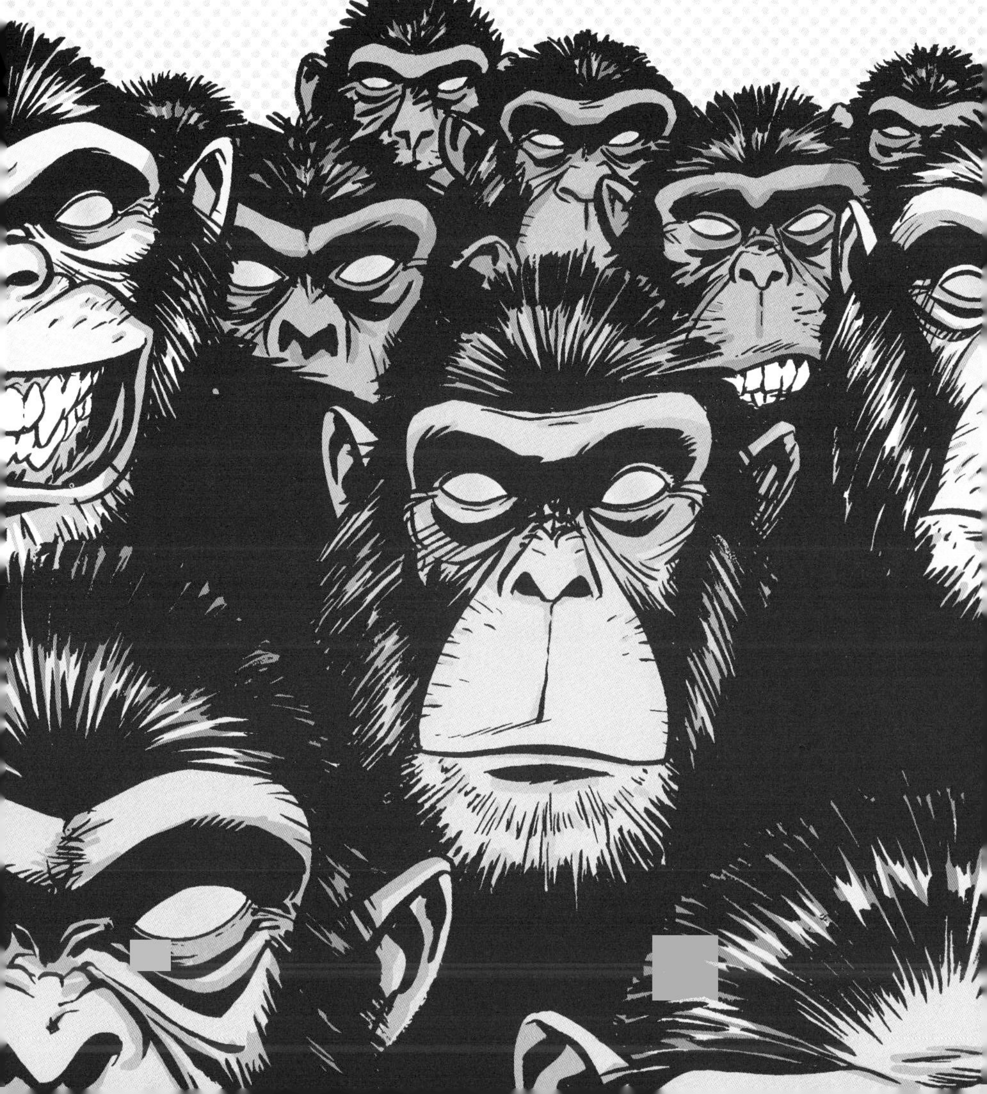

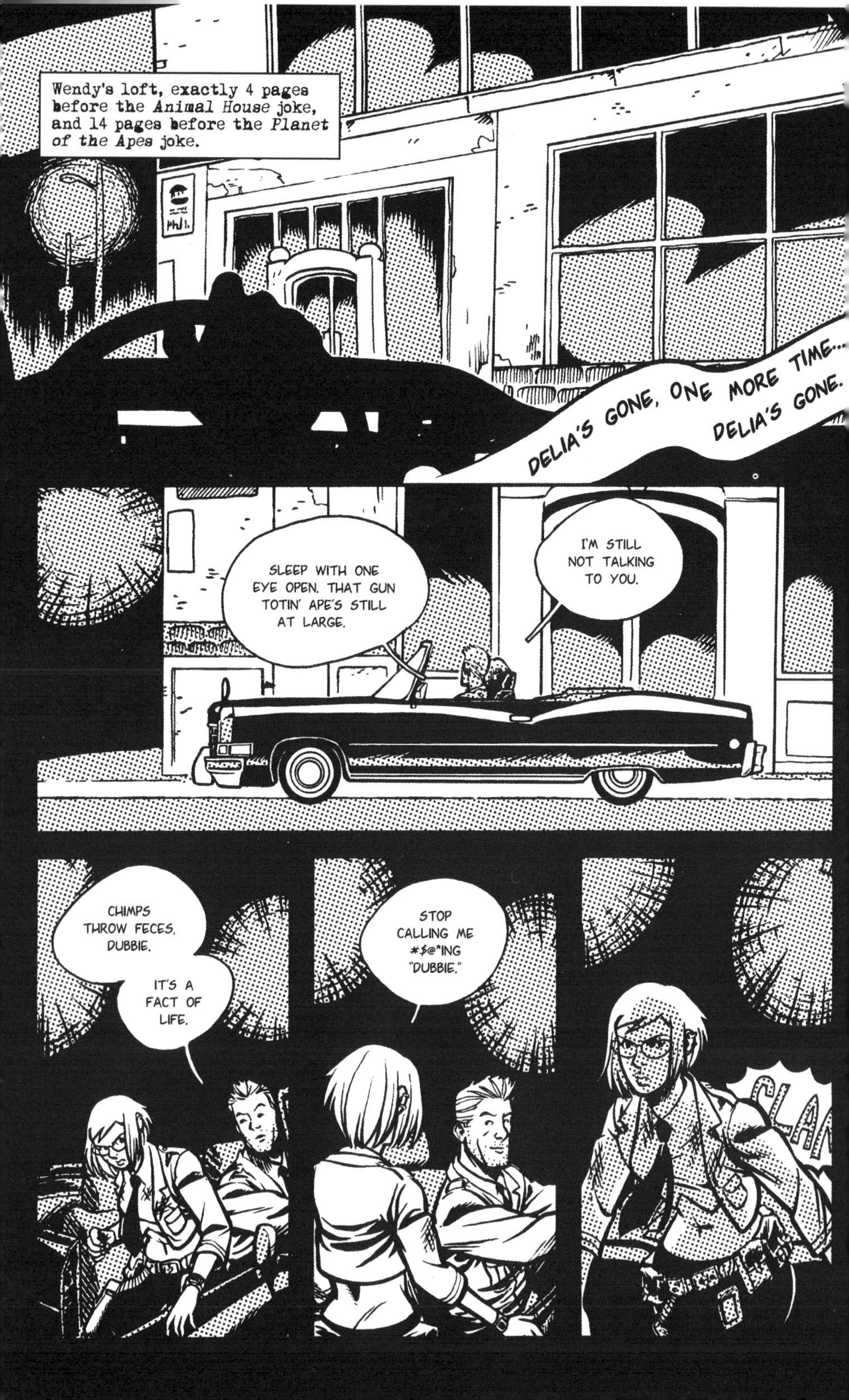
Wendy's loft, exactly 4 pages before the *Animal House* joke, and 14 pages before the *Planet of the Apes* joke.
DELIA'S GONE, ONE MORE TIME... DELIA'S GONE.
SLEEP WITH ONE EYE OPEN. THAT GUN TOTIN' APE'S STILL AT LARGE.
I'M STILL NOT TALKING TO YOU.
CHIMPS THROW FECES, DUBBIE.
IT'S A FACT OF LIFE.
STOP CALLING ME #$@*ING "DUBBIE."

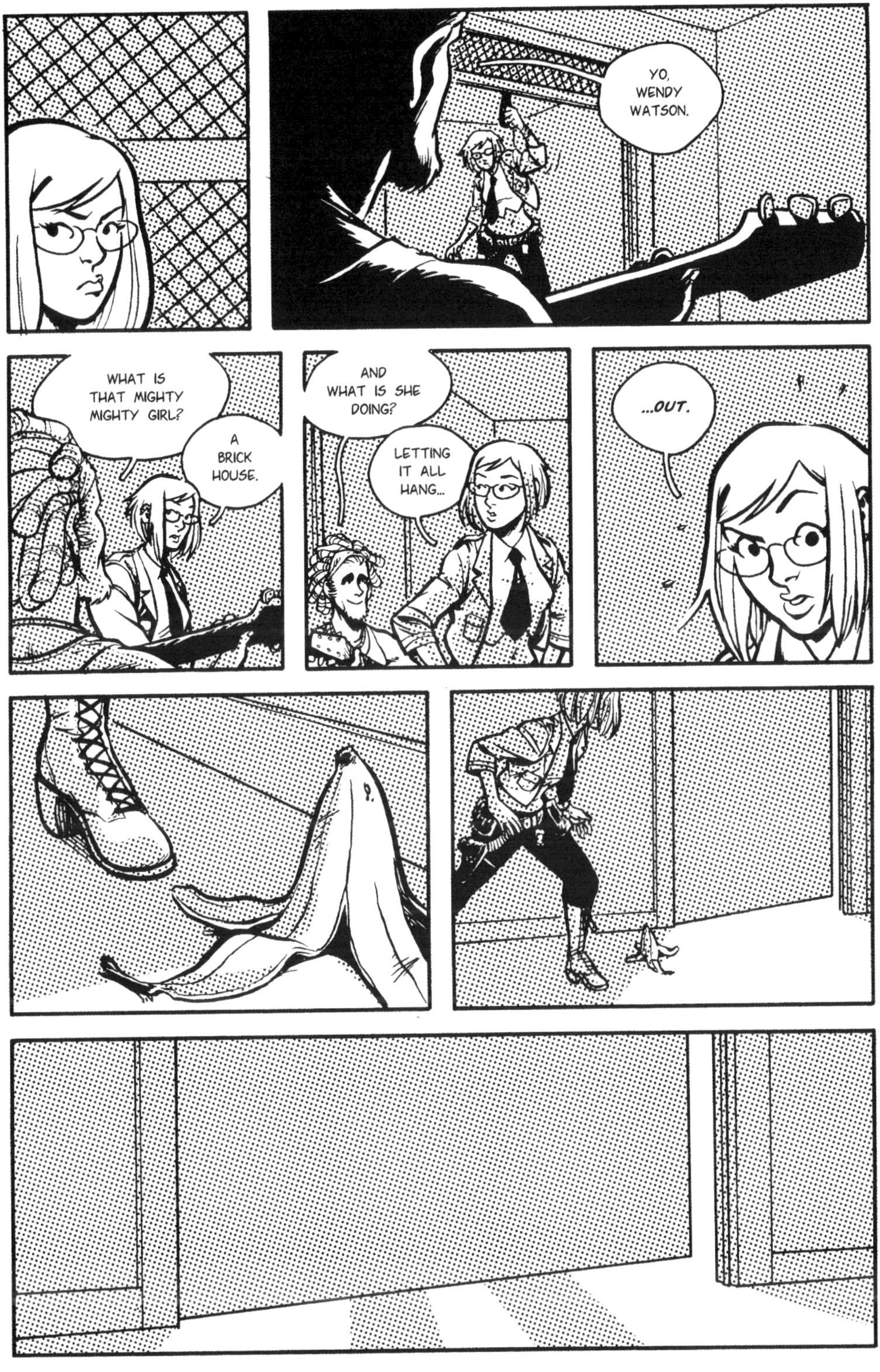
YO, WENDY WATSON.
WHAT IS THAT MIGHTY MIGHTY GIRL?
A BRICK HOUSE.
AND WHAT IS SHE DOING?
LETTING IT ALL HANG...
...OUT.

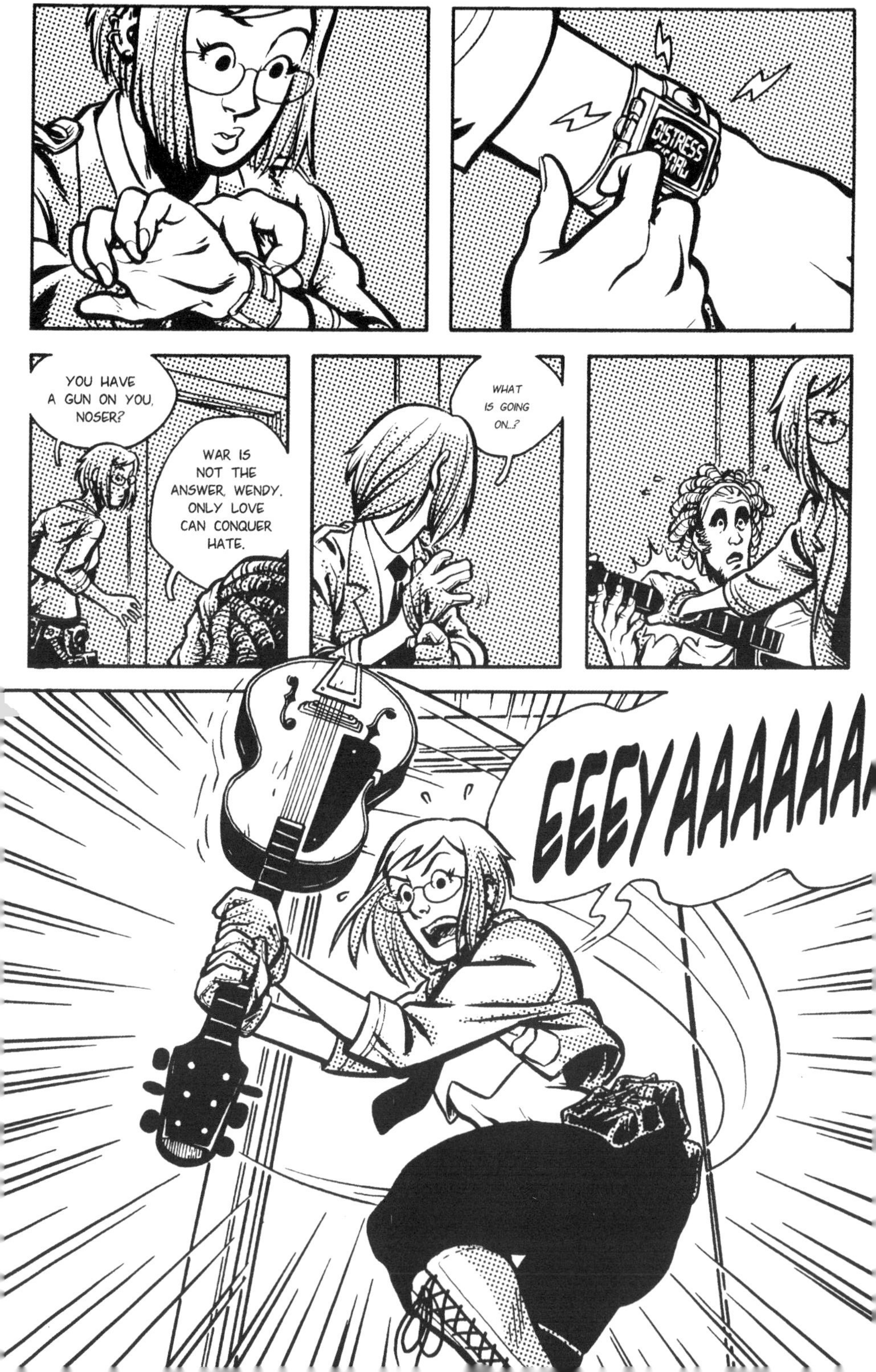
DISTRESS SIGNAL
YOU HAVE A GUN ON YOU, NOSER?
WAR IS NOT THE ANSWER, WENDY. ONLY LOVE CAN CONQUER HATE.
WHAT IS GOING ON...?
EEEYAAAAAA

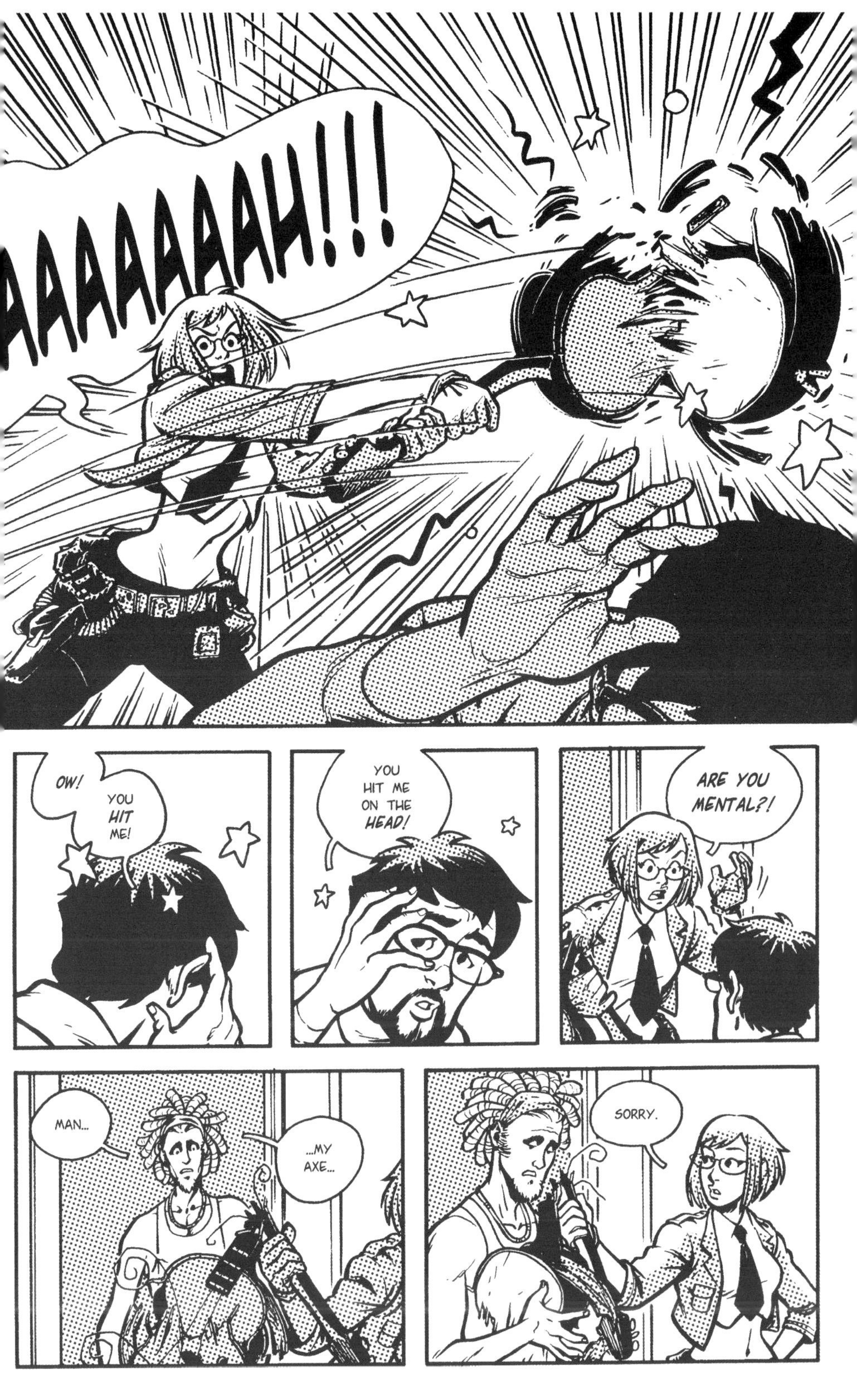
AAAAAAAAH!!!
OW!
YOU HIT ME!
YOU HIT ME ON THE HEAD!
ARE YOU MENTAL?!
MAN...
...MY AXE...
SORRY.

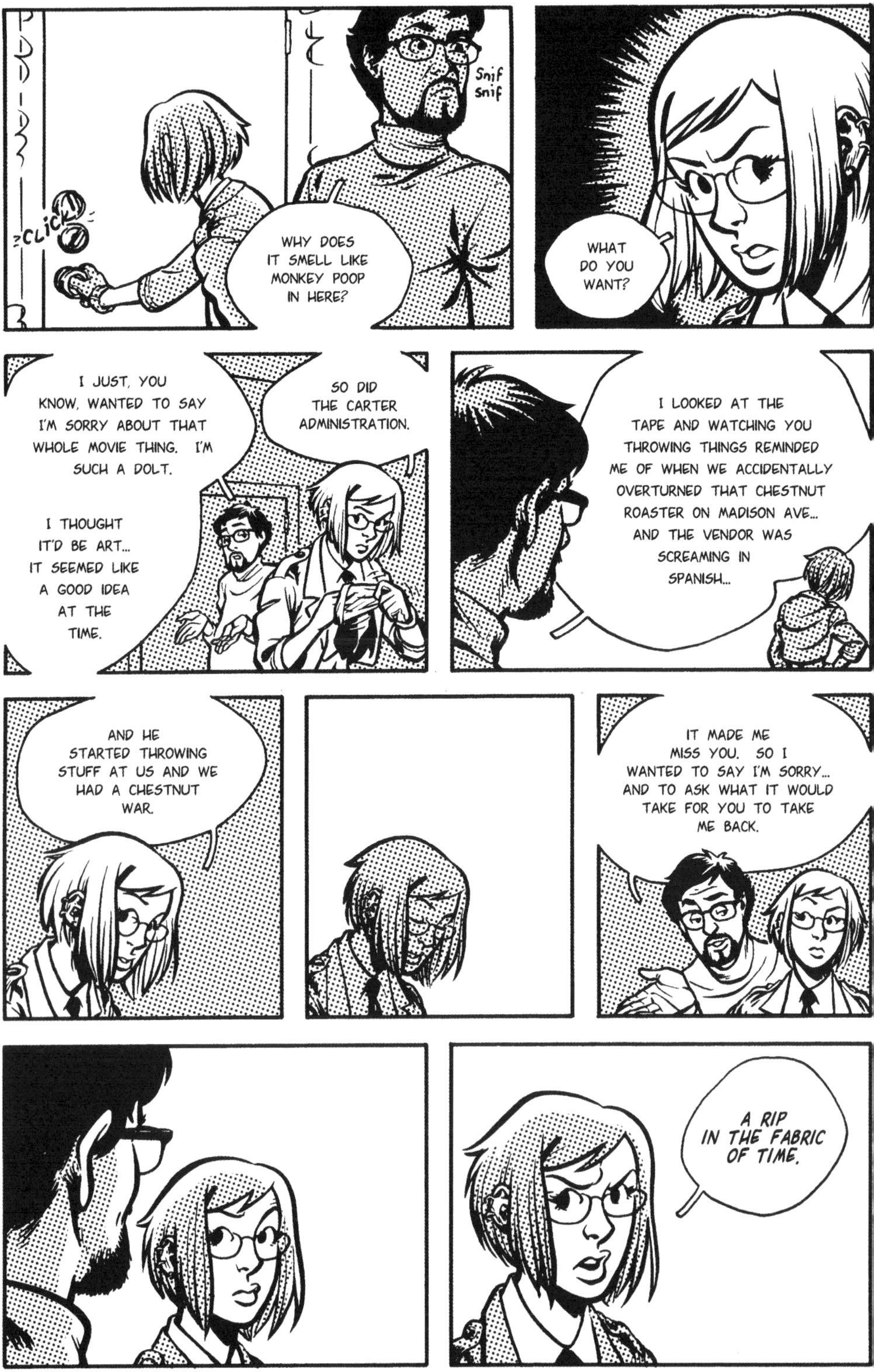
CLICK
Snif snif
WHY DOES IT SMELL LIKE MONKEY POOP IN HERE?
WHAT DO YOU WANT?
I JUST, YOU KNOW, WANTED TO SAY I'M SORRY ABOUT THAT WHOLE MOVIE THING. I'M SUCH A DOLT.
I THOUGHT IT'D BE ART... IT SEEMED LIKE A GOOD IDEA AT THE TIME.
SO DID THE CARTER ADMINISTRATION.
I LOOKED AT THE TAPE AND WATCHING YOU THROWING THINGS REMINDED ME OF WHEN WE ACCIDENTALLY OVERTURNED THAT CHESTNUT ROASTER ON MADISON AVE... AND THE VENDOR WAS SCREAMING IN SPANISH...
AND HE STARTED THROWING STUFF AT US AND WE HAD A CHESTNUT WAR.
IT MADE ME MISS YOU. SO I WANTED TO SAY I'M SORRY... AND TO ASK WHAT IT WOULD TAKE FOR YOU TO TAKE ME BACK.
A RIP IN THE FABRIC OF TIME.

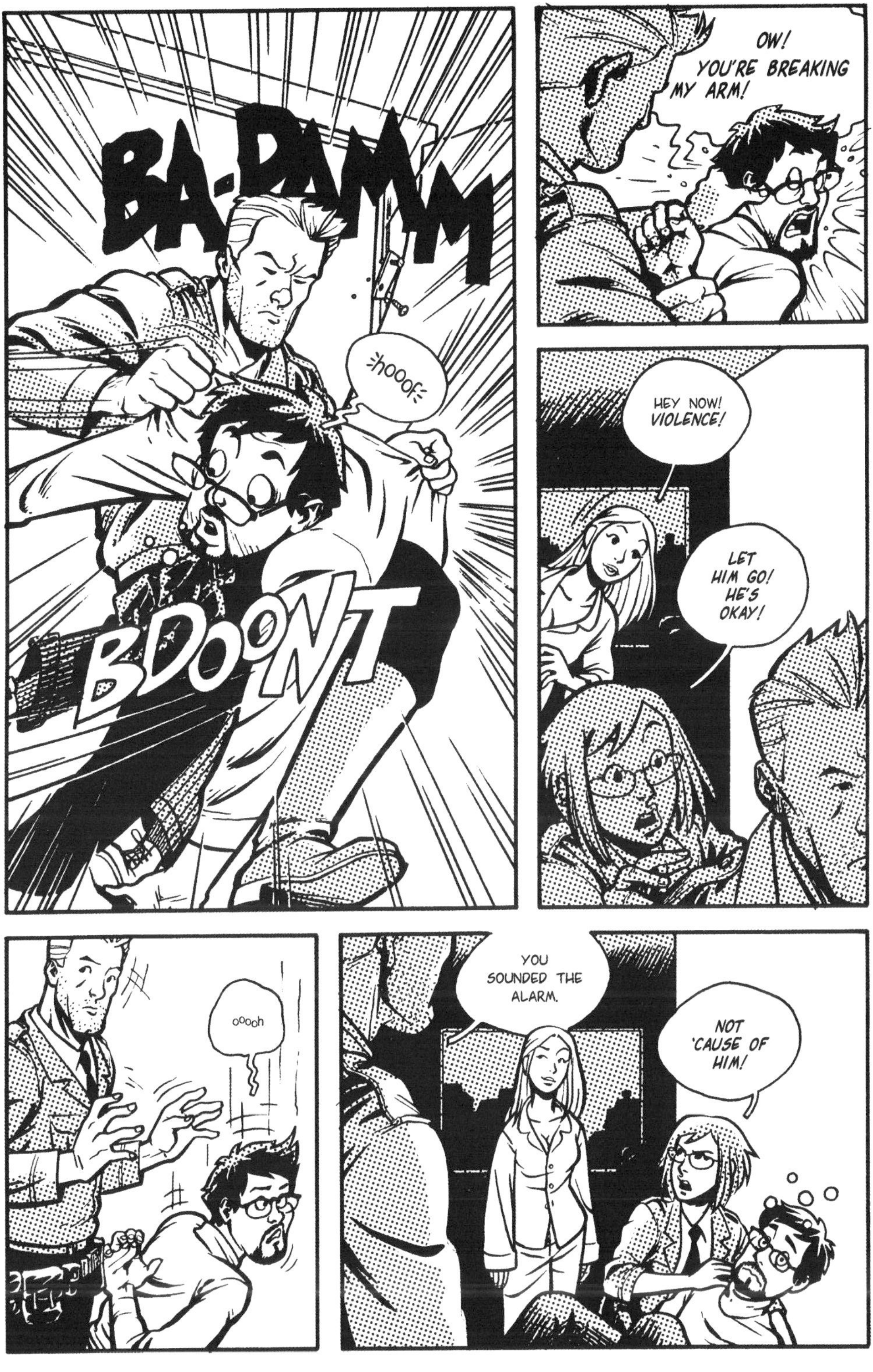
BA-DAMM
hooof
BDOOINT
OW!
YOU'RE BREAKING MY ARM!
HEY NOW! VIOLENCE!
LET HIM GO! HE'S OKAY!
ooooh
YOU SOUNDED THE ALARM.
NOT 'CAUSE OF HIM!

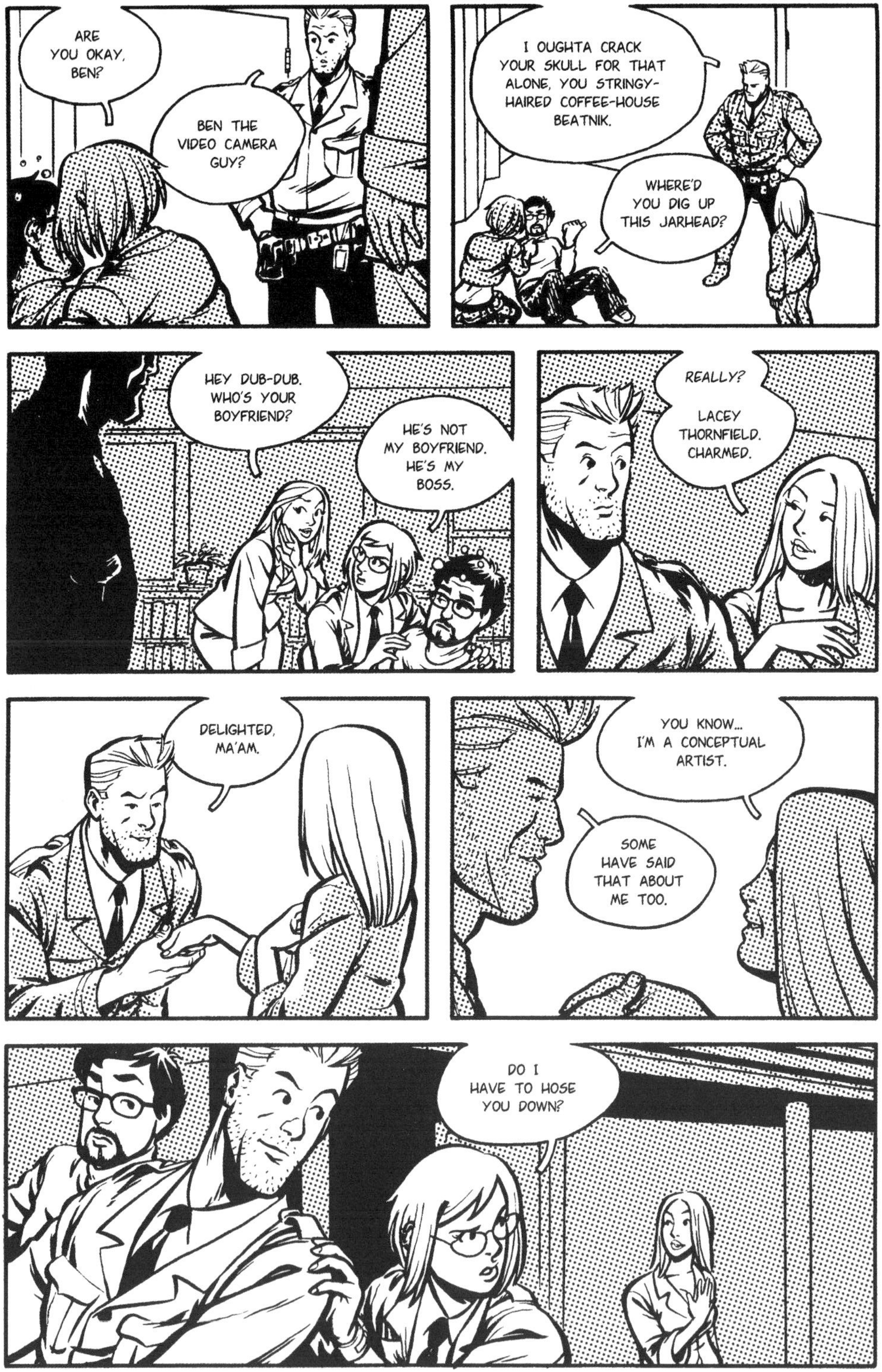
ARE YOU OKAY, BEN?
BEN THE VIDEO CAMERA GUY?
I OUGHTA CRACK YOUR SKULL FOR THAT ALONE, YOU STRINGY-HAIRED COFFEE-HOUSE BEATNIK.
WHERE'D YOU DIG UP THIS JARHEAD?
HEY DUB-DUB. WHO'S YOUR BOYFRIEND?
HE'S NOT MY BOYFRIEND. HE'S MY BOSS.
REALLY?
LACEY THORNFIELD. CHARMED.
DELIGHTED, MA'AM.
YOU KNOW... I'M A CONCEPTUAL ARTIST.
SOME HAVE SAID THAT ABOUT ME TOO.
DO I HAVE TO HOSE YOU DOWN?

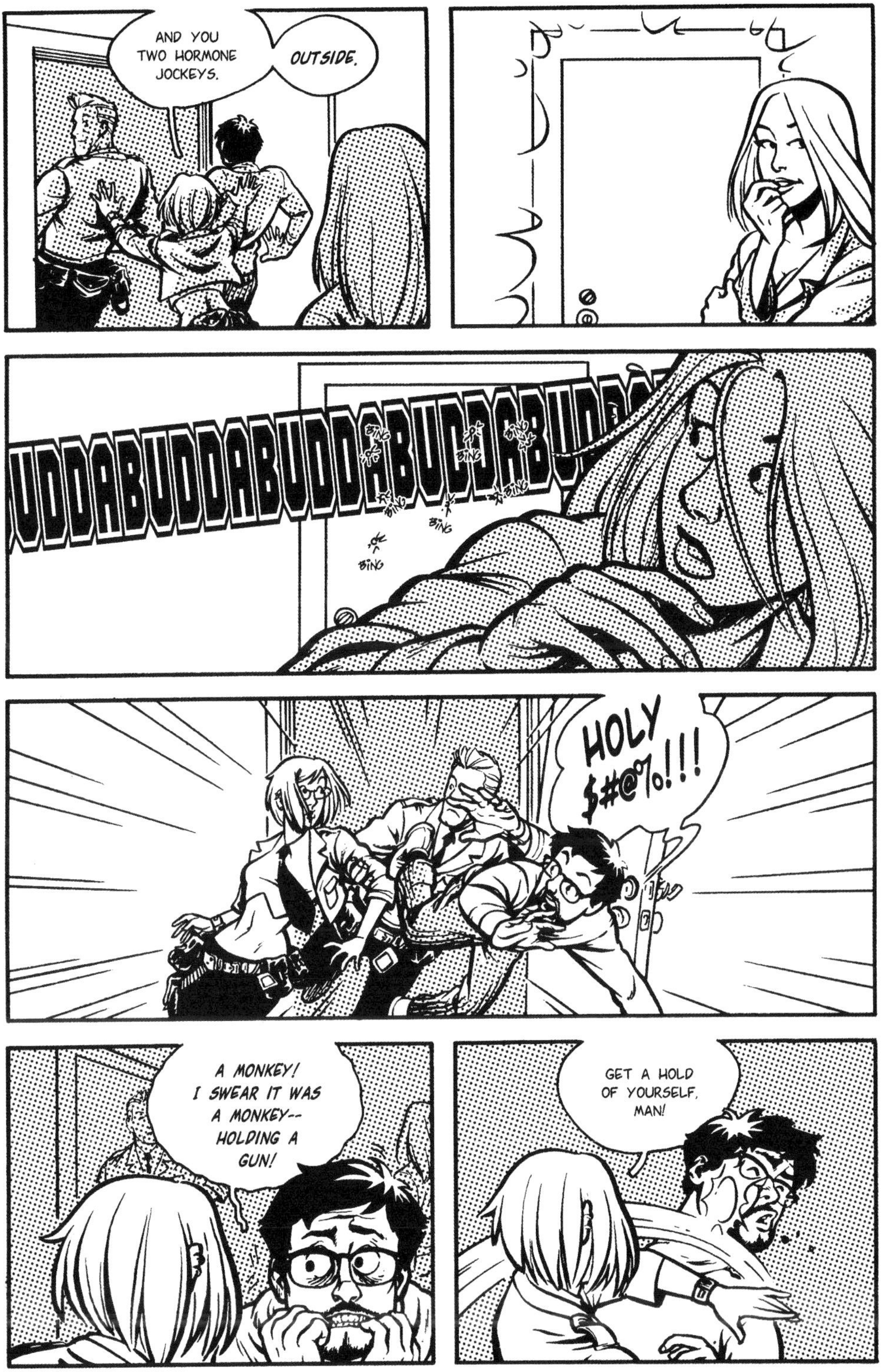
AND YOU TWO HORMONE JOCKEYS.
OUTSIDE.
BUDDABUDDABUDDABUDDABU
BING
BING
BING
BING
BING
BING
BING
HOLY $#@%!!!
A MONKEY! I SWEAR IT WAS A MONKEY-- HOLDING A GUN!
GET A HOLD OF YOURSELF, MAN!

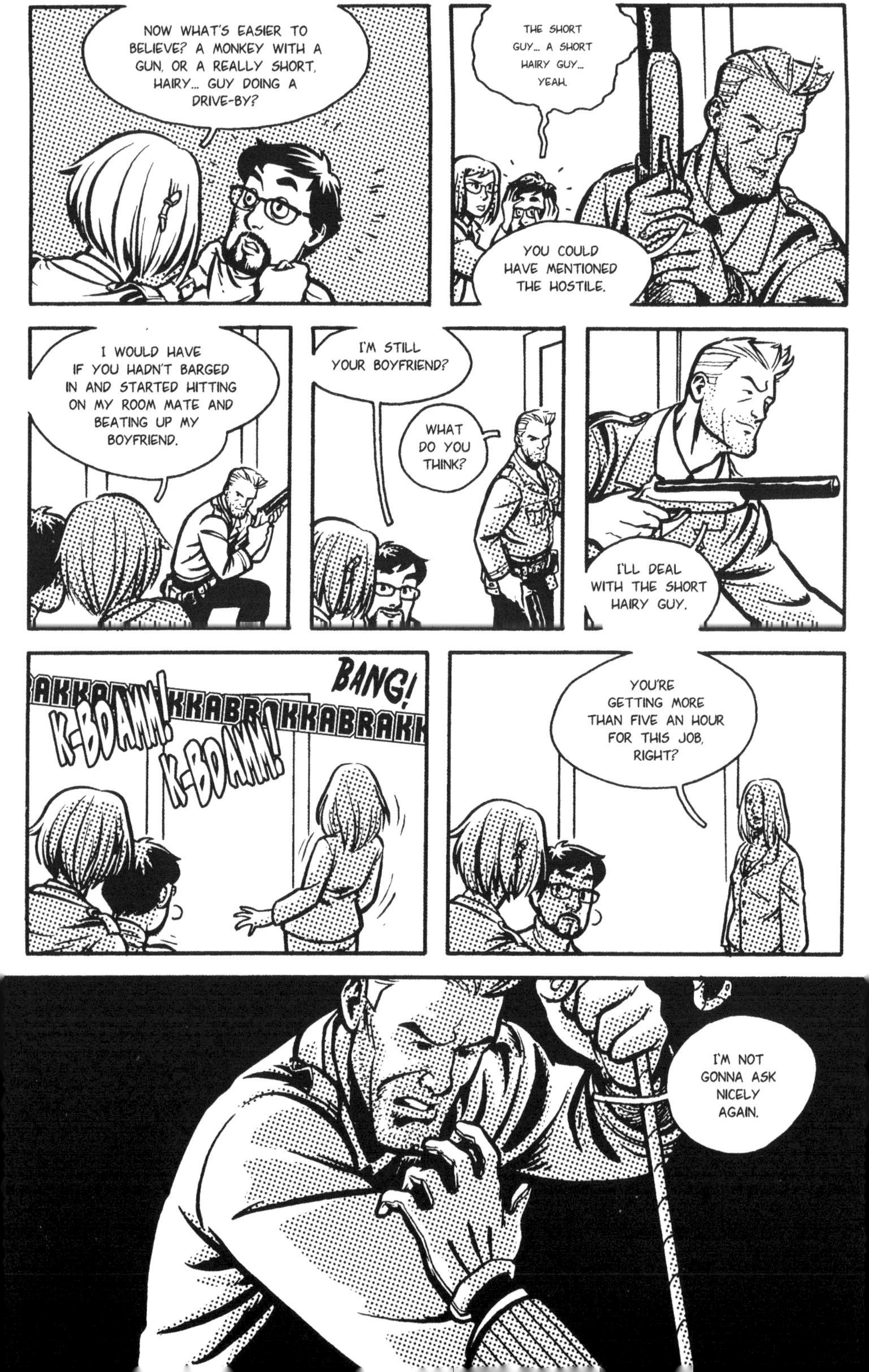
NOW WHAT'S EASIER TO BELIEVE? A MONKEY WITH A GUN, OR A REALLY SHORT, HAIRY... GUY DOING A DRIVE-BY?
THE SHORT GUY... A SHORT HAIRY GUY... YEAH.
YOU COULD HAVE MENTIONED THE HOSTILE.
I WOULD HAVE IF YOU HADN'T BARGED IN AND STARTED HITTING ON MY ROOM MATE AND BEATING UP MY BOYFRIEND.
I'M STILL YOUR BOYFRIEND?
WHAT DO YOU THINK?
I'LL DEAL WITH THE SHORT HAIRY GUY.
BANG!
K-BDAMM!
KKABRAKKABRAKK
K-BDAMM!
YOU'RE GETTING MORE THAN FIVE AN HOUR FOR THIS JOB, RIGHT?
I'M NOT GONNA ASK NICELY AGAIN.

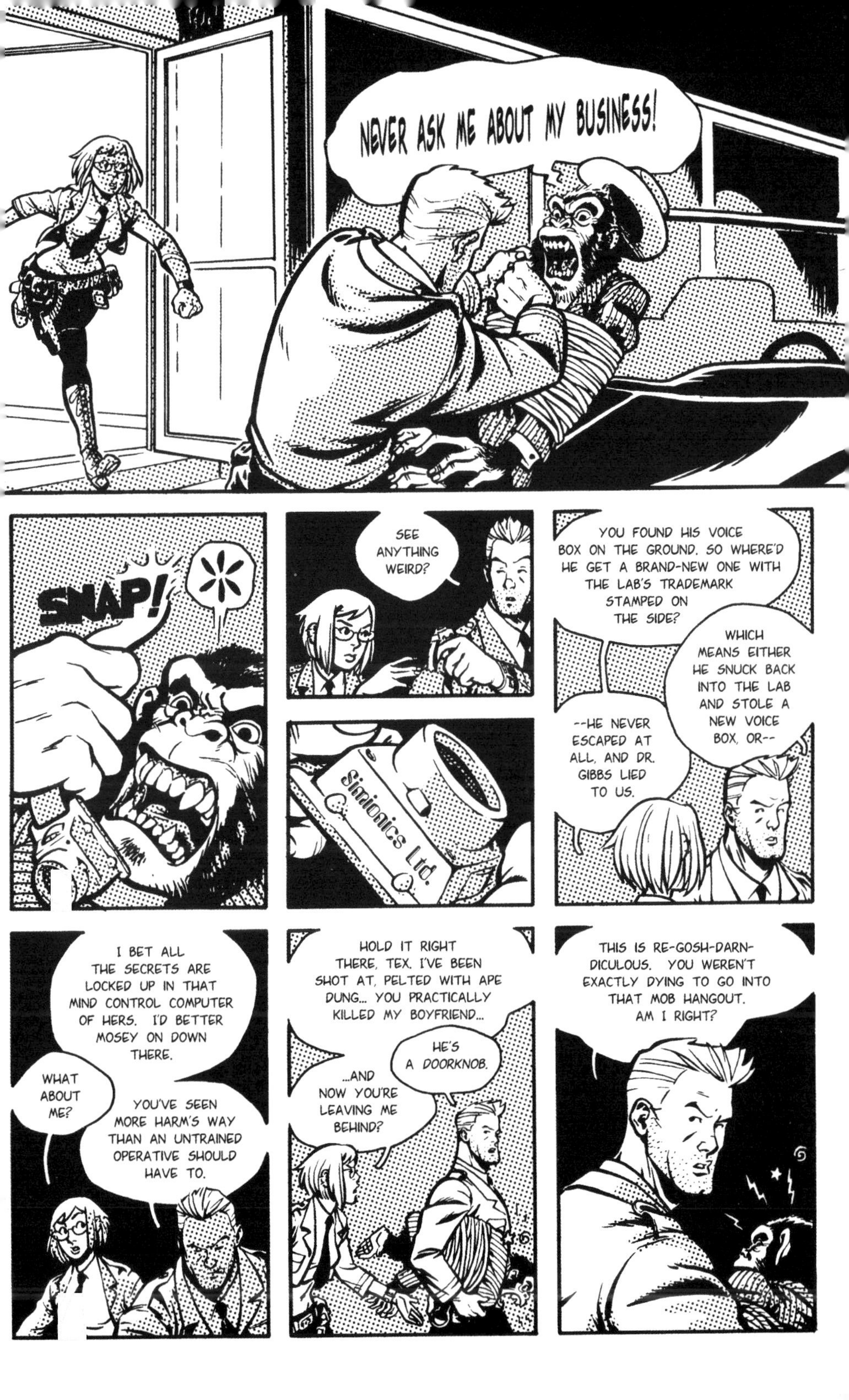
NEVER ASK ME ABOUT MY BUSINESS!
SNAP!
*
SEE ANYTHING WEIRD?
Simionics Ltd.
YOU FOUND HIS VOICE BOX ON THE GROUND. SO WHERE'D HE GET A BRAND-NEW ONE WITH THE LAB'S TRADEMARK STAMPED ON THE SIDE?
WHICH MEANS EITHER HE SNUCK BACK INTO THE LAB AND STOLE A NEW VOICE BOX, OR--
--HE NEVER ESCAPED AT ALL, AND DR. GIBBS LIED TO US.
I BET ALL THE SECRETS ARE LOCKED UP IN THAT MIND CONTROL COMPUTER OF HERS. I'D BETTER MOSEY ON DOWN THERE.
WHAT ABOUT ME?
YOU'VE SEEN MORE HARM'S WAY THAN AN UNTRAINED OPERATIVE SHOULD HAVE TO.
HOLD IT RIGHT THERE, TEX. I'VE BEEN SHOT AT, PELTED WITH APE DUNG... YOU PRACTICALLY KILLED MY BOYFRIEND...
HE'S A DOORKNOB.
...AND NOW YOU'RE LEAVING ME BEHIND?
THIS IS RE-GOSH-DARN-DICULOUS. YOU WEREN'T EXACTLY DYING TO GO INTO THAT MOB HANGOUT. AM I RIGHT?

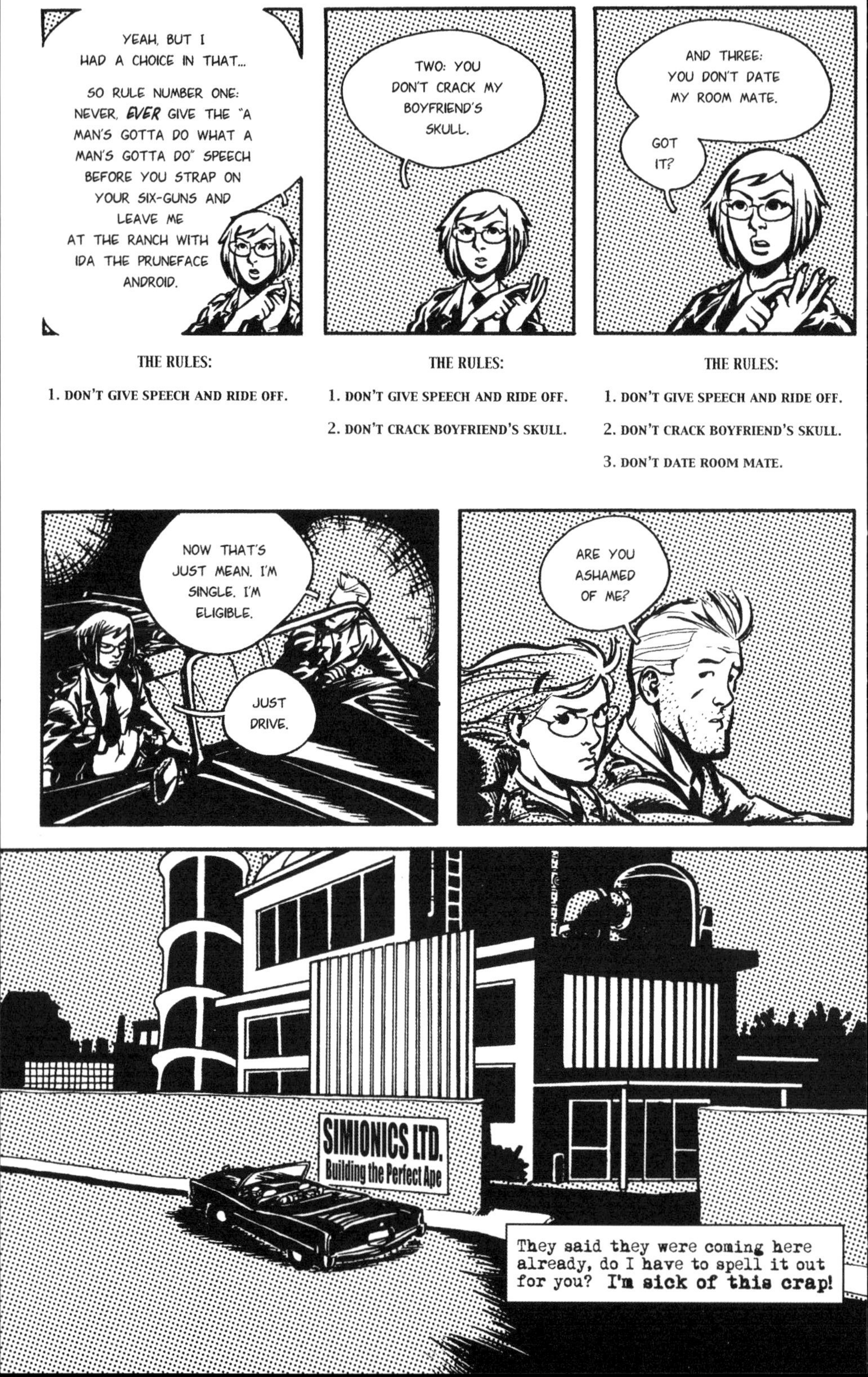
YEAH, BUT I HAD A CHOICE IN THAT...
SO RULE NUMBER ONE: NEVER, EVER GIVE THE "A MAN'S GOTTA DO WHAT A MAN'S GOTTA DO" SPEECH BEFORE YOU STRAP ON YOUR SIX-GUNS AND LEAVE ME AT THE RANCH WITH IDA THE PRUNEFACE ANDROID.
THE RULES:
1. DON'T GIVE SPEECH AND RIDE OFF.
TWO: YOU DON'T CRACK MY BOYFRIEND'S SKULL.
THE RULES:
1. DON'T GIVE SPEECH AND RIDE OFF.
2. DON'T CRACK BOYFRIEND'S SKULL.
AND THREE: YOU DON'T DATE MY ROOM MATE.
GOT IT?
THE RULES:
1. DON'T GIVE SPEECH AND RIDE OFF.
2. DON'T CRACK BOYFRIEND'S SKULL.
3. DON'T DATE ROOM MATE.
NOW THAT'S JUST MEAN. I'M SINGLE. I'M ELIGIBLE.
JUST DRIVE.
ARE YOU ASHAMED OF ME?
SIMIONICS LTD.
Building the Perfect Ape
They said they were coming here already, do I have to spell it out for you? I'm sick of this crap!

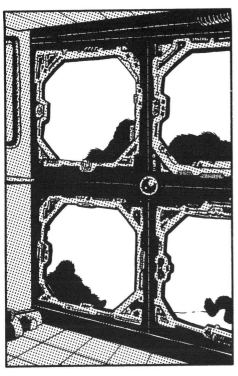
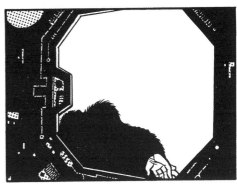

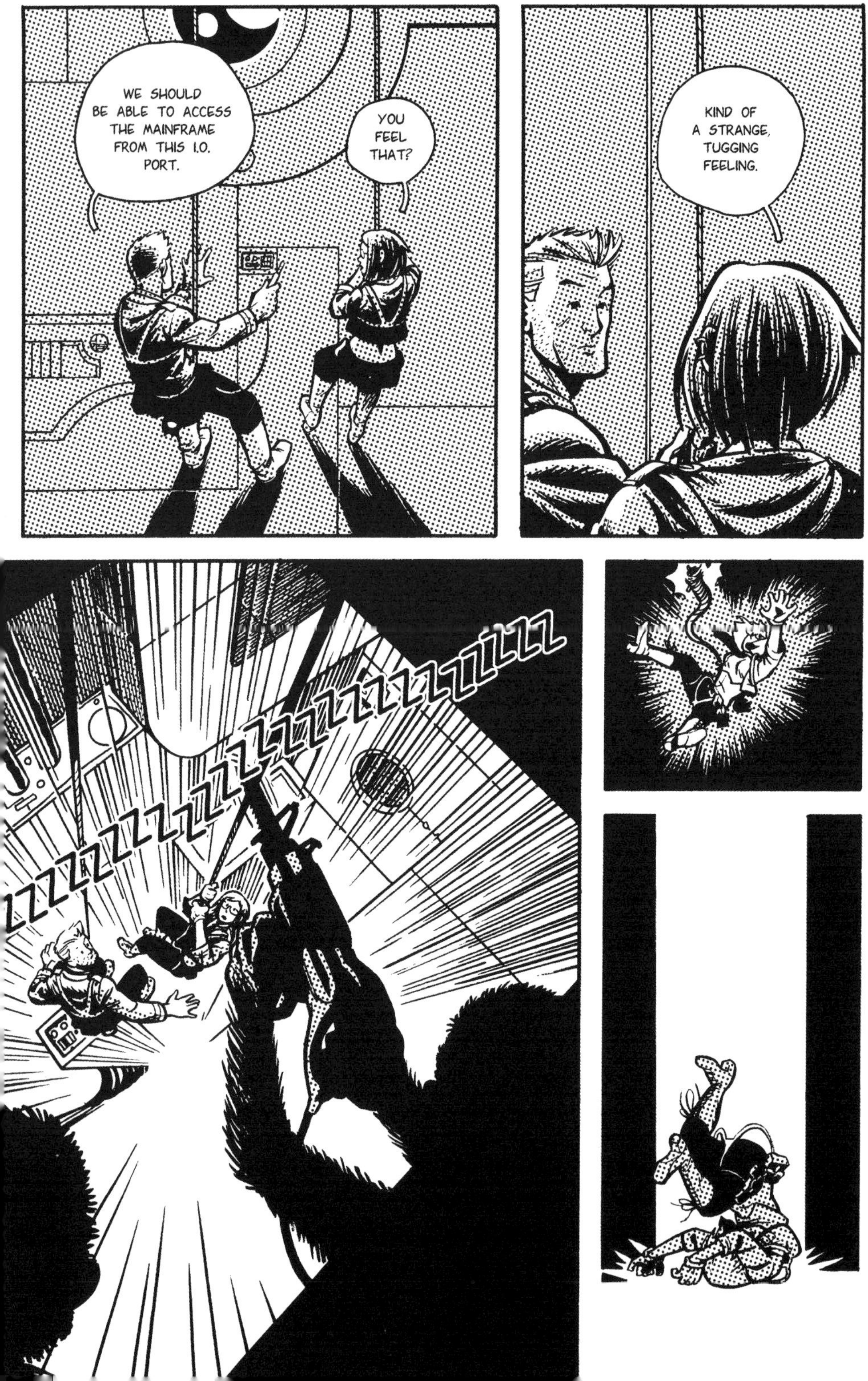
WE SHOULD BE ABLE TO ACCESS THE MAINFRAME FROM THIS I.O. PORT.
YOU FEEL THAT?
KIND OF A STRANGE, TUGGING FEELING.
ZZZZZZZZZZZZZZZZZZZZZZZZZZZZ

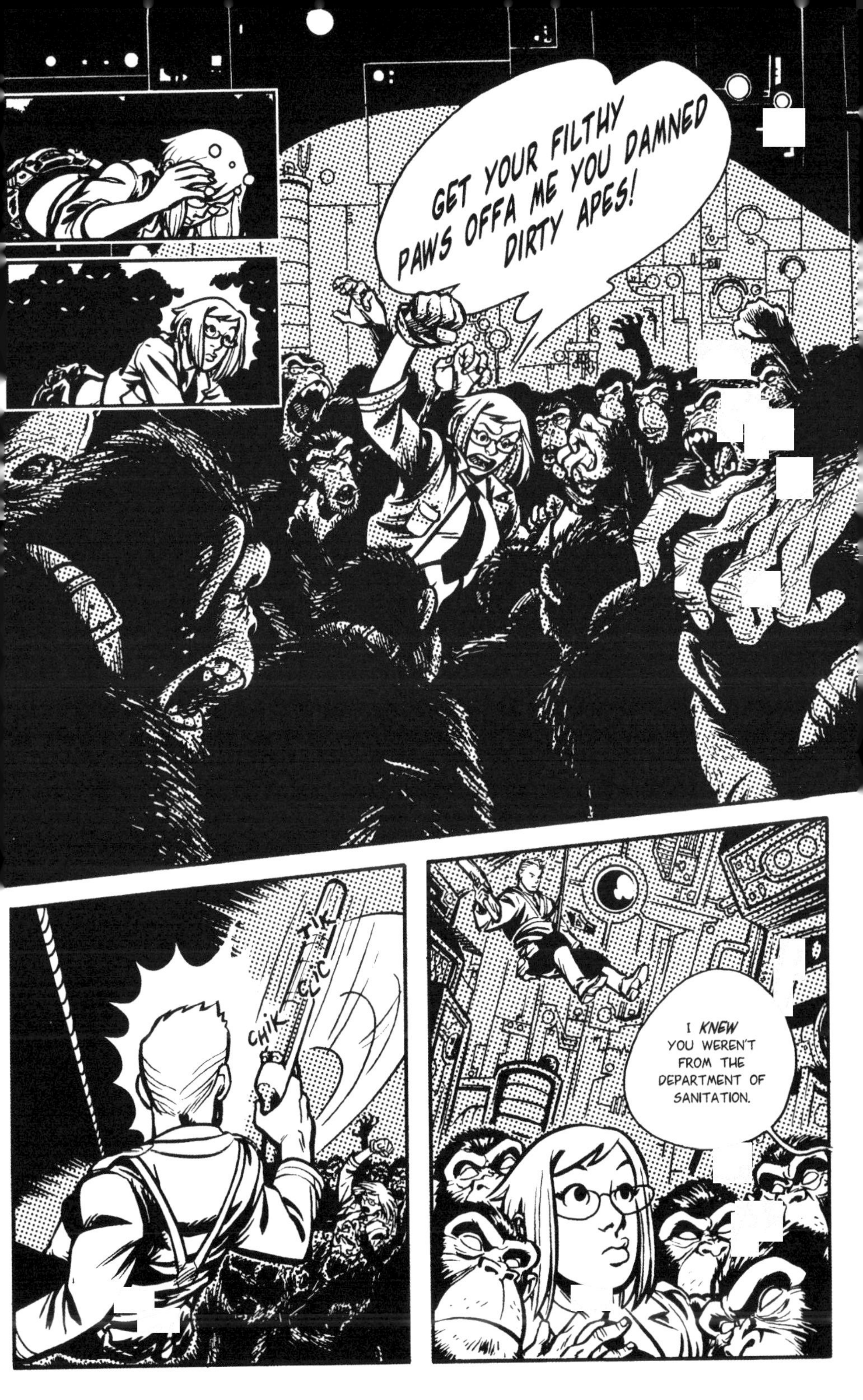
GET YOUR FILTHY PAWS OFFA ME YOU DAMNED DIRTY APES!
CHIK
CLIC
TIK
I *KNEW* YOU WEREN'T FROM THE DEPARTMENT OF SANITATION.

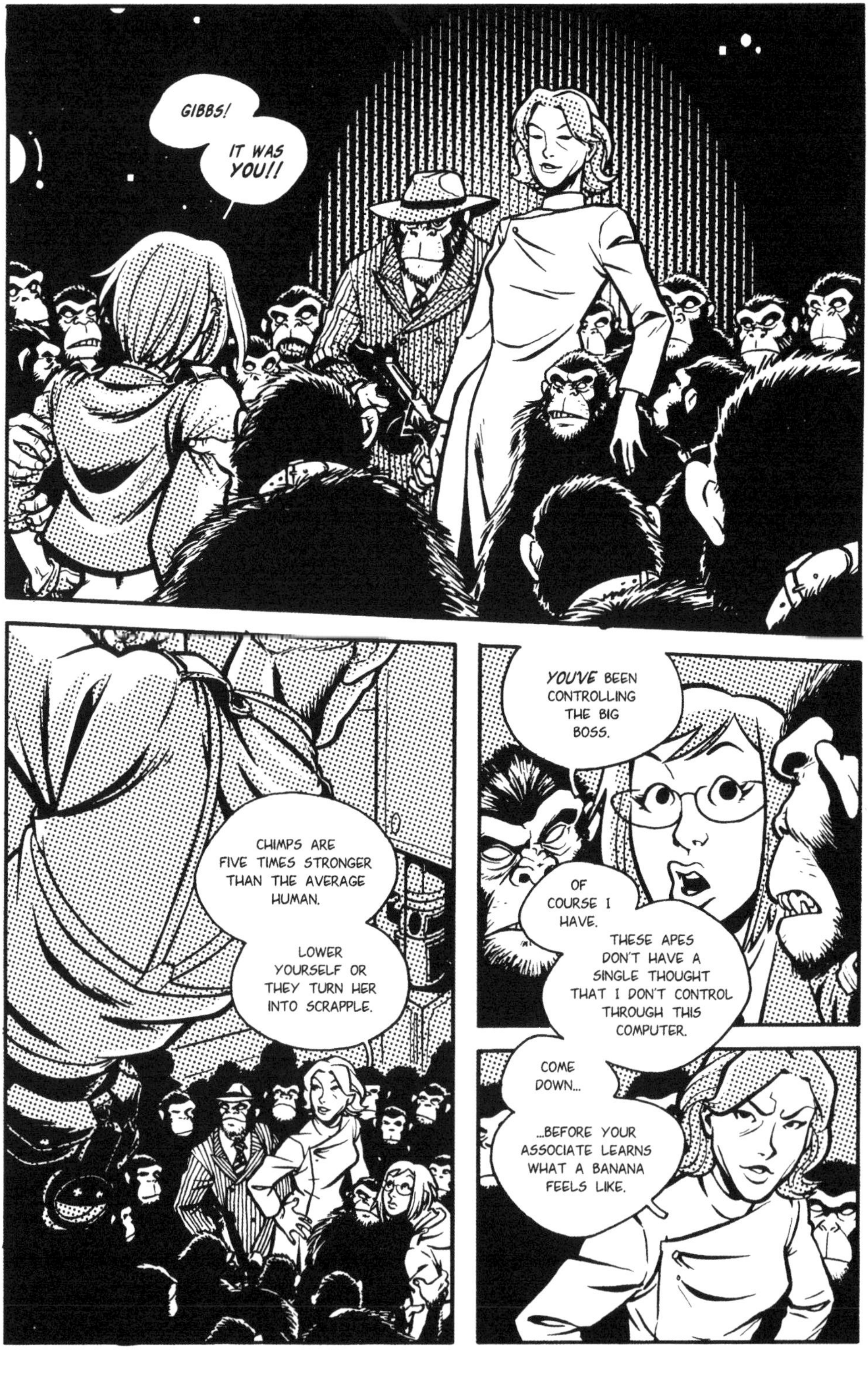
GIBBS!
IT WAS YOU!!
CHIMPS ARE FIVE TIMES STRONGER THAN THE AVERAGE HUMAN.
LOWER YOURSELF OR THEY TURN HER INTO SCRAPPLE.
YOU'VE BEEN CONTROLLING THE BIG BOSS.
OF COURSE I HAVE.
THESE APES DON'T HAVE A SINGLE THOUGHT THAT I DON'T CONTROL THROUGH THIS COMPUTER.
COME DOWN...
...BEFORE YOUR ASSOCIATE LEARNS WHAT A BANANA FEELS LIKE.

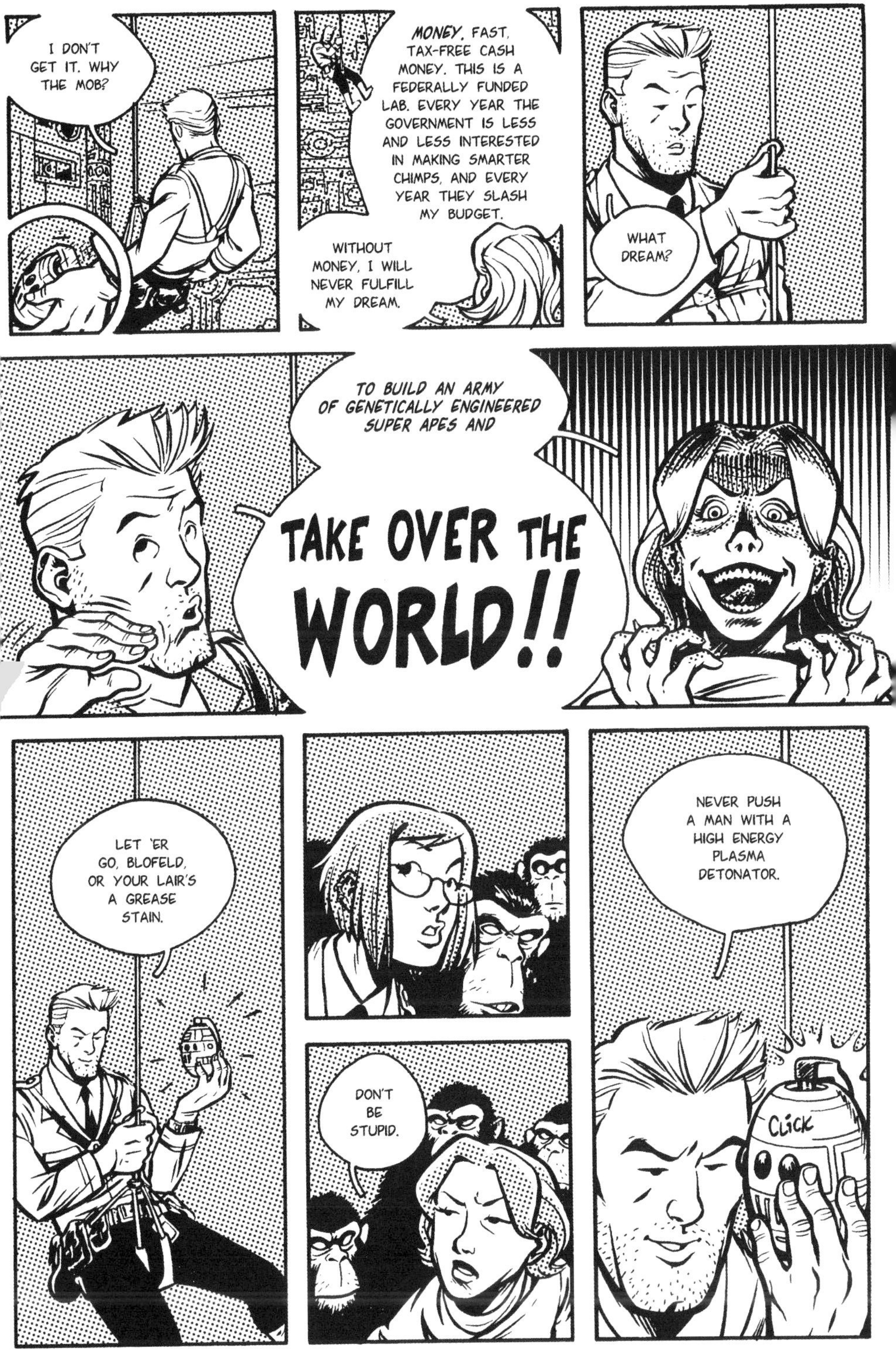
I DON'T GET IT. WHY THE MOB?
MONEY. FAST, TAX-FREE CASH MONEY. THIS IS A FEDERALLY FUNDED LAB. EVERY YEAR THE GOVERNMENT IS LESS AND LESS INTERESTED IN MAKING SMARTER CHIMPS, AND EVERY YEAR THEY SLASH MY BUDGET.
WITHOUT MONEY, I WILL NEVER FULFILL MY DREAM.
WHAT DREAM?
TO BUILD AN ARMY OF GENETICALLY ENGINEERED SUPER APES AND
TAKE OVER THE WORLD!!
LET 'ER GO, BLOFELD, OR YOUR LAIR'S A GREASE STAIN.
DON'T BE STUPID.
NEVER PUSH A MAN WITH A HIGH ENERGY PLASMA DETONATOR.
CLICK

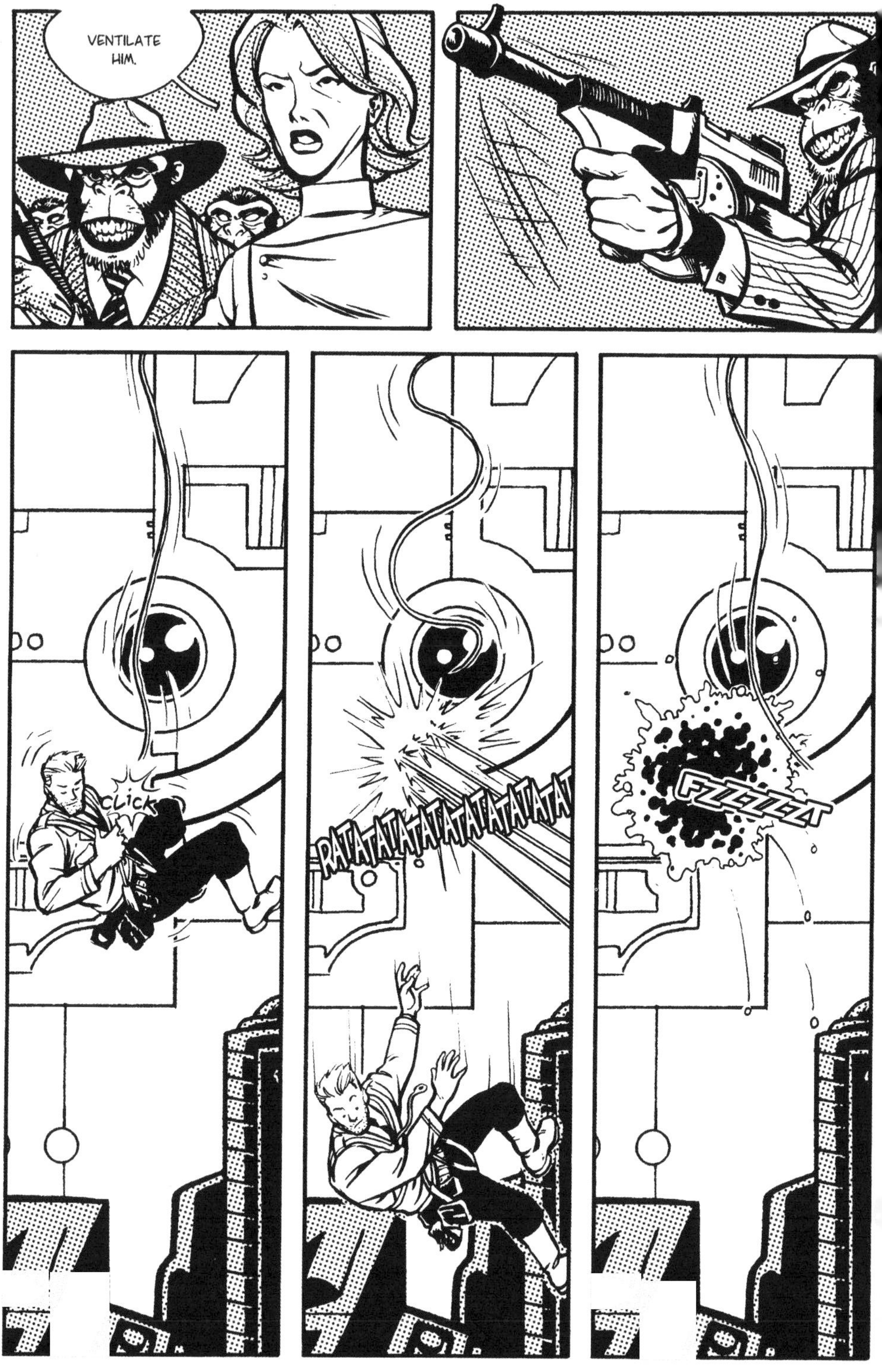
VENTILATE HIM.
CLICK
RATATATATATATATATATATAT
FZZZZZT

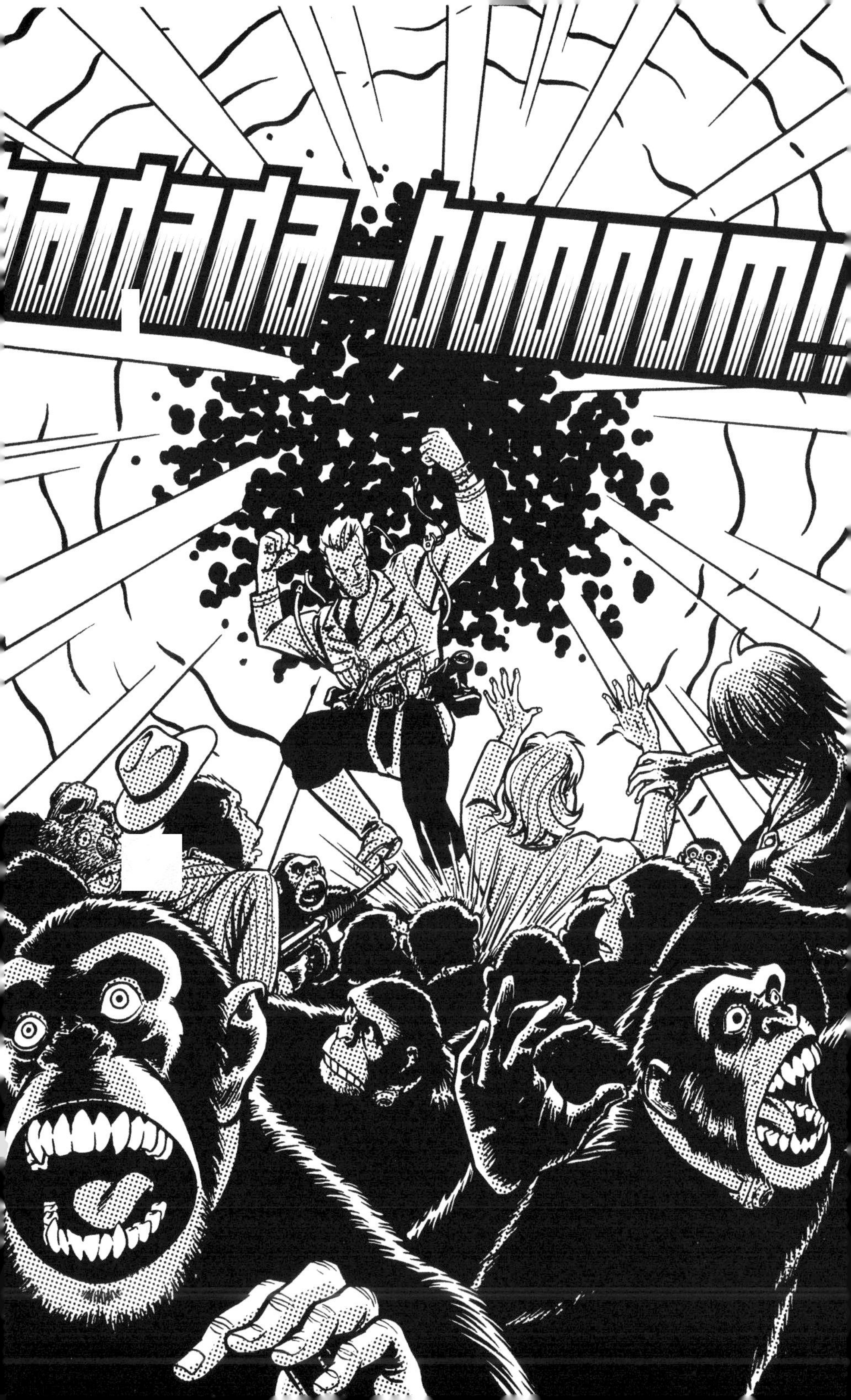

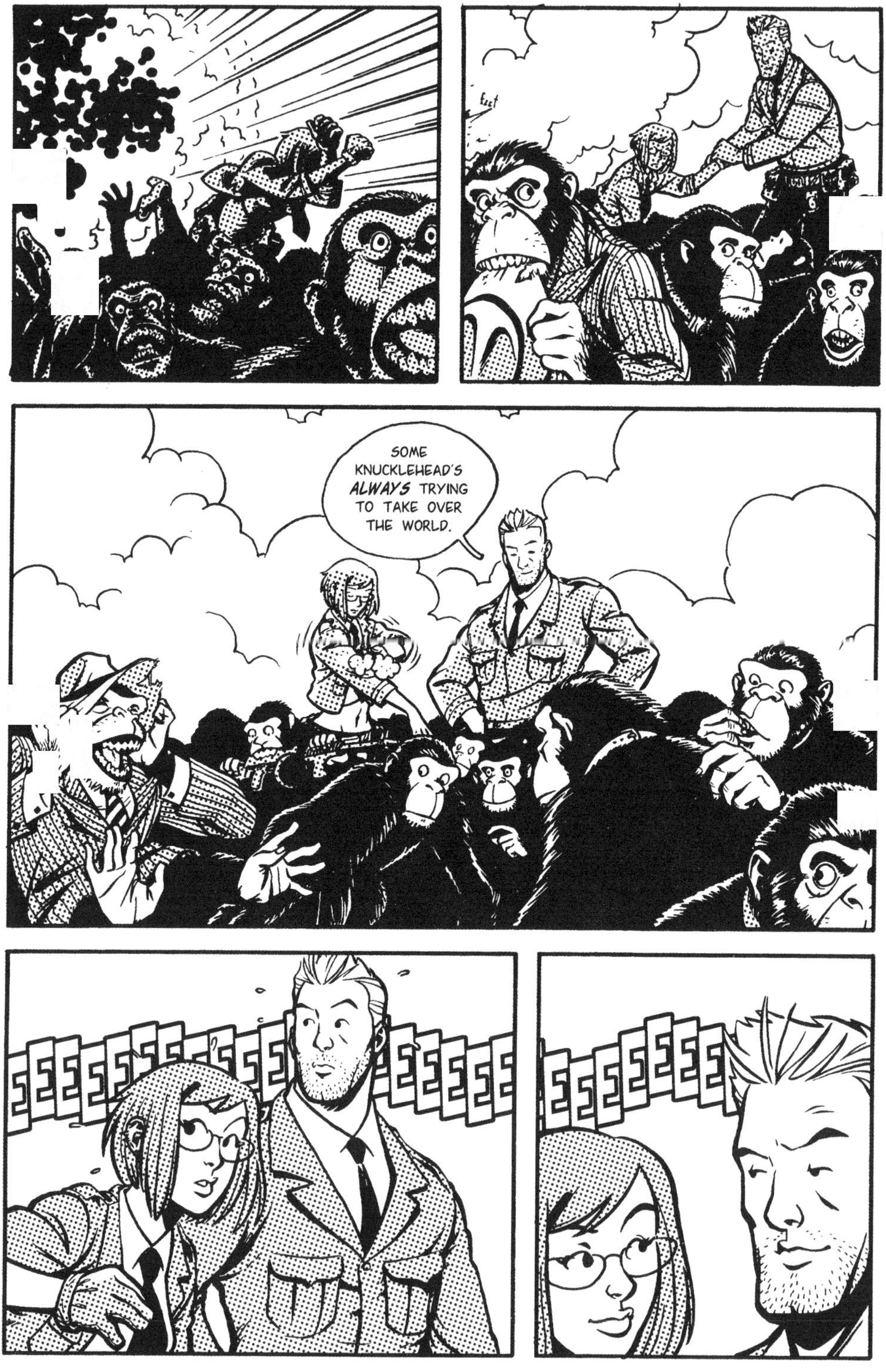
SOME KNUCKLEHEAD'S *ALWAYS* TRYING TO TAKE OVER THE WORLD.

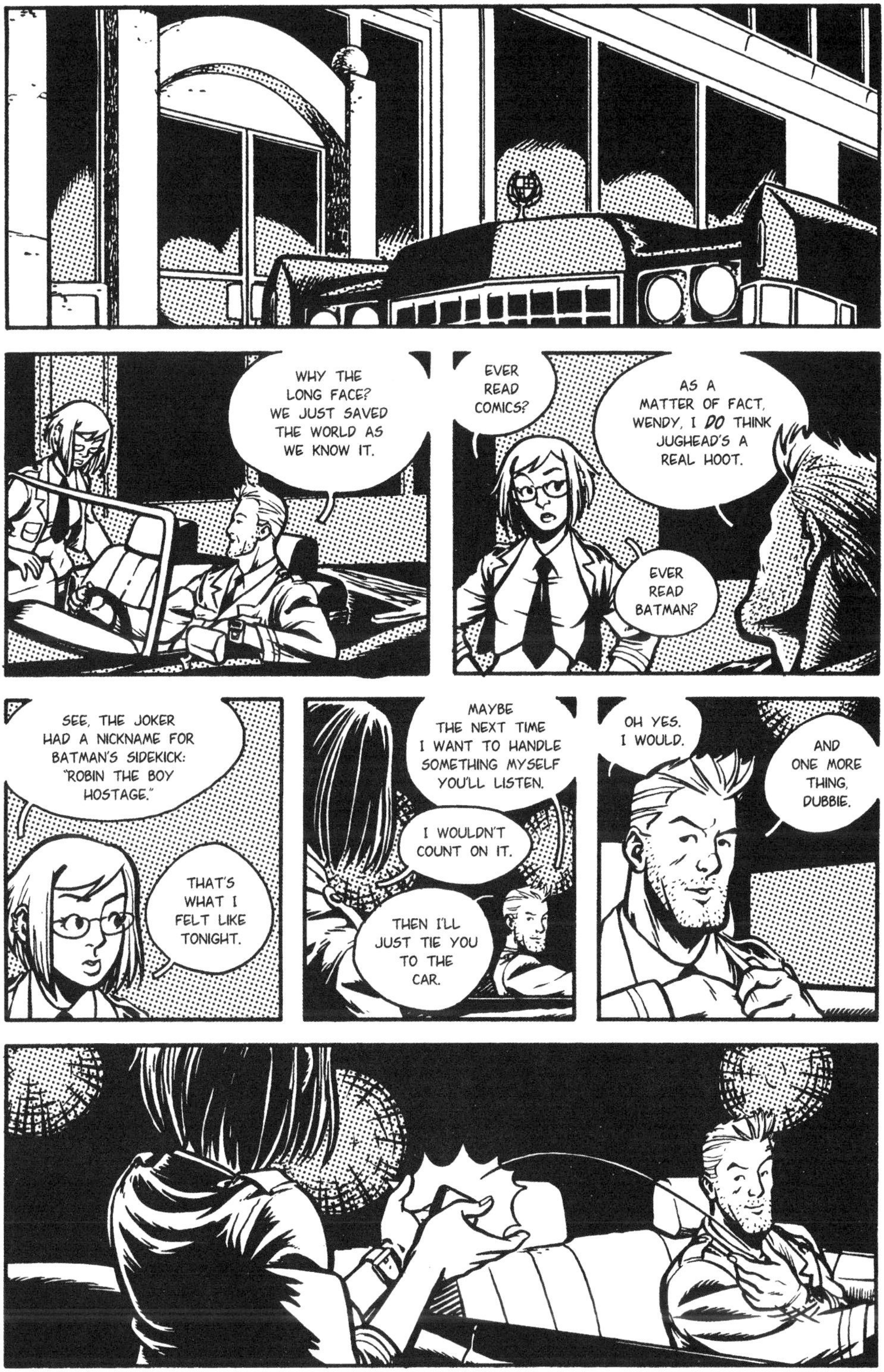
WHY THE LONG FACE? WE JUST SAVED THE WORLD AS WE KNOW IT.
EVER READ COMICS?
AS A MATTER OF FACT, WENDY, I DO THINK JUGHEAD'S A REAL HOOT.
EVER READ BATMAN?
SEE, THE JOKER HAD A NICKNAME FOR BATMAN'S SIDEKICK: "ROBIN THE BOY HOSTAGE."
THAT'S WHAT I FELT LIKE TONIGHT.
MAYBE THE NEXT TIME I WANT TO HANDLE SOMETHING MYSELF YOU'LL LISTEN.
I WOULDN'T COUNT ON IT.
THEN I'LL JUST TIE YOU TO THE CAR.
OH YES. I WOULD.
AND ONE MORE THING, DUBBIE.

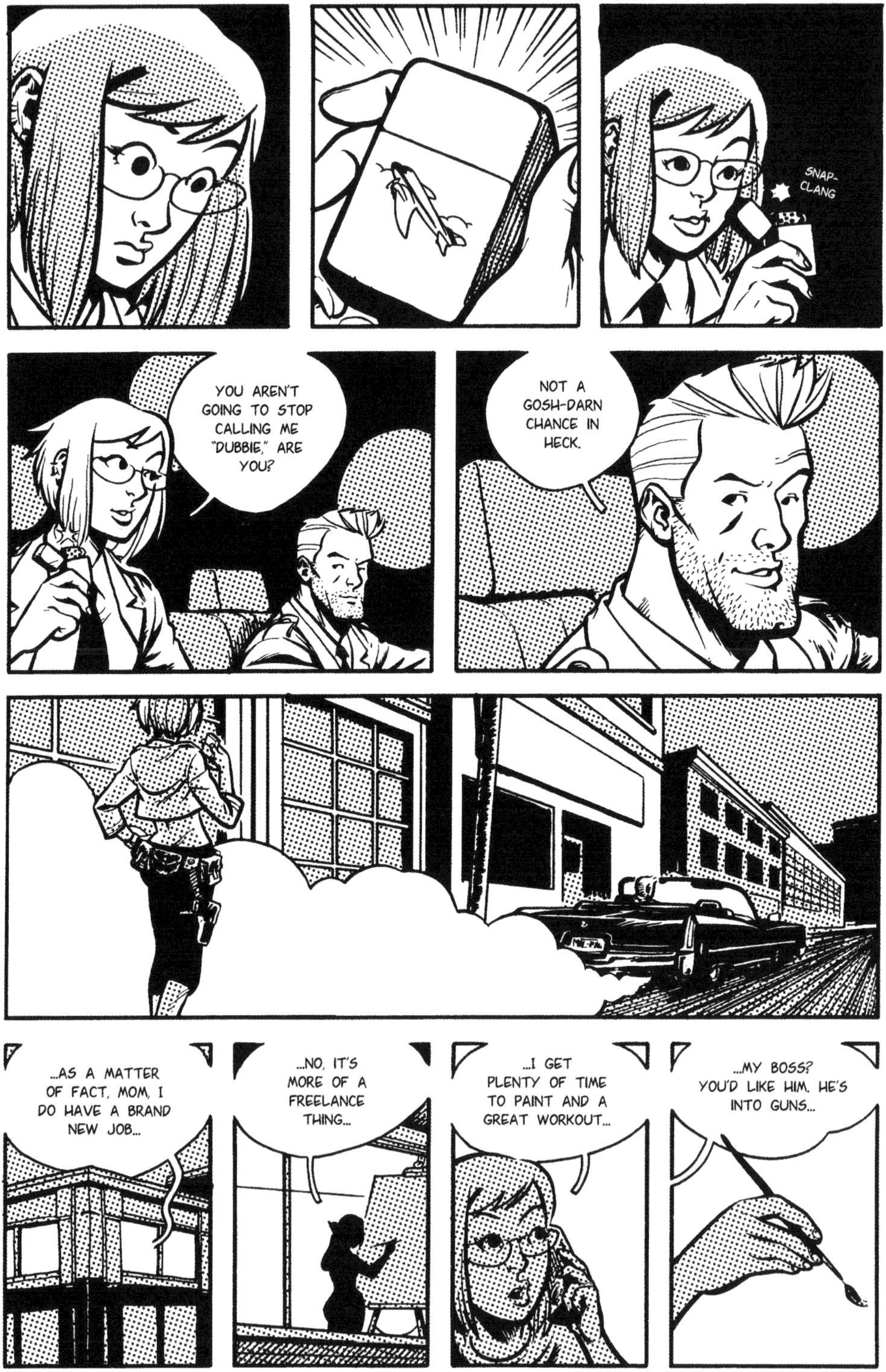
SNAP-CLANG
YOU AREN'T GOING TO STOP CALLING ME "DUBBIE," ARE YOU?
NOT A GOSH-DARN CHANCE IN HECK.
...AS A MATTER OF FACT, MOM, I DO HAVE A BRAND NEW JOB...
...NO, IT'S MORE OF A FREELANCE THING...
...I GET PLENTY OF TIME TO PAINT AND A GREAT WORKOUT...
...MY BOSS? YOU'D LIKE HIM. HE'S INTO GUNS...

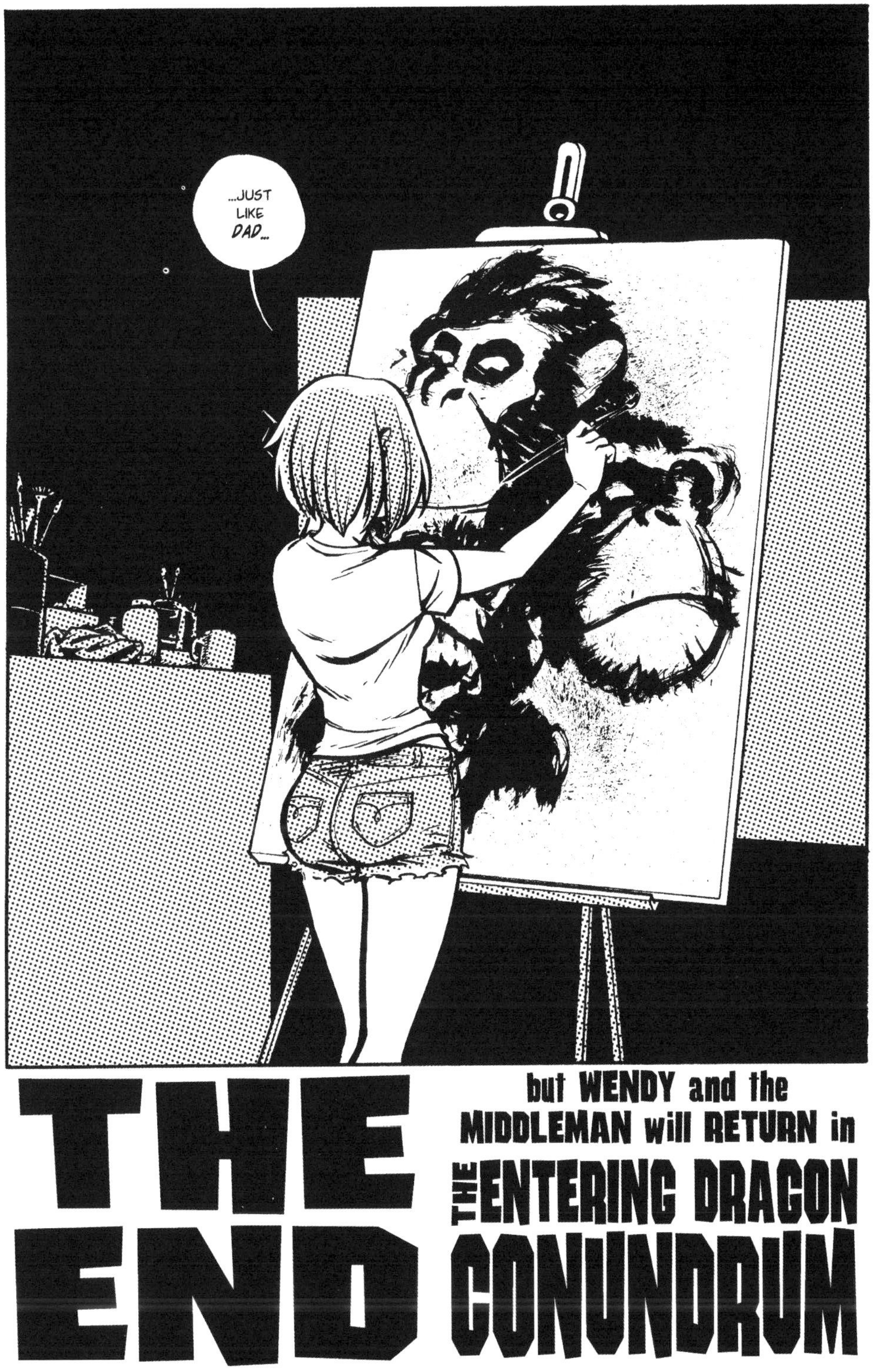
...JUST LIKE DAD...

THE END

but WENDY and the MIDDLEMAN will RETURN in

THE ENTERING DRAGON CONUNDRUM

Photo by Steven Sylvain

SKETCHBOOK

Text by Javier Grillo-Marxuach
Images by Les McClaine

One of the best things about this project was the speed with which Les picked up on the core concepts of my script and translated them into images. With the only exception being Wendy, who took us a while to nail down, almost every character came together in a relatively short amount of time. Here, then, is the evolution of the characters and concepts of "The Middleman."

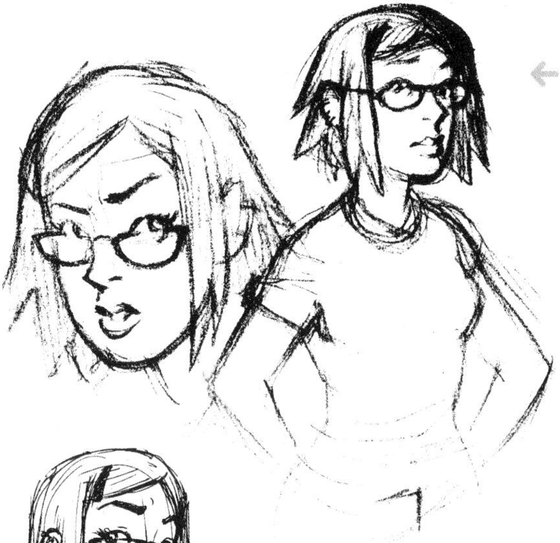

Les's first take on Wendy - much to my chagrin, I asked Les to rework his concept of the character several times thinking his original take was too childlike - I was young and foolish.

Ultimately, the Wendy you see today owes much of her looks and bearing to this first draft.

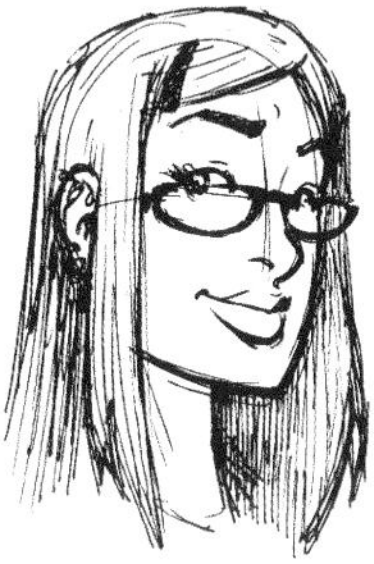

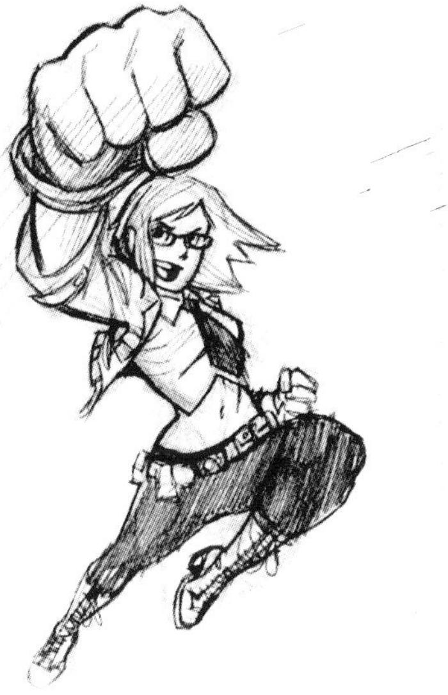

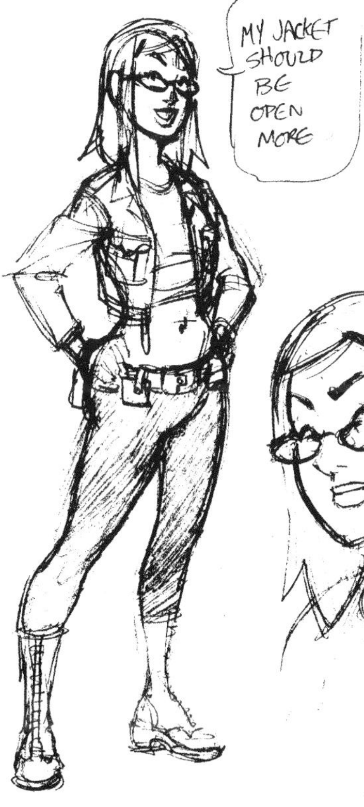
MY JACKET SHOULD BE OPEN MORE

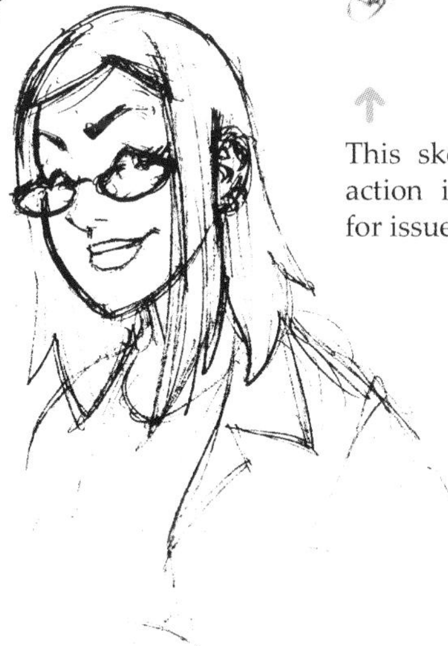

This sketch of Wendy in action inspired the cover for issue #3.

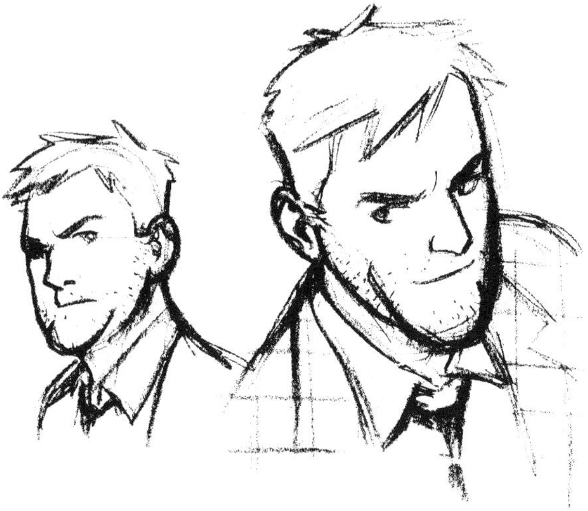

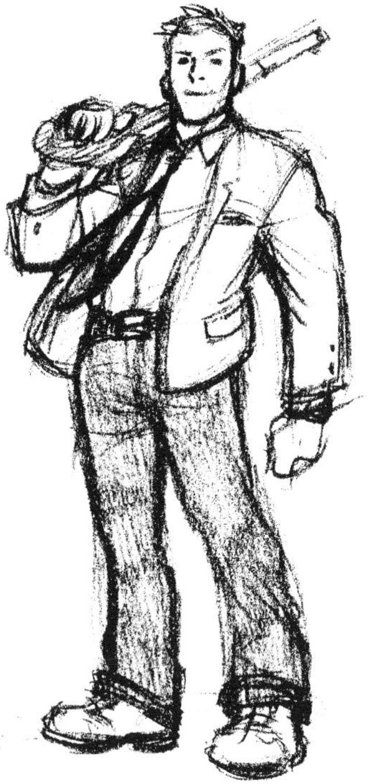

Les's first sketches of The Middleman - too much Steve McQueen, not enough Jonny Quest.

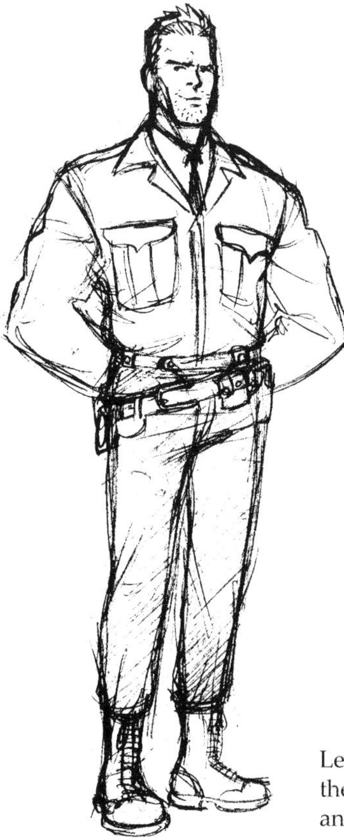

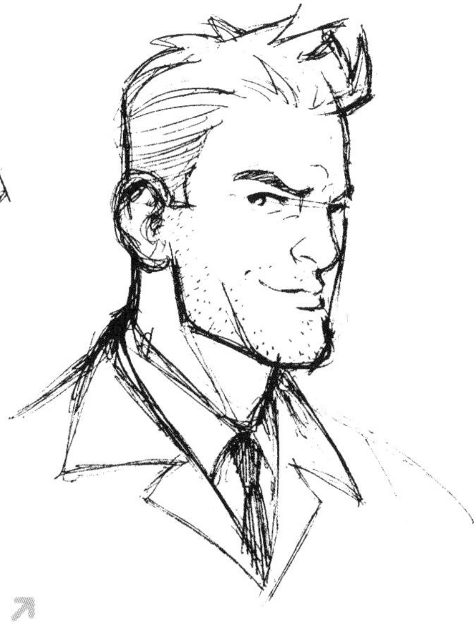

Les's second take on The Middleman nailed the "Dirk Squarejaw" aspect of the character and became our template.

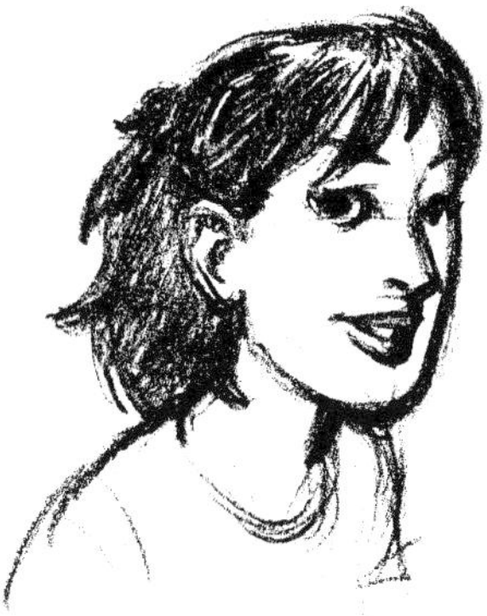

With the exception of Lacey (left), whom I wanted to be more of a sexpot and a contrast to Wendy, Les's first take on the supporting cast was dead on.

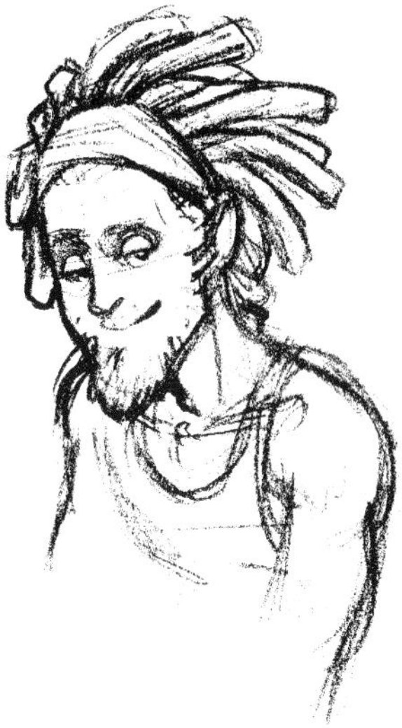

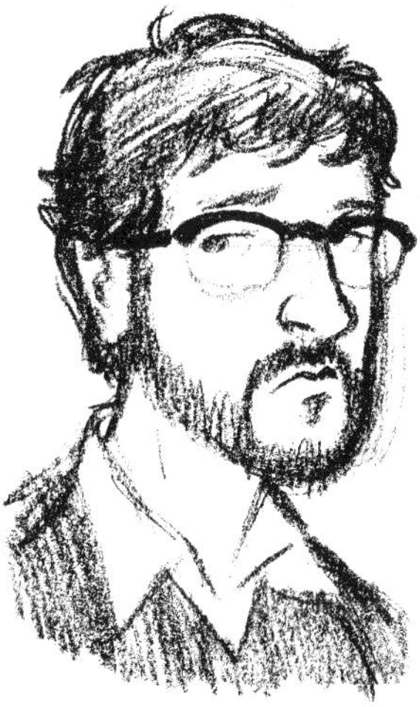

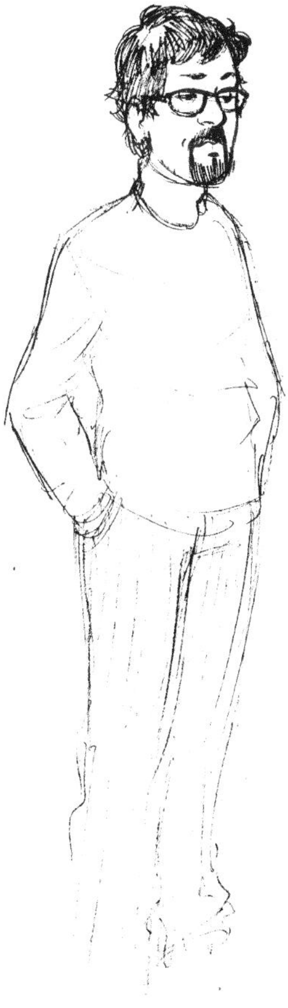

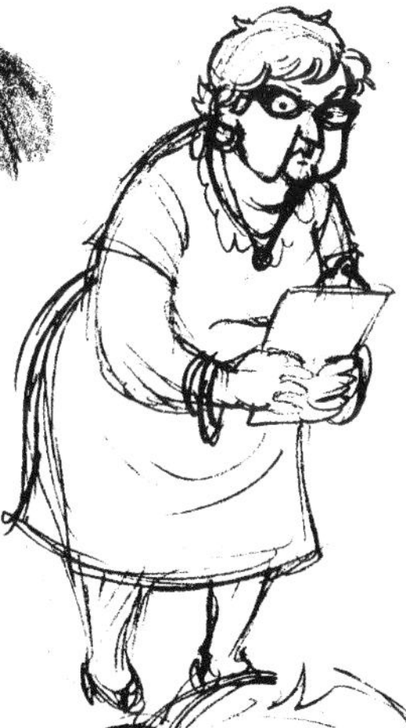

The only revision on the second take on Ben was a slight shave.

Ida was perfect from sketch #1.

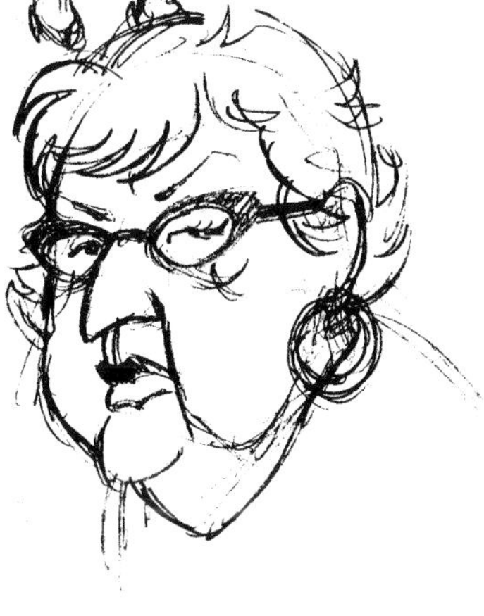

Lacey in her revised form - did I mention I wanted her to be a sexpot? I think Les heard me.

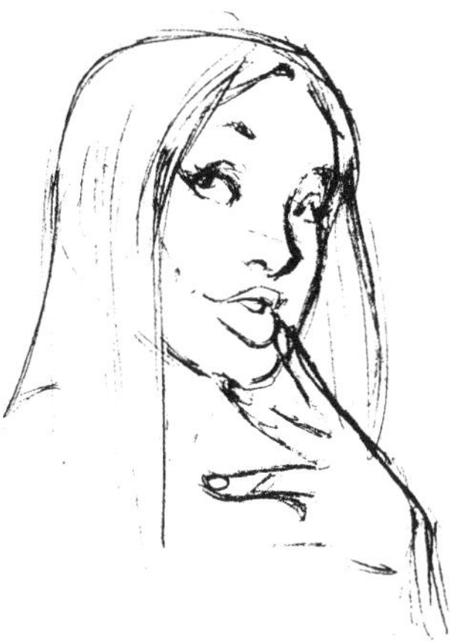

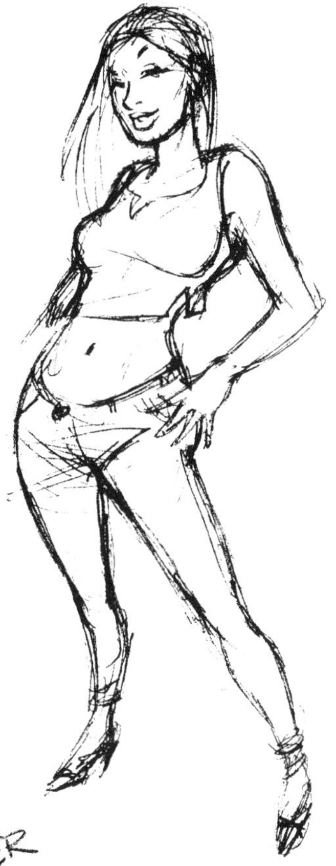

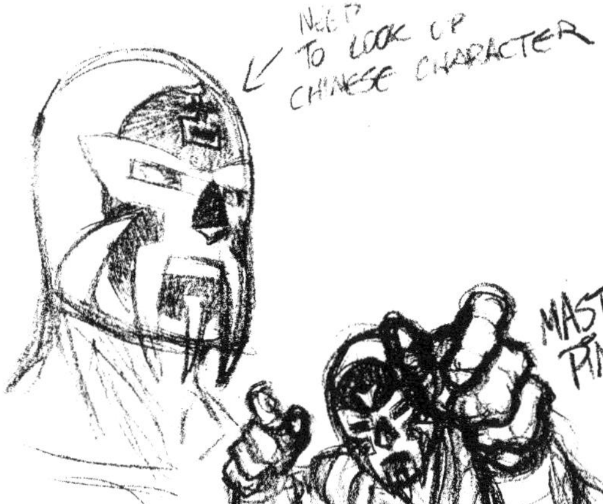
NEED TO LOOK UP CHINESE CHARACTER

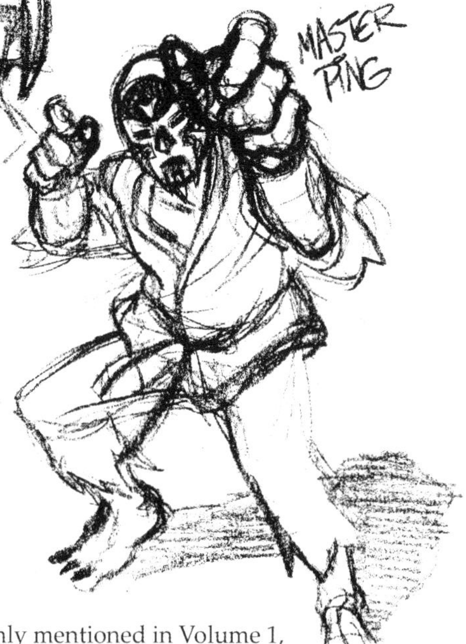
MASTER PING

Though only mentioned in Volume 1, Sensei Ping will be a major character in Volume 2.

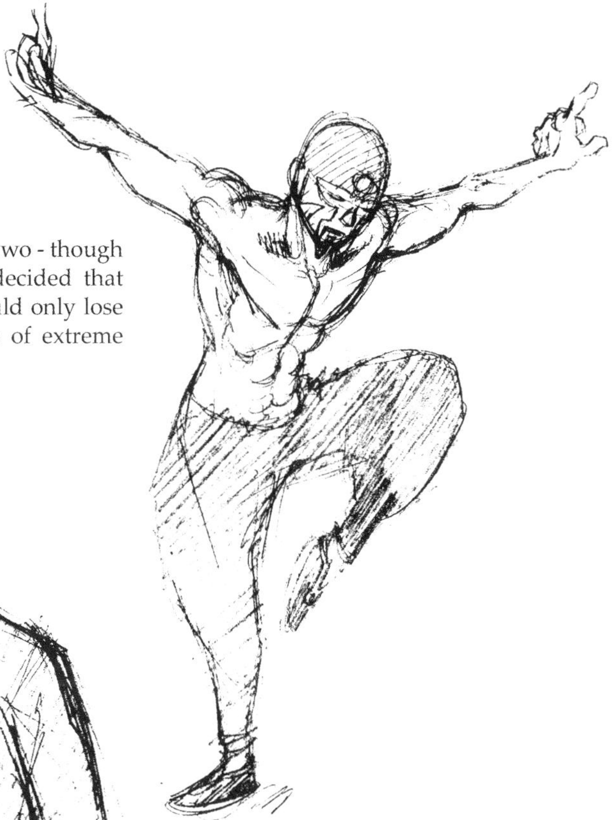

Sensei Ping, take two - though spot on, I later decided that the character would only lose his shirt in times of extreme action.

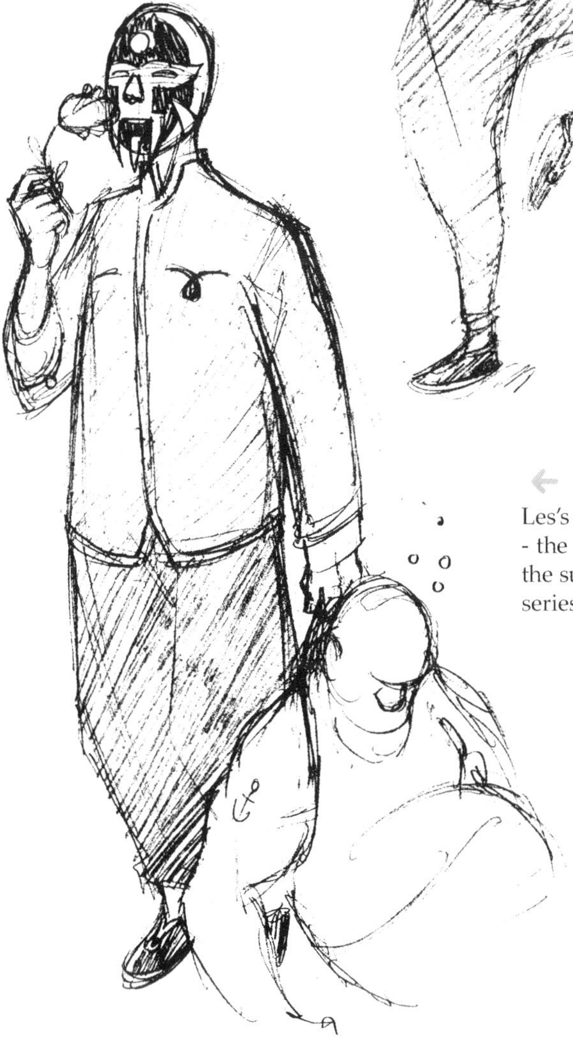

Les's final take on Sensei Ping - the pot-bellied sailor will be the subject of his own spin-off series.

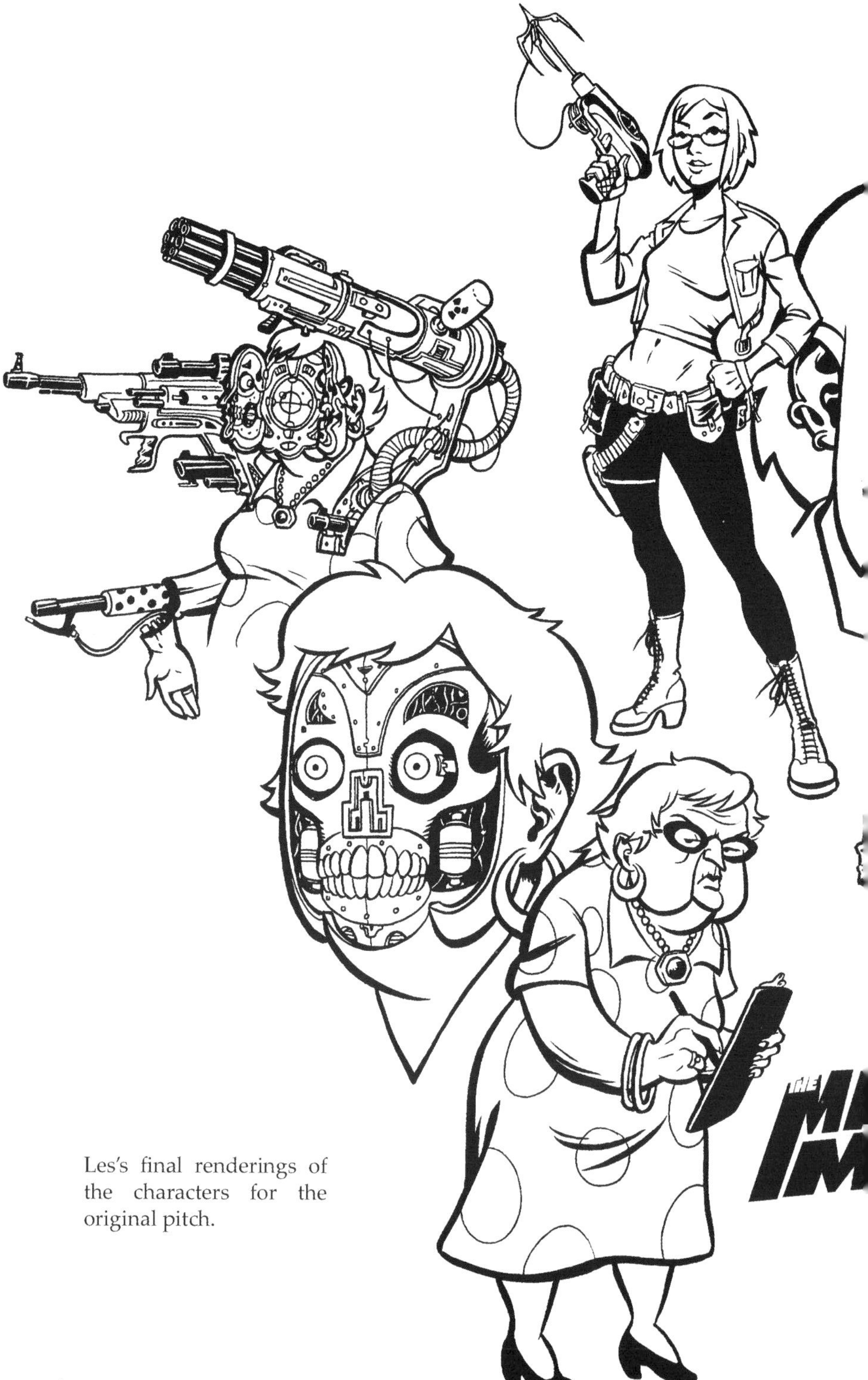

Les's final renderings of the characters for the original pitch.

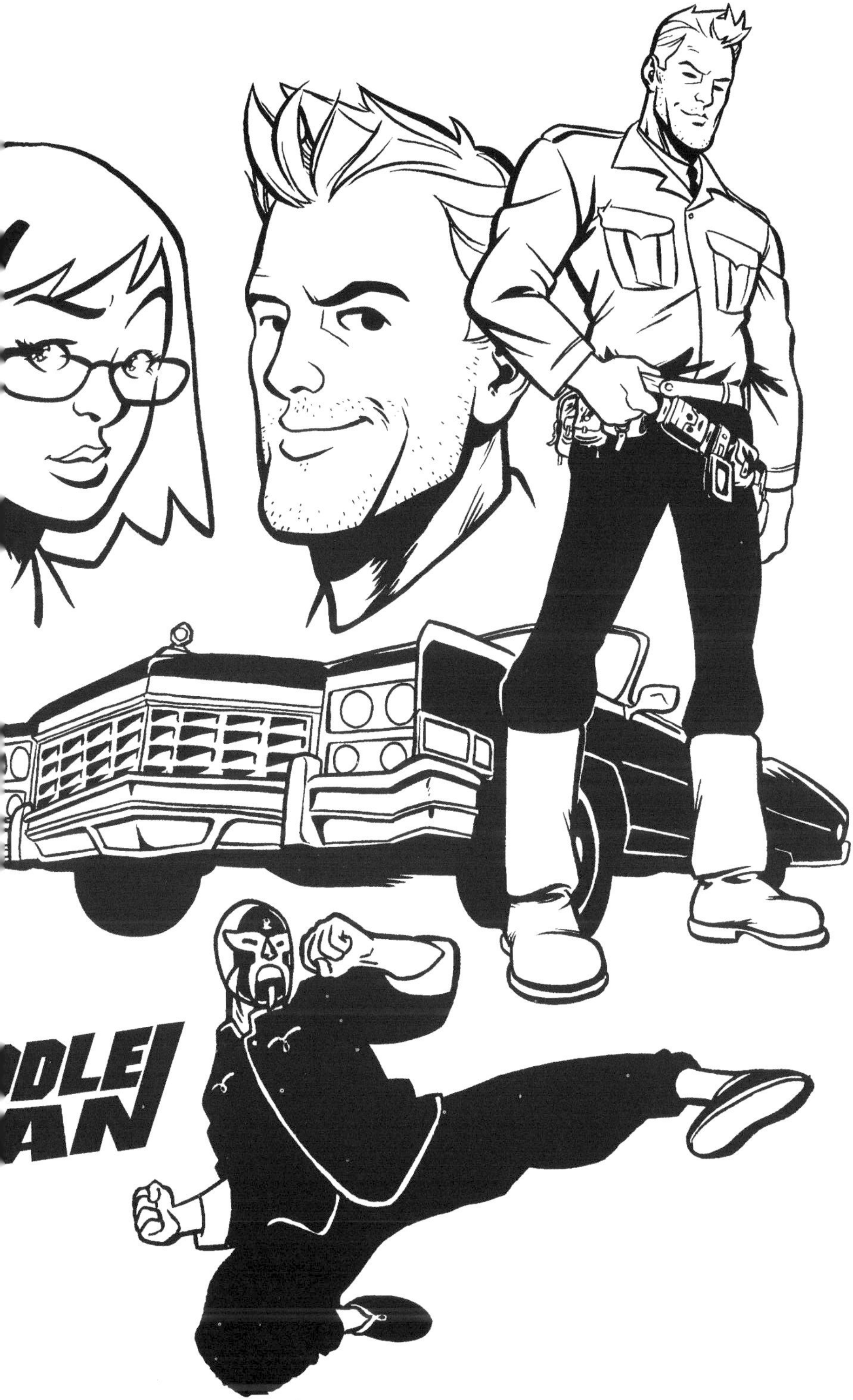

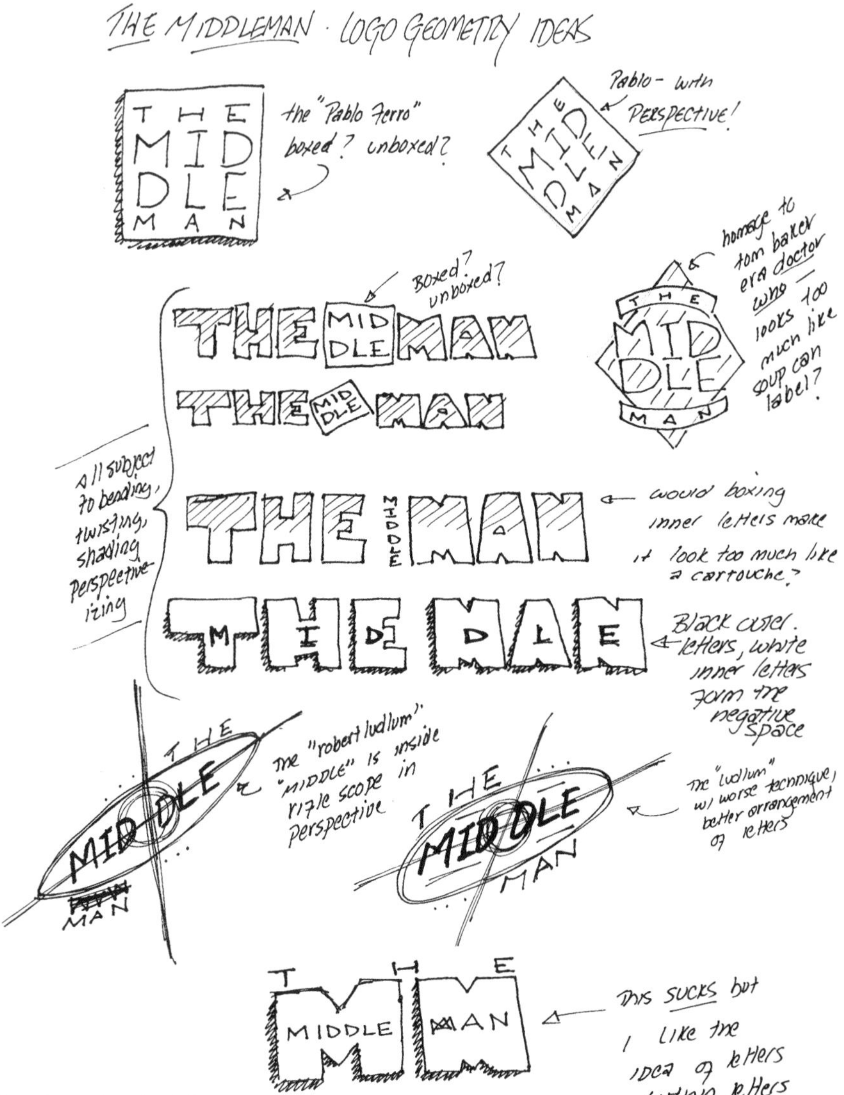
THE MIDDLEMAN · LOGO GEOMETRY IDEAS
THE MID DLE MAN
the "Pablo Ferro" boxed? unboxed?
Pablo - with PERSPECTIVE!
homage to tom baker era doctor who — looks too much like soup can label?
Boxed? unboxed?
All subject to bending, twisting, shading perspective-izing
would boxing inner letters make it look too much like a cartouche?
Black outer letters, white inner letters form the negative space
The "robert ludlum" "MIDDLE" is inside rifle scope in perspective
The "ludlum" w/ worse technique, better arrangement of letters
This SUCKS but I like the idea of letters within letters

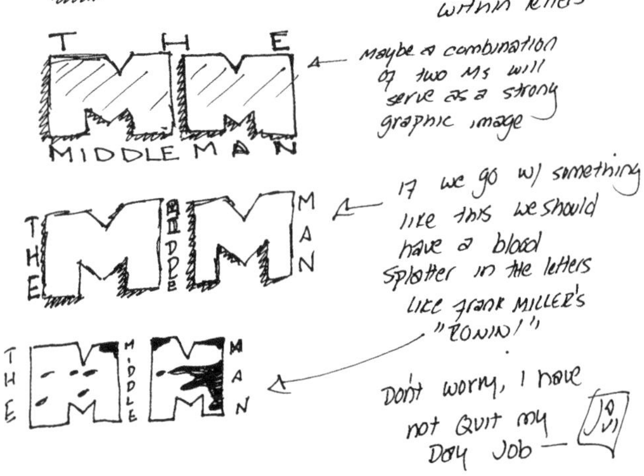
maybe a combination of two Ms will serve as a strong graphic image
If we go w/ something like this we should have a blood splotter in the letters like Frank Miller's "RONIN!"
Don't worry, I have not Quit my Day Job

Proving why I stick to writing, these were my proposed concepts for the logo. I soon vowed never to send Les another one of my sketches for fear of violent reprisal.

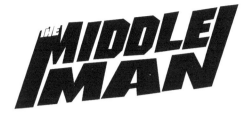

Les's first version of the logo.

The final logo for Volume One - after I asked Les to give the original a little "Empire Strikes Back."

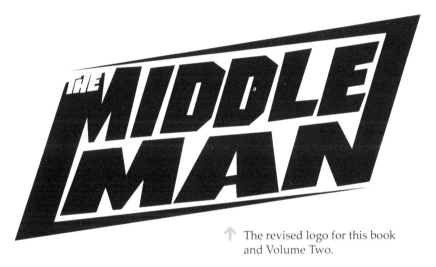

The revised logo for this book and Volume Two.

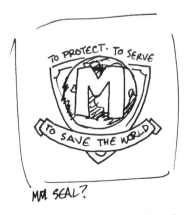

TO PROTECT · TO SERVE
M
TO SAVE THE WORLD
MM SEAL?

FIGHTING EVIL
M
SO YOU DON'T HAVE TO

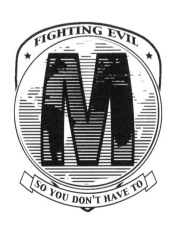

Les's first take on the Middleman Badge went unchanged to its final version.

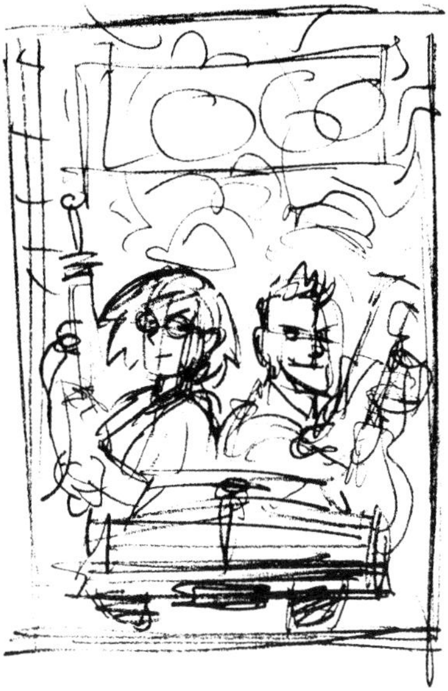

Les's sketch for the cover used to pitch the book.

Pitch cover final.

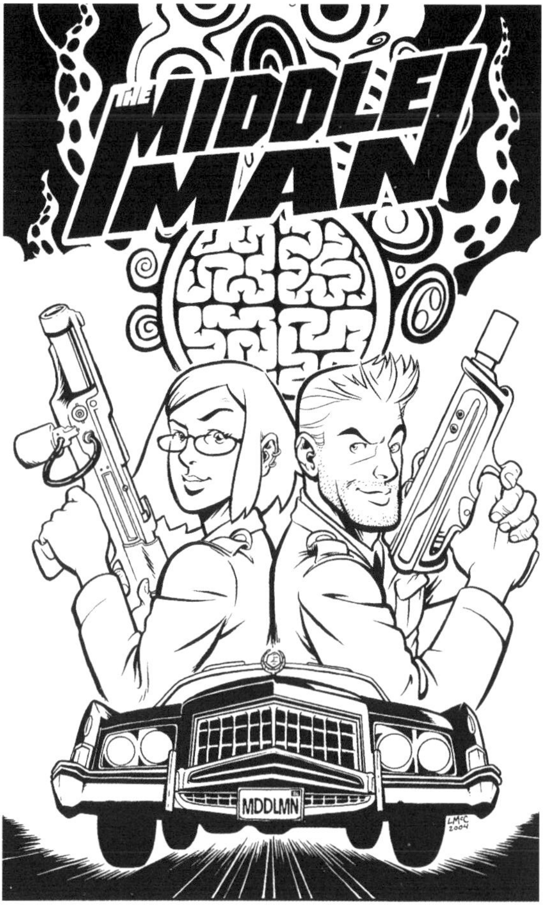
THE
MIDDLE
MAN
MDDLMN
LMcC
2004

PAGE 12

← Les's layout for the last page of the pitch - or page 12 of issue #1, notice the difference in the final panel...

↓ ...we felt the need to end the pitch on a large image of our hero!

SORRY.

SO WHAT'S IT GONNA BE? KEEP THE SECRET OR DEATH?

WHAT DO YOU THINK?

MA'AM, SPECIFICITY IS THE SOUL OF ALL GOOD COMMUNICATION.

YES. DUH!

OUTSTANDING.

YOU'RE GOOD UNDER PRESSURE.

ARE YOU HITTING ON ME?

JUST MAKING AN OBSERVATION.

HELLO! NUTJOB. PARTY OF ONE.

NO, MA'AM.

I'M JUST

THE MIDDLEMAN.

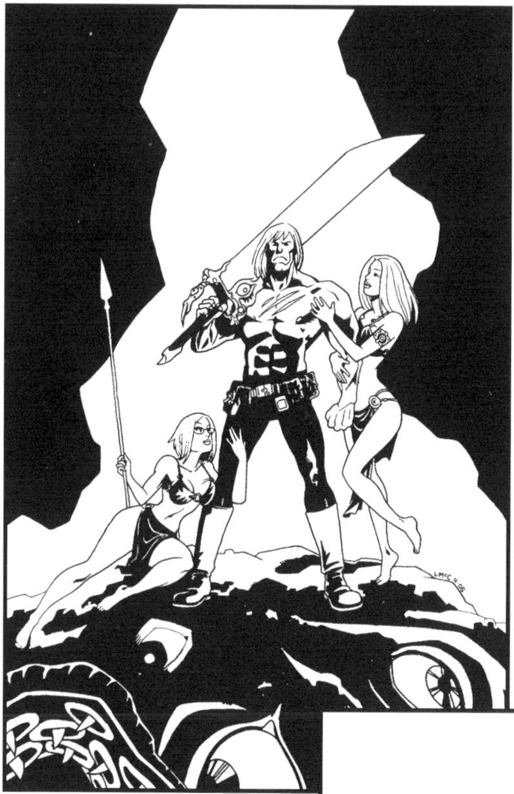

For a Comicon variant cover, we decided to create an unique "Completely Inaccurate Variant Cover." It truly has nothing to do with the book...

......but Les's rendition of "Barbarian Middleman" inspired a series of stories titled "Legends of the Middleman" showing the adventures of several Middlemen through history, look for it in the Volume 2 trade paperback!

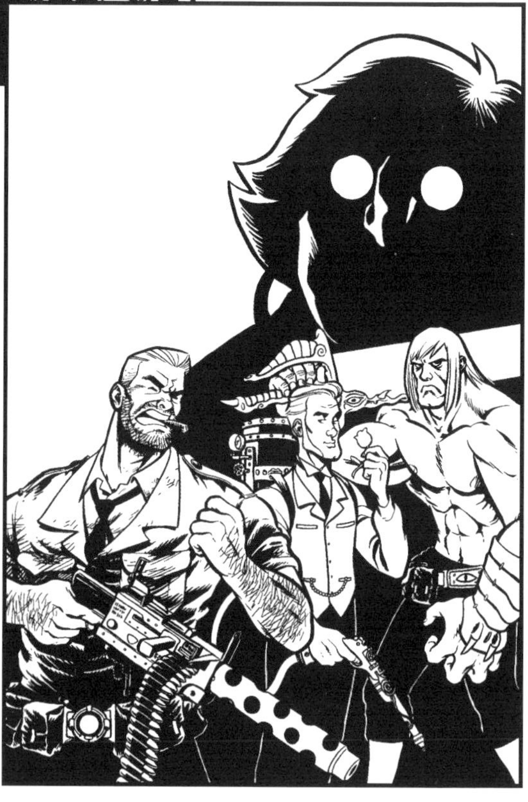

A character spread used in promotional posters for
the launch at the 2005 San Diego Comicon.

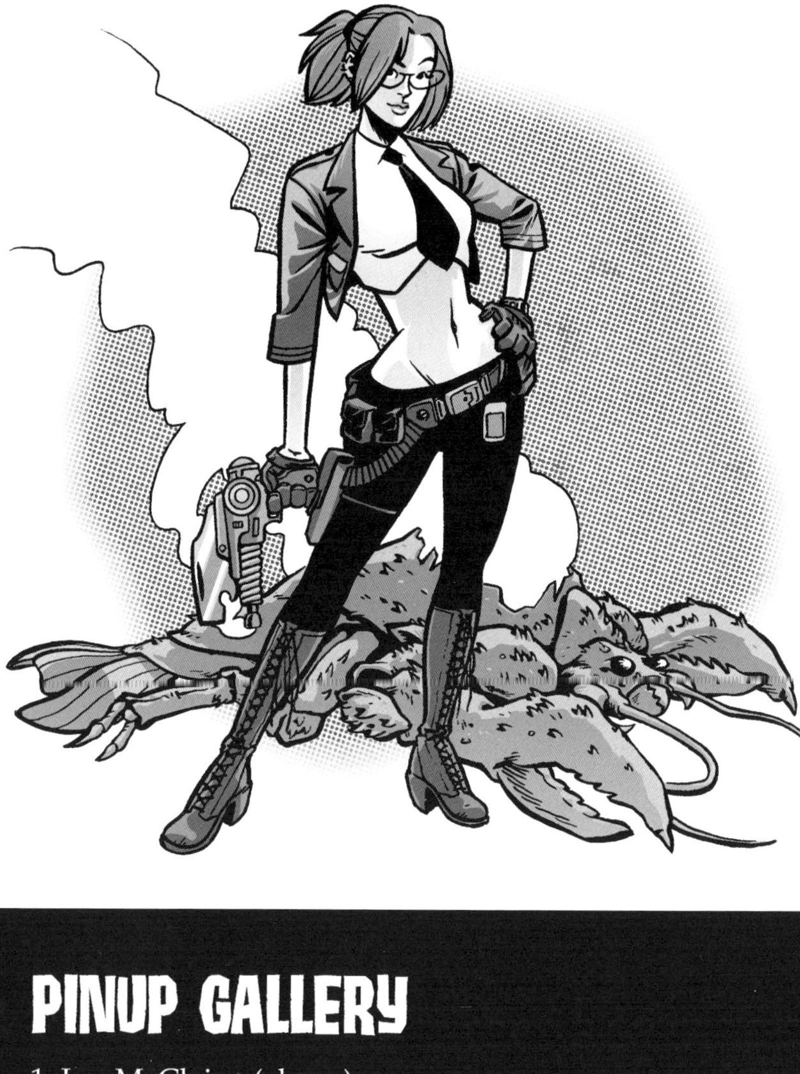

PINUP GALLERY

1. Les McClaine (above)
2. Steve Bryant
3. Ryan Cody
4. Joshua Boulet
5. Keith Howell
6. Nicc Balce
7. Tom Kurzanski

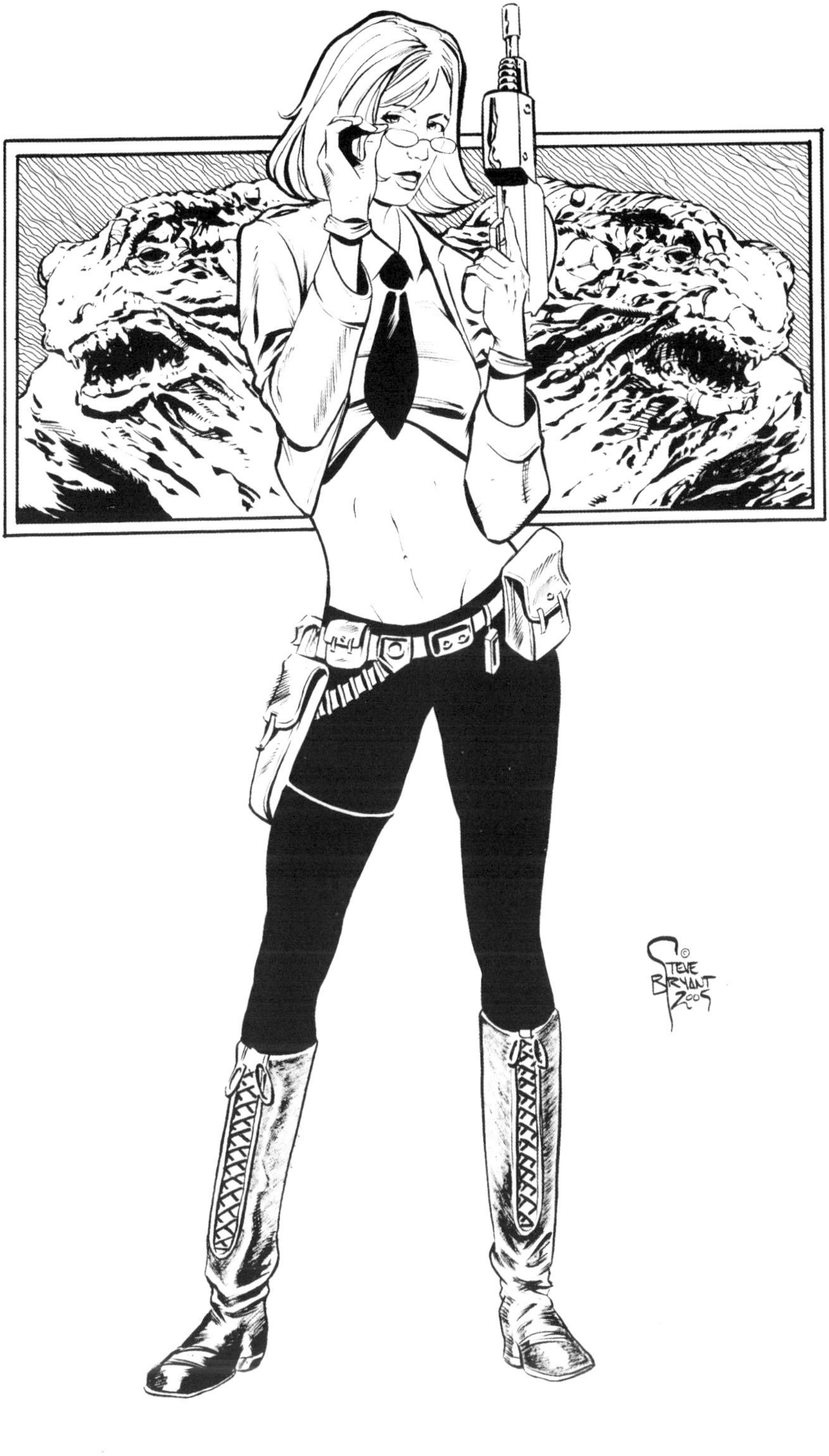
©
STEVE
BRYANT
2005

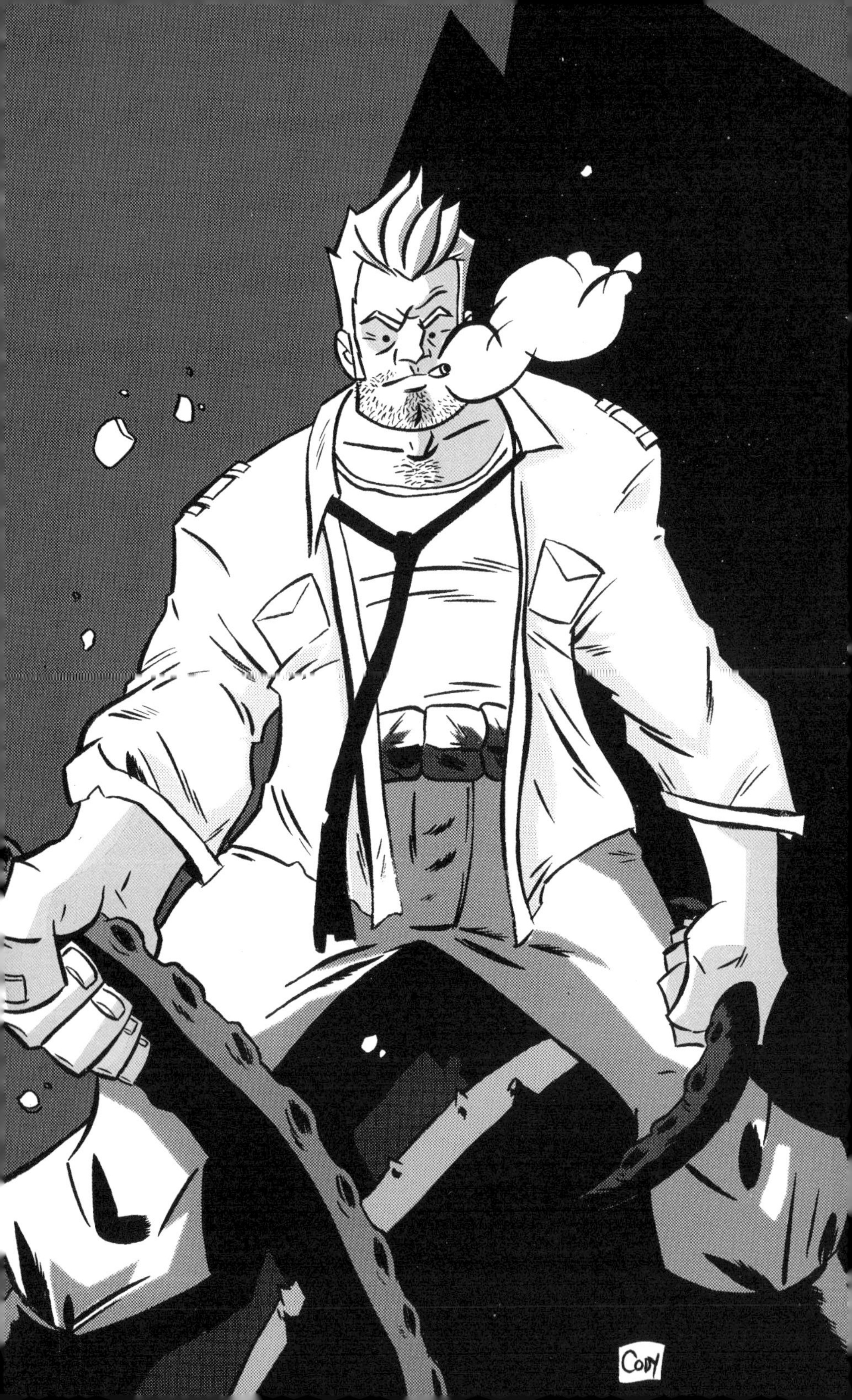
CODY

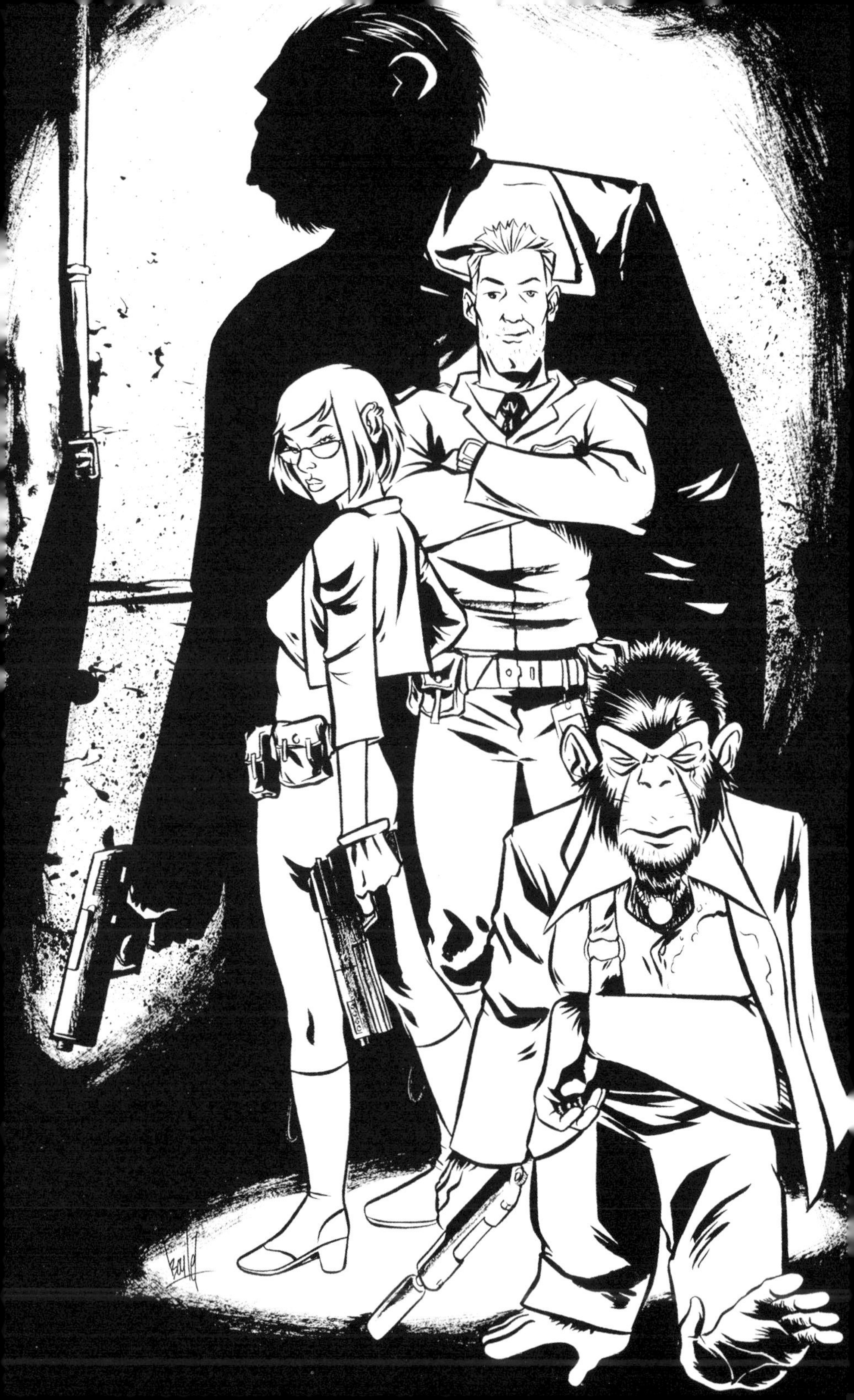

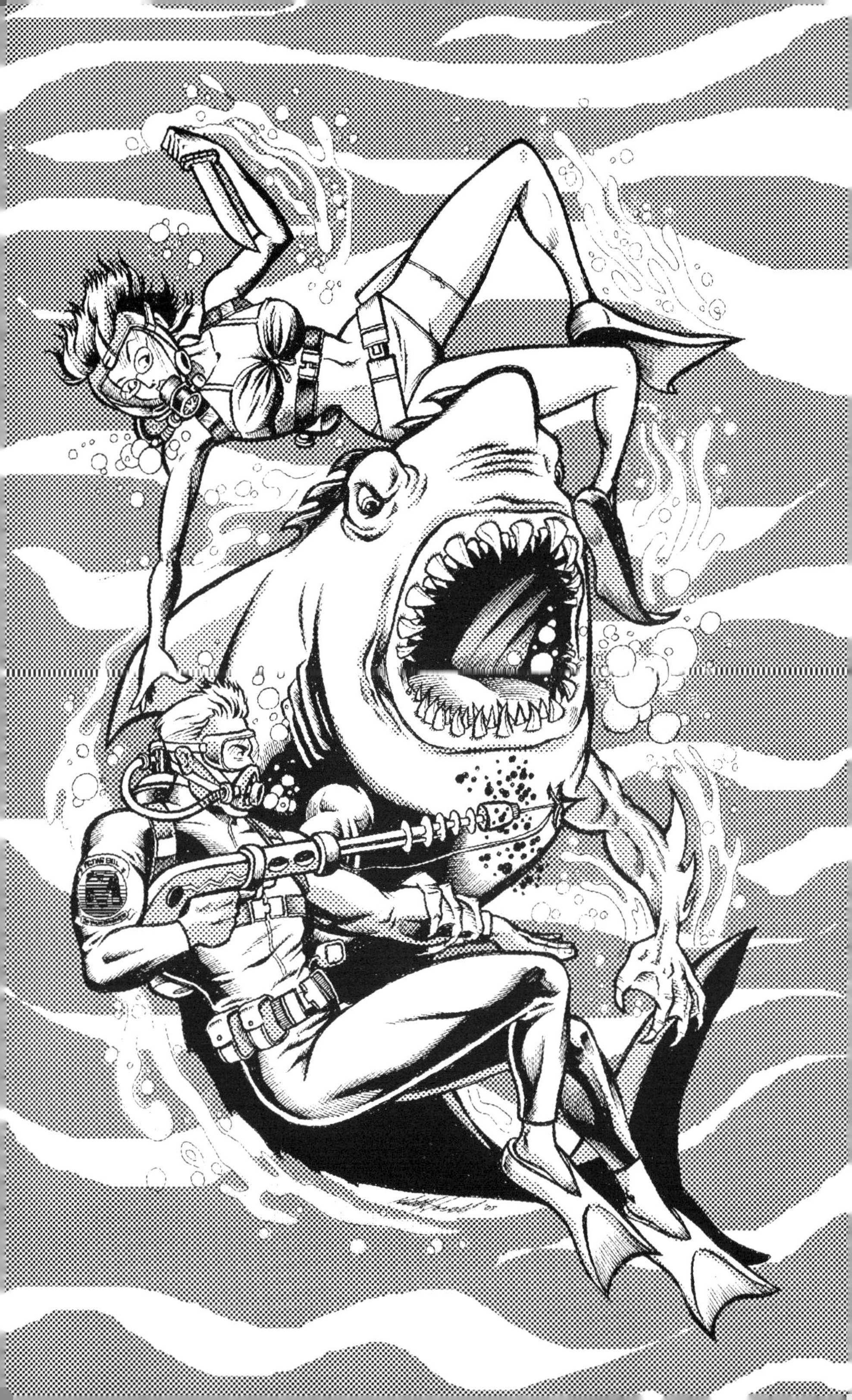

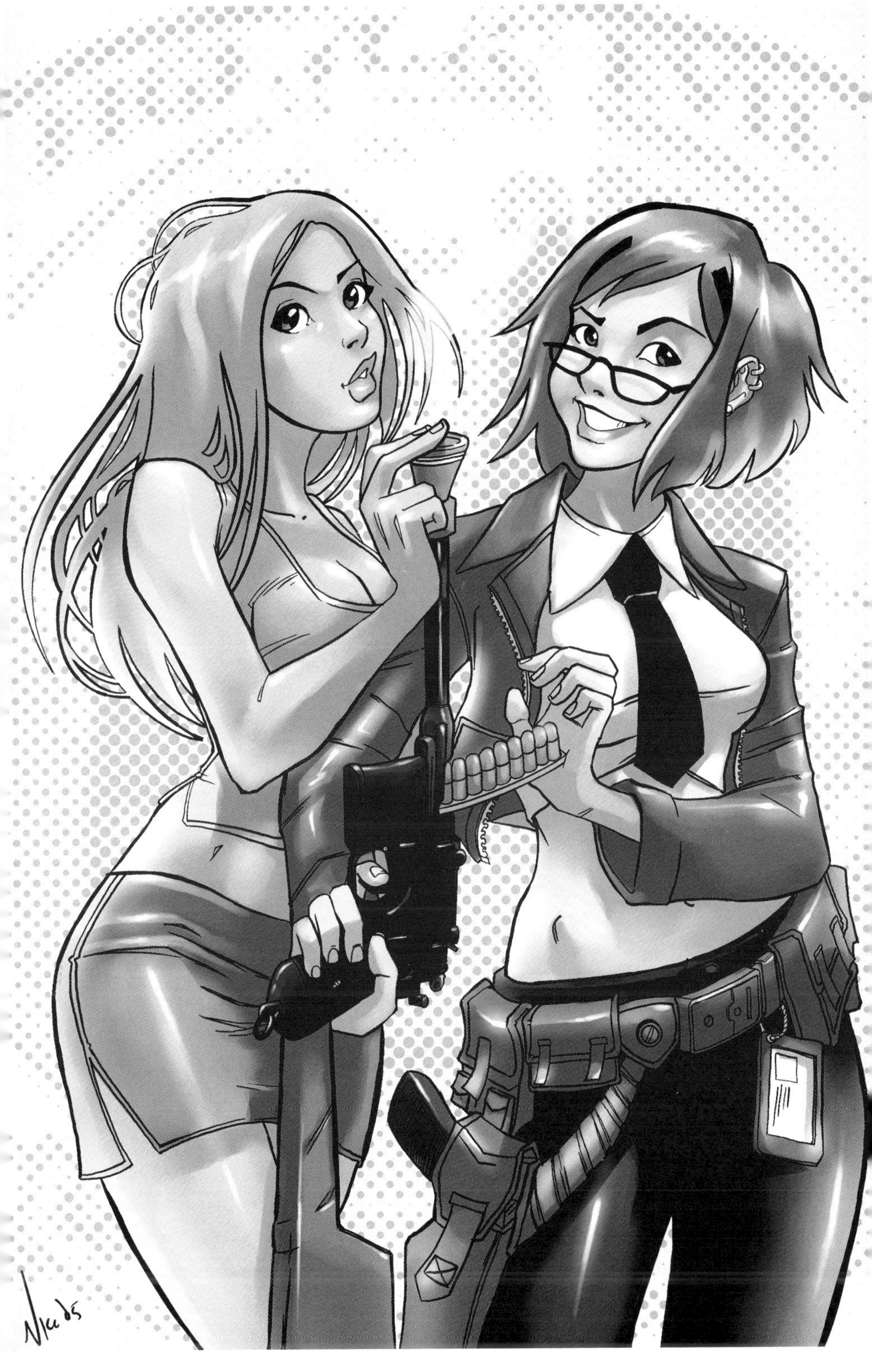

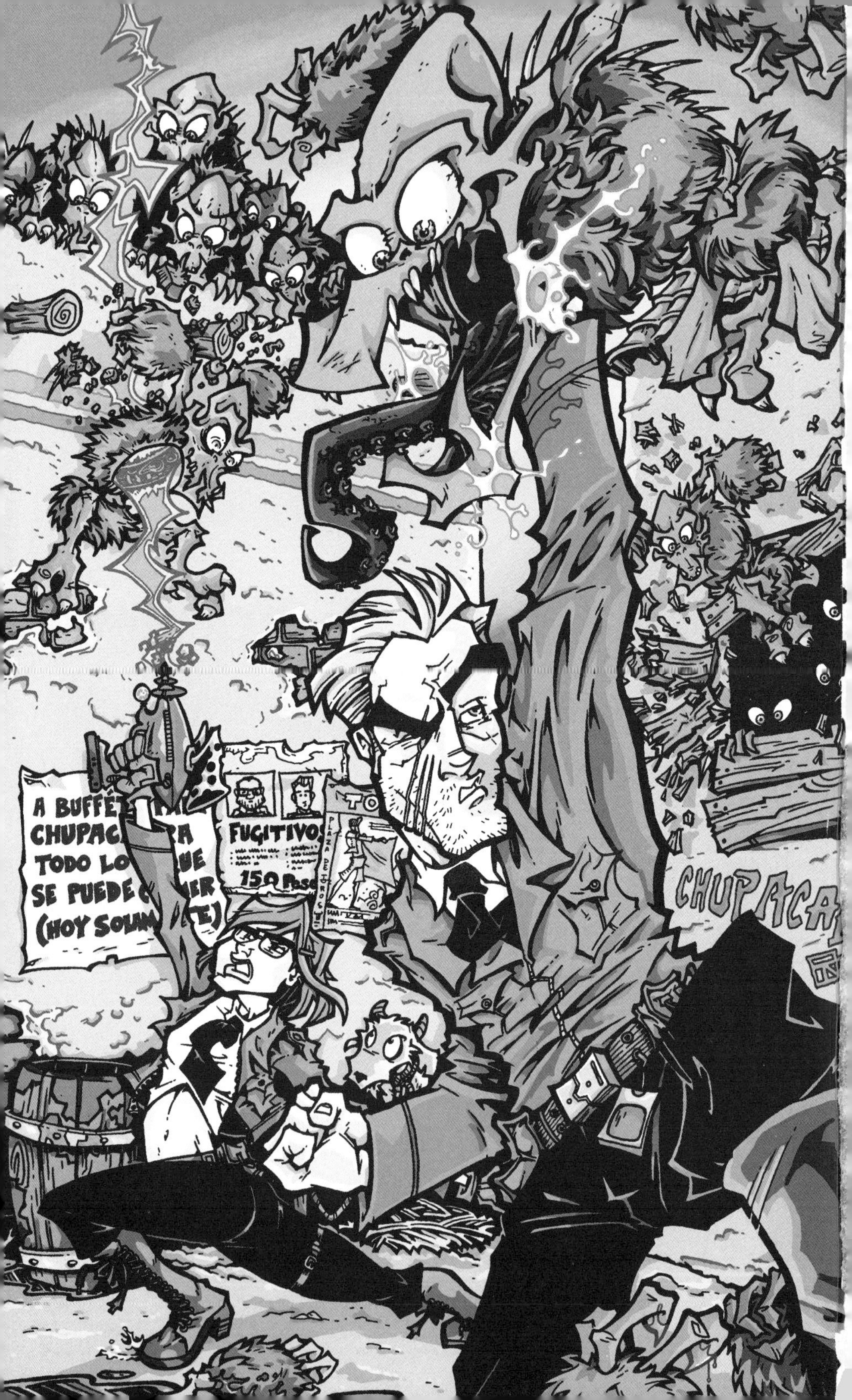
A BUFFÉ
CHUPAC
TODO LO
SE PUEDE
(HOY SOLAM
FUGITIVOS
150
PLAZA DE TOROS
CHUPACA